EVENING TIM

Edited by FRASER GIBSON and STUART SANDLER
Published by Newsquest (Herald and Times) Ltd.,
200 Renfield Street, Glasgow, G2 3QB.

ISBN: 978-0-903216-16-6

BIG GAME DATES

INTERNATIONAL FRIENDLY

England v Scotland .... Wednesday, August 14, 2013

WORLD CUP QUALIFIERS

Scotland v Belgium .... Friday, September 6, 2013
Macedonia v Scotland .... Tuesday, September 10, 2013
Scotland v Croatia..................................... Tuesday, October 15, 2013

SCOTTISH COMMUNITIES LEAGUE CUP

FIRST ROUND... Saturday, August 3, 2013
SECOND ROUND .... Tuesday, Wednesday, August 27/28, 2013
THIRD ROUND........... Tuesday/Wednesday, September 24/25, 2013
FOURTH ROUND............ Tuesday/Wednesday, October 29/30, 2013
SEMI-FINALS .... Saturday/Sunday, February 1/2, 2014
FINAL ....Sunday, March 16, 2014

RAMSDENS CUP

FIRST ROUND.. Saturday, July 27, 2013
SECOND ROUND .... Tuesday/Wednesday, August 20/21, 2013
THIRD ROUND...................................... Saturday, September 7, 2013
SEMI-FINALS .... Sunday, October 13, 2013
FINAL ....Sunday, April 6, 2014

SCOTTISH CUP

ROUND ONE....................................... Saturday, September 14, 2013
ROUND TWO .... Saturday, October 5, 2013
ROUND THREE.......................................Saturday, November 2, 2013
ROUND FOUR..................................... Saturday, November 30, 2013
ROUND FIVE .... Saturday, February 8, 2014
QUARTER-FINALS....................................... Saturday, March 8, 2014
SEMI-FINALS .... Saturday/Sunday, April 12/13, 2014
FINAL ....Saturday, May 17, 2014

SCOTTISH FOOTBALL LEAGUE PLAY-OFFS

SEMI-FINALS ....Wednesday/Saturday, May 7/10, 2014
FINALS....................................Wednesday/Sunday, May 14/18, 2014

UEFA CHAMPIONS LEAGUE

FIRST QUALIFYING ROUND .... July 2/3 and July 9/10, 2013
SECOND QUALIFYING ROUND......July 16/17 and July 23/24, 2013
THIRD QUALIFYING ROUND....................................July 30/31, 2013
....August 6/7, 2013
PLAY-OFF ROUND.................August 20/21 and August 27/28, 2013
GROUP STAGE .... September 17/18, October 1/2, 2013
....October 22/23, November 5/6, 2013
....November 26/27, December 10/11, 2013
ROUND OF 16..February 18/19/25/26, 2014

.... March, 11/12/18/19, 2014
QUARTER-FINALS.......... April 1/2 and April 8/9, 2014
SEMI-FINALS .... April 22/23 and April 29/30, 2014
FINAL .... May 24, 2014, (Estadio da Luz, Lisbon)

EUROPA LEAGUE

FIRST QUALIFYING ROUND .... July 4 and July 11, 2013
SECOND QUALIFYING ROUND.......... July 18 and July 25, 2013
THIRD QUALIFYING ROUND.......... August 1 and August 8, 2013
PLAY-OFF ROUND.......... August 22 and August 29, 2013
GROUP STAGE .... September 19 and October 3, 2013
.... October 24 and November 7, 2013
.... November 28 and December 12, 2013
ROUND OF 32.......... February 20 and February 27, 2014
ROUND OF 16.......... March 13 and March 20, 2014
QUARTER-FINALS.......... April 3 and April 10, 2014
SEMI-FINALS .... April 24 and May 1, 2014
FINAL .... May 14, 2014 (Juventus Stadium, Turin)

FINAL LEAGUE TABLES 2012-2013

CLYDESDALE BANK PREMIER LEAGUE

	P	W	D	L	F	A	Pt
Celtic	38	24	7	7	92	35	79
Motherwell	38	18	9	11	67	51	63
St Johnstne	38	14	14	10	45	44	56
Inverness	38	13	15	10	64	60	54
Ross Co	38	13	14	11	47	48	53
Dundee Utd	38	11	14	13	51	62	47
Hibernian	38	13	12	13	49	52	51
Aberdeen	38	11	15	12	41	43	48
Kilmarnock	38	11	12	15	52	53	45
Hearts	38	11	11	16	40	49	44
St Mirren	38	9	14	15	47	60	41
Dundee	38	7	9	22	28	66	30

IRN-BRU DIVISION TWO

	P	W	D	L	F	A	Pt
QoS	36	29	5	2	92	23	92
Alloa Ath	36	20	7	9	62	35	67
Brechin	36	19	4	13	72	59	61
Forfar Ath	36	17	3	16	67	74	54
Arbroath	36	15	7	14	47	57	52
Stenhsemr	36	12	13	11	59	59	49
Ayr Utd	36	12	5	19	53	65	41
Stranraer	36	10	7	19	43	71	37
East Fife	36	8	8	20	50	65	32
Albion Rovs	36	7	3	26	45	82	24

IRN-BRU DIVISION ONE

	P	W	D	L	F	A	Pt
Partick Th	36	23	9	4	76	28	78
Morton	36	20	7	9	73	47	67
Falkirk	36	15	8	13	52	48	53
Livingston	36	14	10	12	58	56	52
Hamilton	36	14	9	13	52	45	51
Raith Rovs	36	11	13	12	45	48	46
Dumbarton	36	13	4	19	58	83	43
Cowdenbth	36	8	12	16	51	65	36
Dunfermline	36	14	7	15	62	59	34
Airdrie Utd	36	5	7	24	41	89	22

IRN-BRU DIVISION THREE

	P	W	D	L	F	A	Pt
Rangers	36	25	8	3	87	29	83
Peterhead	36	17	8	11	52	28	59
Queen's P	36	16	8	12	60	54	56
Berwick	36	14	7	15	59	55	49
Elgin City	36	13	10	13	67	69	49
Montrose	36	12	11	13	60	68	47
Stirling Alb	36	12	9	15	59	58	45
Annan Ath	36	11	10	15	54	65	43
Clyde	36	12	4	20	42	66	40
E Stirling	36	8	5	23	49	97	20

WESTERN REGION SJFA LEAGUES 2012-2013

STAGECOACH SUPER PREMIER DIVISION

	P	W	D	L	F	A	Pts
Auchinleck	22	20	2	0	62	14	62
Petershill	22	11	6	5	41	23	39
Clydebank	22	11	3	8	34	32	36
Glenafton	22	10	2	10	26	37	32
Irvine Meadow	22	9	3	10	36	37	30
Arthurlie	22	8	5	9	40	40	29
Rob Roy	22	8	5	9	49	50	29
Pollok	22	7	6	9	25	35	27
Cumnock	22	7	4	11	36	40	25
Ashfield	22	7	4	11	35	40	25
Beith	22	7	3	12	36	50	24
Shotts BA	22	2	7	13	23	45	13

STAGECOACH SUPER LEAGUE FIRST DIVISION

	P	W	D	L	F	A	Pts
Hurlford	26	16	3	7	52	43	51
Kilbirnie	26	15	5	6	58	37	50
Largs Th	26	14	3	9	59	39	45
Thorniewood	26	13	5	8	44	31	44
Yoker	26	11	7	8	67	49	40
Rutherglen	26	12	4	10	51	42	40
Renfrew	26	11	4	11	48	40	37
Cumbernauld	26	11	4	11	53	63	37
Kilsyth	26	10	6	10	44	42	36
Maybole	26	9	8	9	43	48	35
Perthshire	26	10	4	12	57	48	34
Kello Rovs	26	9	2	15	43	69	29
Ardrossan WR	26	5	7	14	52	80	22
Whitletts Vics	26	3	4	19	30	70	13

STAGECOACH CENTRAL DISTRICT LEAGUE FIRST DIVISION

	P	W	D	L	F	A	Pts
Greenock	26	17	5	4	66	33	56
Lesmahagow	26	15	6	5	73	37	51
Larkhall	26	16	2	8	80	52	50
Shettleston	26	15	4	7	57	34	49
St Anthony's	26	14	7	5	49	28	49
Lanark	26	14	3	9	56	41	45
Carluke Rovs	26	13	4	9	58	47	43
Benburb	26	11	4	11	57	51	37
Bellshill Ath	26	10	6	10	56	50	36
Dunipace	26	11	3	12	51	46	36
Neilston	26	10	4	12	51	51	34
Port Glasgow	26	6	2	18	39	65	20
St Roch's	26	3	1	22	21	96	10
East Kilbride	26	1	1	24	20	103	4

STAGECOACH CENTRAL DISTRICT LEAGUE SECOND DIVISION

	P	W	D	L	F	A	Pts
Cambuslang	20	15	1	4	65	20	46
Maryhill	20	14	2	4	52	32	44
Johnstone Brgh	20	11	2	7	55	40	35
Wishaw	20	10	4	6	42	36	34
Rossvale	20	9	4	7	34	35	31
Vale of Clyde	20	8	4	8	39	30	28
Vale of Leven	20	8	4	8	37	38	28
Blantyre Vics	20	8	2	10	32	32	26
Forth	20	4	6	10	26	38	18
Royal Albert	20	5	2	13	32	62	17
Newmains	20	2	1	17	13	64	7

AUCHINLECK Talbot boss Tommy Sloan led his team to a league and cup double

STAGECOACH AYRSHIRE DISTRICT LEAGUE

	P	W	D	L	F	A	Pts
Kilwinning	22	18	2	2	76	22	56
Troon	22	16	3	3	66	23	51
Lugar Boswell	22	16	2	4	60	27	50
Ardeer	22	12	2	8	55	26	38
Irvine Vics	22	11	3	8	37	38	36
Saltcoats Vics	22	9	3	10	43	44	30
Girvan	22	8	3	11	52	43	27
Annbank	22	8	2	12	41	45	26
Darvel	22	7	4	11	43	57	25
Dalry	22	6	2	14	39	76	20
Craigmark B	22	6	1	15	39	69	19
Muirkirk	22	1	1	20	16	97	4

SCOTTISH PROFESSIONAL FOOTBALL LEAGUE PREMIER DIVISION 2013-2014

FIXTURES SUBJECT TO CHANGE FOR LIVE TV COVERAGE, AND CORRECT AT TIME OF GOING TO PRESS

Saturday August 3, 2013
Aberdeen v Kilmarnock
Celtic v Ross County
Inverness CT v St Mirren
Partick Thistle v Dundee United
St Johnstone v Hearts

Sunday August 4, 2013
Hibernian v Motherwell

Saturday August 10, 2013
Celtic P-P St Mirren
Dundee United v Inverness CT
Hearts v Hibernian
Kilmarnock v St Johnstone
Ross County v Partick Thistle

Sunday August 11, 2013
Motherwell v Aberdeen

Saturday August 17, 2013
Aberdeen v Celtic
Hibernian v Dundee United
Inverness CT v Motherwell
Partick Thistle v Hearts
St Johnstone v Ross County
St Mirren v Kilmarnock

Saturday August 24, 2013
Celtic v Inverness CT
Dundee United v St Johnstone
Hearts v Aberdeen
Kilmarnock v Hibernian
Motherwell v Partick Thistle
Ross County v St Mirren

Saturday August 31, 2013
Aberdeen v St Johnstone
Dundee United v Celtic
Hibernian v Ross County
Inverness CT v Hearts
Motherwell v Kilmarnock
St Mirren v Partick Thistle

Saturday September 14, 2013
Hearts v Celtic
Kilmarnock v Inverness CT
Partick Thistle v Aberdeen
Ross County v Dundee United
St Johnstone v Hibernian
St Mirren v Motherwell

Saturday September 21, 2013
Aberdeen v Inverness CT
Celtic v St Johnstone
Dundee United v Motherwell
Hibernian v St Mirren
Partick Thistle v Kilmarnock
Ross County v Hearts

Saturday September 28, 2013
Hearts v Dundee United
Inverness CT v Hibernian
Kilmarnock v Celtic
Motherwell v Ross County
St Johnstone v Partick Thistle
St Mirren v Aberdeen

Saturday October 5, 2013
Celtic v Motherwell
Dundee United v Kilmarnock
Hearts v St Mirren
Partick Thistle v Hibernian
Ross County v Aberdeen
St Johnstone v Inverness CT

Saturday October 19, 2013
Aberdeen v Dundee United
Hibernian v Celtic
Inverness CT v Partick Thistle
Kilmarnock v Ross County
Motherwell v Hearts
St Mirren v St Johnstone

Saturday October 26, 2013
Dundee United v St Mirren
Hibernian v Aberdeen
Kilmarnock v Hearts
Partick Thistle v Celtic
Ross County v Inverness CT
St Johnstone v Motherwell

Saturday November 2, 2013
Aberdeen v Partick Thistle
Celtic v Dundee United
Hearts v St Johnstone
Inverness CT v Kilmarnock
Motherwell v Hibernian
St Mirren v Ross County

Saturday November 9, 2013
Aberdeen v Hearts
Hibernian v Inverness CT
Motherwell v Dundee United
Partick Thistle v St Mirren
Ross County v Celtic
St Johnstone v Kilmarnock

Saturday November 23, 2013
Celtic v Aberdeen
Dundee United v Partick Thistle
Hearts v Ross County
Inverness CT v St Johnstone
Kilmarnock v Motherwell
St Mirren v Hibernian

Saturday December 7, 2013
Dundee United v Hearts
Hibernian v Partick Thistle
Motherwell v Celtic
Ross County v Kilmarnock
St Johnstone v Aberdeen
St Mirren v Inverness CT

Saturday December 14, 2013
Aberdeen v St Mirren
Celtic v Hibernian
Hearts v Inverness CT
Kilmarnock v Dundee United
Partick Thistle v St Johnstone
Ross County v Motherwell

Saturday December 21, 2013
Celtic v Hearts
Dundee United v Ross County
Hibernian v St Johnstone
Inverness CT v Aberdeen
Kilmarnock v Partick Thistle
Motherwell v St Mirren

Thursday December 26, 2013
Aberdeen v Motherwell
Hearts v Kilmarnock
Partick Thistle v Inverness CT
Ross County v Hibernian
St Johnstone v Celtic
St Mirren v Dundee United

Sunday December 29, 2013
Aberdeen v Ross County
Hibernian v Kilmarnock
Inverness CT v Celtic
Partick Thistle v Motherwell
St Johnstone v Dundee United
St Mirren v Hearts

Wednesday January 1, 2014
Celtic v Partick Thistle
Dundee United v Aberdeen
Hibernian v Hearts
Inverness CT v Ross County
Kilmarnock v St Mirren
Motherwell v St Johnstone

Saturday January 4, 2014
Dundee United v Hibernian
Hearts v Partick Thistle
Kilmarnock v Aberdeen
Motherwell v Inverness CT
Ross County v St Johnstone
St Mirren v Celtic

Saturday January 11, 2014
Aberdeen v Hibernian
Celtic v Kilmarnock
Hearts v Motherwell
Inverness CT v Dundee United
Partick Thistle v Ross County
St Johnstone v St Mirren

Saturday January 18, 2014
Aberdeen v Inverness CT
Celtic v Motherwell
Hibernian v St Mirren
Partick Thistle v Kilmarnock
Ross County v Dundee United
St Johnstone v Hearts

Saturday January 25, 2014
Dundee United v St Johnstone
Hibernian v Celtic
Kilmarnock v Inverness CT
Motherwell v Aberdeen
Ross County v Hearts
St Mirren v Partick Thistle

Saturday February 1, 2014
Aberdeen v Celtic
Hearts v St Mirren
Inverness CT v Hibernian
Kilmarnock v Ross County
Partick Thistle v Dundee United
St Johnstone v Motherwell

Saturday February 15, 2014
Celtic v St Johnstone
Dundee United v Kilmarnock
Hibernian v Ross County
Inverness CT v Hearts
Motherwell v Partick Thistle
St Mirren v Aberdeen

Saturday February 22, 2014
Dundee United v Motherwell
Hearts v Celtic
Kilmarnock v Hibernian
Partick Thistle v Aberdeen
Ross County v St Mirren
St Johnstone v Inverness CT

Saturday March 1, 2014
Aberdeen v St Johnstone
Celtic v Inverness CT
Hibernian v Dundee United
Motherwell v Hearts
Ross County v Partick Thistle
St Mirren v Kilmarnock

Saturday March 15, 2014
Dundee United v St Mirren
Hearts v Aberdeen
Inverness CT v Motherwell
Kilmarnock v Celtic
Partick Thistle v Hibernian
St Johnstone v Ross County

Saturday March 22, 2014
Aberdeen v Kilmarnock
Celtic v St Mirren
Hearts v Dundee United
Inverness CT v Partick Thistle
Motherwell v Ross County
St Johnstone v Hibernian

Wednesday March 26, 2014
Dundee United v Inverness CT
Hibernian v Motherwell
Kilmarnock v Hearts
Partick Thistle v Celtic
Ross County v Aberdeen
St Mirren v St Johnstone

Saturday March 29, 2014
Aberdeen v Dundee United
Celtic v Ross County
Hearts v Hibernian
Inverness CT v St Mirren
Motherwell v Kilmarnock
St Johnstone v Partick Thistle

Saturday April 5, 2014
Dundee United v Celtic
Hibernian v Aberdeen
Kilmarnock v St Johnstone
Partick Thistle v Hearts
Ross County v Inverness CT
St Mirren v Motherwell

LEAGUE WILL NOW SPLIT IN TWO FOR FINAL FIVE GAMES. DATES TO BE ARRANGED.

SPFL FIRST DIVISION 2013-2014

Saturday August 10, 2013
Alloa Ath v Livingston
Dumbarton v Falkirk
Morton v Cowdenbeath
QoS v Dundee
Raith Rovers v Hamilton A

Saturday August 17, 2013
Cowdenbeath v Raith Rovers
Dundee v Alloa Ath
Falkirk v Morton
Hamilton A v Dumbarton
Livingston v QoS

Saturday August 24, 2013
Alloa Ath v Cowdenbeath
Dumbarton v Morton
Hamilton A v QoS
Livingston v Falkirk
Raith Rovers v Dundee

Saturday August 31, 2013
Cowdenbeath v Dumbarton
Dundee v Livingston
Falkirk v Hamilton A
Morton v Raith Rovers
QoS v Alloa Ath

Saturday September 14, 2013
Alloa Ath v Dumbarton
Cowdenbeath v Falkirk
Dundee v Hamilton A
Livingston v Morton
QoS v Raith Rovers

Saturday September 21, 2013
Dumbarton v Livingston
Falkirk v Dundee
Hamilton A v Cowdenbeath
Morton v QoS
Raith Rovers v Alloa Ath

Saturday September 28, 2013
Alloa Ath v Hamilton A
Dundee v Morton
Livingston v Cowdenbeath
QoS v Dumbarton
Raith Rovers v Falkirk

Saturday October 5, 2013
Cowdenbeath v Dundee
Dumbarton v Raith Rovers
Falkirk v QoS
Hamilton A v Livingston
Morton v Alloa Ath

Saturday October 12, 2013
Alloa Ath v Falkirk
Dumbarton v Dundee
Morton v Hamilton A
QoS v Cowdenbeath
Raith Rovers v Livingston

Saturday October 19, 2013
Cowdenbeath v Morton
Dundee v QoS
Falkirk v Dumbarton
Hamilton A v Raith Rovers
Livingston v Alloa Ath

Saturday October 26, 2013
Alloa Ath v QoS
Dumbarton v Cowdenbeath
Hamilton A v Falkirk
Livingston v Dundee
Raith Rovers v Morton

Saturday November 9, 2013
Cowdenbeath v Alloa Ath
Dundee v Raith Rovers
Falkirk v Livingston
Morton v Dumbarton
QoS v Hamilton A

Saturday November 16, 2013
Alloa Ath v Raith Rovers
Cowdenbeath v Hamilton A
Dundee v Falkirk
Livingston v Dumbarton
QoS v Morton

Saturday November 23, 2013
Dumbarton v Alloa Ath
Falkirk v Cowdenbeath
Hamilton A v Dundee
Morton v Livingston
Raith Rovers v QoS

Saturday December 7, 2013
Cowdenbeath v Livingston
Dumbarton v QoS
Falkirk v Raith Rovers
Hamilton A v Alloa Ath
Morton v Dundee

Saturday December 14, 2013
Alloa Ath v Morton
Dundee v Cowdenbeath
Livingston v Hamilton A
QoS v Falkirk
Raith Rovers v Dumbarton

Thursday December 26, 2013
Alloa Ath v Dundee
Dumbarton v Hamilton A
Morton v Falkirk
QoS v Livingston
Raith Rovers v Cowdenbeath

Saturday December 28, 2013
Cowdenbeath v QoS
Dundee v Dumbarton
Falkirk v Alloa Ath
Hamilton A v Morton
Livingston v Raith Rovers

Thursday January 2, 2014
Alloa Ath v Cowdenbeath
Dumbarton v Morton
Hamilton A v QoS
Livingston v Falkirk
Raith Rovers v Dundee

Saturday January 11, 2014
Cowdenbeath v Dumbarton
Dundee v Livingston
Falkirk v Hamilton A
Morton v Raith Rovers
QoS v Alloa Ath

Saturday January 18, 2014
Alloa Ath v Dumbarton
Cowdenbeath v Falkirk
Dundee v Hamilton A
Livingston v Morton
QoS v Raith Rovers

Saturday January 25, 2014
Dumbarton v Livingston
Falkirk v Dundee
Hamilton A v Cowdenbeath
Morton v QoS
Raith Rovers v Alloa Ath

Saturday, February 1, 2014
Cowdenbeath v Raith Rovers
Dundee v Alloa Ath
Falkirk v Morton
Hamilton A v Dumbarton
Livingston v QoS

Saturday February 15, 2014
Alloa Ath v Livingston
Dumbarton v Falkirk
Morton v Cowdenbeath
QoS v Dundee
Raith Rovers v Hamilton A

Saturday February 22, 2014
Cowdenbeath v Dundee
Dumbarton v Raith Rovers
Falkirk v QoS
Hamilton A v Livingston
Morton v Alloa Ath

Saturday March 1, 2014
Alloa Ath v Hamilton A
Dundee v Morton
Livingston v Cowdenbeath
QoS v Dumbarton
Raith Rovers v Falkirk

Saturday March 8, 2014
Cowdenbeath v Alloa Ath
Dundee v Raith Rovers
Falkirk v Livingston
Morton v Dumbarton
QoS v Hamilton A

Saturday March 15, 2014
Alloa Ath v QoS
Dumbarton v Cowdenbeath
Hamilton A v Falkirk
Livingston v Dundee
Raith Rovers v Morton

Saturday March 22, 2014
Alloa Ath v Falkirk
Dumbarton v Dundee
Morton v Hamilton A
QoS v Cowdenbeath
Raith Rovers v Livingston

Tuesday March 25, 2014
Cowdenbeath v Morton
Dundee v QoS
Falkirk v Dumbarton
Hamilton A v Raith Rovers
Livingston v Alloa Ath

Saturday March 29, 2014
Alloa Ath v Raith Rovers
Cowdenbeath v Hamilton A
Dundee v Falkirk
Livingston v Dumbarton
QoS v Morton

Saturday April 5, 2014
Dumbarton v Alloa Ath
Falkirk v Cowdenbeath
Hamilton A v Dundee
Morton v Livingston
Raith Rovers v QoS

Saturday April 12, 2014
Alloa Ath v Morton
Dundee v Cowdenbeath
Livingston v Hamilton A
QoS v Falkirk
Raith Rovers v Dumbarton

Saturday April 19, 2014
Cowdenbeath v Livingston
Dumbarton v QoS
Falkirk v Raith Rovers
Hamilton A v Alloa Ath
Morton v Dundee

Saturday April 26, 2014
Alloa Ath v Dundee
Dumbarton v Hamilton A
Morton v Falkirk
QoS v Livingston
Raith Rovers v
Cowdenbeath

Saturday May 3, 2014
Cowdenbeath v QoS
Dundee v Dumbarton
Falkirk v Alloa Ath
Hamilton A v Morton
Livingston v Raith Rovers

SPFL SECOND DIVISION 2013-2014

Saturday August 10, 2013
Arbroath v Ayr Utd
East Fife v Dunfermline Ath
Forfar Ath v Airdrie
Rangers v Brechin C
Stenhousemuir v Stranraer

Saturday August 17, 2013
Airdrie v Stenhousemuir
Ayr Utd v Forfar Ath
Brechin C v East Fife
Dunfermline Ath v Arbroath
Stranraer v Rangers

Saturday August 24, 2013
Airdrie v Rangers
Brechin C v Forfar Ath
East Fife v Arbroath
Stenhousemuir v Dunfermline Ath
Stranraer v Ayr Utd

Saturday August 31, 2013
Arbroath v Brechin C
Ayr Utd v Airdrie
Dunfermline Ath v Stranraer
Forfar Ath v Stenhousemuir
Rangers v East Fife

Saturday September 14, 2013
Airdrie v Stranraer
Brechin C v Dunfermline Ath
East Fife v Forfar Ath
Rangers v Arbroath
Stenhousemuir v Ayr Utd

Saturday September 21, 2013
Arbroath v Stenhousemuir
Ayr Utd v Brechin C
Dunfermline Ath v Airdrie
Forfar Ath v Rangers
Stranraer v East Fife

Saturday September 28, 2013
Arbroath v Forfar Ath
Brechin C v Stranraer
Dunfermline Ath v Ayr Utd
East Fife v Airdrie
Rangers v Stenhousemuir

Saturday October 5, 2013
Airdrie v Brechin C
Ayr Utd v Rangers
Forfar Ath v Dunfermline Ath
Stenhousemuir v East Fife
Stranraer v Arbroath

Saturday October 12, 2013
Arbroath v Airdrie
East Fife v Ayr Utd
Forfar Ath v Stranraer
Rangers v Dunfermline Ath
Stenhousemuir v Brechin C

Saturday October 19, 2013
Airdrie v Forfar Ath
Ayr Utd v Arbroath
Brechin C v Rangers
Dunfermline Ath v East Fife
Stranraer v Stenhousemuir

Saturday, October 26, 2013
Airdrie v Ayr Utd
Brechin C v Arbroath
East Fife v Rangers
Stenhousemuir v Forfar Ath
Stranraer v Dunfermline Ath

Saturday November 9, 2013
Arbroath v East Fife
Ayr Utd v Stranraer
Dunfermline Ath v Stenhousemuir
Forfar Ath v Brechin C
Rangers v Airdrie

Saturday November 16, 2013
Airdrie v Dunfermline Ath
Brechin C v Ayr Utd
East Fife v Stranraer
Rangers v Forfar Ath
Stenhousemuir v Arbroath

Saturday November 23, 2013
Arbroath v Rangers
Ayr Utd v Stenhousemuir
Dunfermline Ath v Brechin C
Forfar Ath v East Fife
Stranraer v Airdrie

Saturday December 7, 2013
Arbroath v Stranraer
Brechin C v Airdrie
Dunfermline Ath v Forfar Ath
East Fife v Stenhousemuir
Rangers v Ayr Utd

Saturday December 14, 2013
Airdrie v East Fife
Ayr Utd v Dunfermline Ath
Forfar Ath v Arbroath
Stenhousemuir v Rangers
Stranraer v Brechin C

Thursday December 26, 2013
Arbroath v Dunfermline Ath
East Fife v Brechin C
Forfar Ath v Ayr Utd
Rangers v Stranraer
Stenhousemuir v Airdrie

Saturday December 28, 2013
Airdrie v Arbroath
Ayr Utd v East Fife
Brechin C v Stenhousemuir
Dunfermline Ath v Rangers
Stranraer v Forfar Ath

Thursday January 2, 2014
Airdrie v Rangers
Brechin C v Forfar Ath
East Fife v Arbroath
Stenhousemuir v Dunfermline Ath
Stranraer v Ayr Utd

Saturday January 11, 2014
Arbroath v Brechin C
Ayr Utd v Airdrie
Dunfermline Ath v Stranraer
Forfar Ath v Stenhousemuir
Rangers v East Fife

Saturday January 18, 2014
Arbroath v Stenhousemuir
Ayr Utd v Brechin C
Dunfermline Ath v Airdrie
Forfar Ath v Rangers
Stranraer v East Fife

Saturday January 25, 2014
Airdrie v Stranraer
Brechin C v Dunfermline Ath
East Fife v Forfar Ath
Rangers v Arbroath
Stenhousemuir v Ayr Utd

Saturday February 1, 2014
Arbroath v Ayr Utd
East Fife v Dunfermline Ath
Forfar Ath v Airdrie
Rangers v Brechin C
Stenhousemuir v Stranraer

Saturday February 8, 2014
Airdrie v Stenhousemuir
Ayr Utd v Forfar Ath
Brechin C v East Fife
Dunfermline Ath v Arbroath
Stranraer v Rangers

Saturday February 15, 2014
Airdrie v Brechin C
Ayr Utd v Rangers
Forfar Ath v Dunfermline Ath
Stenhousemuir v East Fife
Stranraer v Arbroath

Saturday February 22, 2014
Arbroath v Forfar Ath
Brechin C v Stranraer
Dunfermline Ath v Ayr Utd
East Fife v Airdrie
Rangers v Stenhousemuir

Saturday March 1, 2014
Airdrie v Ayr Utd
Brechin C v Arbroath
East Fife v Rangers
Stenhousemuir v Forfar Ath
Stranraer v Dunfermline Ath

Saturday March 8, 2014
Arbroath v East Fife
Ayr Utd v Stranraer
Dunfermline Ath v Stenhousemuir
Forfar Ath v Brechin C
Rangers v Airdrie

Saturday March 15, 2014
Arbroath v Airdrie
East Fife v Ayr Utd
Forfar Ath v Stranraer
Rangers v Dunfermline Ath
Stenhousemuir v Brechin C

Saturday March 22, 2014
Airdrie v Forfar Ath
Ayr Utd v Arbroath
Brechin C v Rangers
Dunfermline Ath v East Fife
Stranraer v Stenhousemuir

Saturday March 29, 2014
Arbroath v Rangers
Ayr Utd v Stenhousemuir
Dunfermline Ath v Brechin C
Forfar Ath v East Fife
Stranraer v Airdrie

Saturday April 5, 2014
Airdrie v Dunfermline Ath
Brechin C v Ayr Utd
East Fife v Stranraer
Rangers v Forfar Ath
Stenhousemuir v Arbroath

Saturday April 12, 2014
Arbroath v Stranraer
Brechin C v Airdrie
Dunfermline Ath v Forfar Ath
East Fife v Stenhousemuir
Rangers v Ayr Utd

Saturday April 19, 2014
Airdrie v East Fife
Ayr Utd v Dunfermline Ath
Forfar Ath v Arbroath
Stenhousemuir v Rangers
Stranraer v Brechin C

Saturday April 26, 2014
Arbroath v Dunfermline Ath
East Fife v Brechin C
Forfar Ath v Ayr Utd
Rangers v Stranraer
Stenhousemuir v Airdrie

Saturday May 3, 2014
Airdrie v Arbroath
Ayr Utd v East Fife
Brechin C v Stenhousemuir
Dunfermline Ath v Rangers
Stranraer v Forfar Ath

SPFL THIRD DIVISION 2013-14

Saturday August 10, 2013
Clyde v Berwick R
Elgin City v Albion Rovers
Montrose v Stirling A
Peterhead v Annan Ath
Queen's P v E Stirling

Saturday August 17, 2013
Albion Rovers v Clyde
Annan Ath v Montrose
Berwick R v Queen's P
E Stirling v Elgin City
Stirling A v Peterhead

Saturday August 24, 2013
Annan Ath v Albion Rovers
Clyde v Queen's P
Montrose v Berwick R
Peterhead v Elgin City
Stirling A v E Stirling

Saturday August 31, 2013
Albion Rovers v Montrose
Berwick R v Annan Ath
E Stirling v Peterhead
Elgin City v Clyde
Queen's P v Stirling A

Saturday September 14, 2013
Albion Rovers v Berwick R
Clyde v E Stirling
Elgin City v Montrose
Peterhead v Queen's P
Stirling A v Annan Ath

Saturday September 21, 2013
Annan Ath v Clyde
Berwick R v Stirling A
E Stirling v Albion Rovers
Montrose v Peterhead
Queen's P v Elgin City

Saturday September 28, 2013
Albion Rovers v Peterhead
Clyde v Montrose
E Stirling v Berwick R
Elgin City v Stirling A
Queen's P v Annan Ath

Saturday October 12, 2013
Annan Ath v E Stirling
Berwick R v Elgin City
Montrose v Queen's P
Peterhead v Clyde
Stirling A v Albion Rovers

Saturday October 19, 2013
Albion Rovers v Elgin City
Annan Ath v Peterhead
Berwick R v Clyde
E Stirling v Queen's P
Stirling A v Montrose

Saturday October 26, 2013
Clyde v Stirling A
Elgin City v Annan Ath
Montrose v E Stirling
Peterhead v Berwick R
Queen's P v Albion Rovers

Saturday November 9, 2013
Albion Rovers v Annan Ath
Berwick R v Montrose
E Stirling v Stirling A
Elgin City v Peterhead
Queen's P v Clyde

Saturday November 16, 2013
Annan Ath v Berwick R
Clyde v Elgin City
Montrose v Albion Rovers
Peterhead v E Stirling
Stirling A v Queen's P

Saturday November 23, 2013
Annan Ath v Stirling A
Berwick R v Albion Rovers
E Stirling v Clyde
Montrose v Elgin City
Queen's P v Peterhead

Saturday November 30, 2013
Albion Rovers v E Stirling
Clyde v Annan Ath
Elgin City v Queen's P
Peterhead v Montrose
Stirling A v Berwick R

Saturday December 7, 2013
Albion Rovers v Stirling A
Clyde v Peterhead
E Stirling v Annan Ath
Elgin City v Berwick R
Queen's P v Montrose

Saturday December 14, 2013
Annan Ath v Queen's P
Berwick R v E Stirling
Montrose v Clyde
Peterhead v Albion Rovers
Stirling A v Elgin City

Thursday December 26, 2013
Clyde v Albion Rovers
Elgin City v E Stirling
Montrose v Annan Ath
Peterhead v Stirling A
Queen's P v Berwick R

Saturday December 28, 2013
Albion Rovers v Queen's P
Annan Ath v Elgin City
Berwick R v Peterhead
E Stirling v Montrose
Stirling A v Clyde

Thursday January 2, 2014
Annan Ath v Albion Rovers
Clyde v Queen's P
Montrose v Berwick R
Peterhead v Elgin City
Stirling A v E Stirling

Saturday January 11, 2014
Albion Rovers v Montrose
Berwick R v Annan Ath
E Stirling v Peterhead
Elgin City v Clyde
Queen's P v Stirling A

Saturday January 18, 2014
Annan Ath v Clyde
Berwick R v Stirling A
E Stirling v Albion Rovers
Montrose v Peterhead
Queen's P v Elgin City

Saturday January 25, 2014
Albion Rovers v Berwick R
Clyde v E Stirling
Elgin City v Montrose
Peterhead v Queen's P
Stirling A v Annan Ath

Saturday February 1, 2014
Clyde v Berwick R
Elgin City v Albion Rovers
Montrose v Stirling A
Peterhead v Annan Ath
Queen's P v E Stirling

Saturday February 8, 2014
Albion Rovers v Clyde
Annan Ath v Montrose
Berwick R v Queen's P
E Stirling v Elgin City
Stirling A v Peterhead

Saturday February 15, 2014
Annan Ath v E Stirling
Berwick R v Elgin City
Montrose v Queen's P
Peterhead v Clyde
Stirling A v Albion Rovers

Saturday February 22, 2014
Albion Rovers v Peterhead
Clyde v Montrose
E Stirling v Berwick R
Elgin City v Stirling A
Queen's P v Annan Ath

Saturday March 1, 2014
Annan Ath v Berwick R
Clyde v Elgin City
Montrose v Albion Rovers
Peterhead v E Stirling
Stirling A v Queen's P

Saturday March 8, 2014
Albion Rovers v Annan Ath
Berwick R v Montrose
E Stirling v Stirling A
Elgin City v Peterhead
Queen's P v Clyde

Saturday March 15, 2014
Clyde v Stirling A
Elgin City v Annan Ath
Montrose v E Stirling
Peterhead v Berwick R
Queen's P v Albion Rovers

Saturday March 22, 2014
Albion Rovers v Elgin City
Annan Ath v Peterhead
Berwick R v Clyde
E Stirling v Queen's P
Stirling A v Montrose

Saturday March 29, 2014
Annan Ath v Stirling A
Berwick R v Albion Rovers
E Stirling v Clyde
Montrose v Elgin City
Queen's P v Peterhead

Saturday April 5, 2014
Albion Rovers v E Stirling
Clyde v Annan Ath
Elgin City v Queen's P
Peterhead v Montrose
Stirling A v Berwick R

Saturday April 12, 2014
Albion Rovers v Stirling A
Clyde v Peterhead
E Stirling v Annan Ath
Elgin City v Berwick R
Queen's P v Montrose

Saturday April 19, 2014
Annan Ath v Queen's P
Berwick R v E Stirling
Montrose v Clyde
Peterhead v Albion Rovers
Stirling A v Elgin City

Saturday April 26, 2014
Clyde v Albion Rovers
Elgin City v E Stirling
Montrose v Annan Ath
Peterhead v Stirling A
Queen's P v Berwick R

Saturday May 3 2014
Albion Rovers v Queen's P
Annan Ath v Elgin City
Berwick R v Peterhead
E Stirling v Montrose
Stirling A v Clyde

LEADING EXECUTIVES/SECRETARIES

SCOTTISH FA – S. Regan, Chief Executive, Hampden Park, Glasgow, G42 9AY. Tel: 0141 616 6000. Website: scottishfa.co.uk
ENGLISH FA – Alex Horne, General Secretary, 25 Soho Square, London, W1D 4FA. Tel: 0207 745 4545. Website: thefa.com
ENGLISH PREMIER LEAGUE – R. Scudamore, Chief Executive, 11 Connaught Place, London, W2 2ET. Tel: 0207 298 1600. Website: premierleague.com
ENGLISH FOOTBALL LEAGUE – G. Clarke, Chairman, Edward VII Quay, Navigation Way, Preston, PR2 2YF. Tel: 0844 463 1888. Website: football-league.co.uk
FA OF WALES – J. Ford, Chief Executive, 11 / 12 Neptune Court, Vanguard Way, Cardiff, CF24 5PJ. Tel: 02920 435 830. Website: faw.org.uk
NORTHERN IRELAND FA – J. Shaw, President, 20 Windsor Avenue, Belfast, BT9 6EE. Tel: 02890 669458. Website: irishfa.com
IRISH LEAGUE – B. Jameson, Chairman, Benmore House, Unit 2, 343-353 Lisburn Road, Belfast BT9 7EN. Tel: 028 9066 9559. Website: ifapremiership.com
FA OF IRELAND – J. Delaney, Chief Executive, National Sports Campus, Abbotstown, Dublin 15. Website: fai.ie
FIFA – S. Blatter, President, FIFA House, PO Box 8040, Zurich, Switzerland. 00 4143 222 7777. Website: fifa.com
UEFA – M. Platini, President, Route de Geneve 46, CH-1260 Nyon 2, Switzerland. Tel: 00 41 848 00 2727. Website: uefa.com
PFA SCOTLAND F. Wishart, Chief Executive, Woodside House, 20-23 Woodside Place, Glasgow, G3 7QF. 0141 582 1301. Website: www.pfascotland.co.uk
SCOTTISH JUNIOR FA – T. Johnston, Secretary, Hampden Park, Glasgow, G42 9DD. Tel: 0141 620 4560. Website: www.scottishfa.co.uk/sjfa
WEST OF SCOTLAND REGION – S. Robertson. Secretary. 01698 266 725. Website: www.scottishfa.co.uk/sjfa
SCOTTISH WOMEN'S FA – Ms M. McGonigle, Executive Administrator. Hampden Park, Glasgow G42. Tel: 0141 620 4580.

2012-2013 CLYDESDALE BANK MONTHLY AWARDS

AUGUST

Manager of the Month – Derek Adams (Ross County)
Player of the Month – Leigh Griffiths (Hibernian)
Young Player – Tony Watt (Celtic)

SEPTEMBER

Manager of the Month – Steve Lomas (St Johnstone)
Player of the Month – Michael Higdon (Motherwell)
Young Player – Ryan Fraser (Aberdeen)

OCTOBER

Manager of the Month – Craig Brown (Aberdeen)
Player of the Month – Niall McGinn (Aberdeen)
Young Player – Ryan Fraser (Aberdeen)

NOVEMBER

Manager of the Month – Terry Butcher (Inverness CT)
Player of the Month – Billy McKay (Inverness CT)
Young Player – Aaron Doran (Inverness CT)

DECEMBER

Manager of the Month – Neil Lennon (Celtic)
Player of the Month – Jamie Murphy (Motherwell)
Young Player – Joe Shaughnessy (Aberdeen)

CRAIG BROWN called time on a long career in management after helping Aberdeen to eighth spot

2012-2013 CLYDESDALE BANK MONTHLY AWARDS

JANUARY

Manager of the Month – Derek Adams (Ross County)
Player of the Month – Gary Hooper (Celtic)
Young Player – Adam Matthews (Celtic)

FEBRUARY

Manager of the Month – Derek Adams (Ross County)
Player of the Month – Leigh Griffiths (Hibernian)
Young Player – Stuart Armstrong (Dundee Utd)

MARCH

Manager of the Month – Stuart McCall (Motherwell)
Player of the Month – Nicky Law (Motherwell)
Young Player – Josh Meekings (Inverness CT)

APRIL

Manager of the Month – John Brown (Dundee)
Player of the Month – Michael Higdon (Motherwell)
Young Player – Henrik Ojamaa (Motherwell)

PARTICK THISTLE boss Alan Archibald won two awards after taking over mid-season to guide Jags to the top flight

2012-2013 IRN-BRU MONTHLY AWARDS

AUGUST

Manager of the Month

First Division – Jackie McNamara (Partick Thistle)
Second Division – Allan Johnston (Queen of the South)
Third Division – Jim McInally (Peterhead)
Player of the Month – John Boyle (Airdrie United)
Young Player of the Month – Steven Lawless (Partick Th)

SEPTEMBER

Manager of the Month

First Division – Jim Jefferies (Dunfermline Athletic)
Second Division – Allan Johnston (Queen of the South)
Third Division – Gardner Speirs (Queen's Park))
Player of the Month – David Anderson (Queen's Park)
Young Player of the Month – Archie Campbell (Morton)

OCTOBER

Manager of the Month

First Division – Allan Moore (Morton)
Second Division – Paul Hartley (Alloa)
Third Division – Greig McDonald, Shaun Fagan and Marc McCulloch (Stirling Albion)
Player of the Month – Archie Campbell (Morton)
Young Player of the Month – David Hopkirk (Annan)

NOVEMBER

Manager of the Month

First Division – Billy Reid (Hamilton)
Second Division – Ray McKinnon (Brechin City)
Third Division – Stuart Garden (Montrose)
Player of the Month – Nicky Clark (QoS)
Young Player of the Month – Lewis Macleod (Rangers)

DECEMBER

Manager of the Month

First Division – Allan Moore (Morton)
Second Division – Allan Johnston (QoS)
Third Division – Ally McCoist (Rangers)
Player of the Month – Lyle Taylor (Falkirk)
Young Player of the Month – Aidan Connolly (Queen's P)

2012-2013 IRN-BRU MONTHLY AWARDS

JANUARY

Manager of the Month

First Division – Ian Murray (Dumbarton)
Second Division – Allan Johnston (Queen of the South)
Third Division – Gardner Speirs (Queen's Park)
Player of the Month – Jesus Garcia Tena (Livingston)
Young Player of the Month – Stuart Bannigan (Partick Th)

FEBRUARY

Manager of the Month

First Division – Alan Archibald (Partick Thistle)
Second Division – Martyn Corrigan (Stenhousemuir)
Third Division – Greig McDonald (Stirling Albion)
Player of the Month – Peter MacDonald (Morton)
Young Player of the Month – Martin Boyle (Montrose)

MARCH

Manager of the Month

First Division – Alan Archibald (Partick Thistle)
Second Division – Allan Johnston (Queen of the South)
Third Division – Greig McDonald (Stirling Albion)
Player of the Month – Kris Doolan (Partick Thistle)
Young Player of the Month – Craig Moore (Cowdenbeath)

APRIL

Manager of the Month

First Division – Alex Neil (Hamilton Academical)
Second Division – Martyn Corrigan (Stenhousemuir)
Third Division – Jim McInally (Peterhead)
Player of the Month – Steven May (Hamilton Academical)
Young Player of the Month – Steven May (Hamilton Academical)

PFA SCOTLAND TEAMS OF THE SEASON

PREMIER LEAGUE: Darren Randolph (Motherwell); **Adam Matthews** (Celtic), **Shaun Hutchinson** (Motherwell), **Kelvin Wilson** (Celtic), **Charlie Mulgrew** (Celtic); **Andrew Shinnie** (Inverness CT), **Victor Wanyama** (Celtic), **Nicky Law** (Motherwell); **Niall McGinn** (Aberdeen), **Michael Higdon** (Motherwell), **Leigh Griffiths** (Hibs).

FIRST DIVISION: Scott Fox (Partick Th); **Stephen O'Donnell** (Partick Th), **Jordan McMillan** (Partick Th), **Callum Morris** (Dunfermline), **Aaron Sinclair** (Partick Th); **Stefan Scougall** (Livingston), **Michael Tidser** (Morton), **Stuart Bannigan** (Partick Th); **Brian Graham** (Raith Rovs), **Lyle Taylor** (Falkirk), **Chris Erskine** (Partick Th).

SECOND DIVISION: Lee Robinson (QoS); **Chris Mitchell** (QoS), **Mark Durnan** (QoS), **Ben Gordon** (Alloa), **Chris Higgins** (QoS); **Alan Trouten** (Brechin), **Ryan McCord** (Alloa), **Daniel Carmichael** (QoS); **Andy Jackson** (Brechin), **Nicky Clark** (QoS), **Steven Doris** (Arbroath).

THIRD DIVISION: Jamie Barclay (Clyde); **Stephen McNally** (Montrose), **Ricky Little** (Queen's Park), **Lee McCulloch** (Rangers), **Lee Wallace** (Rangers); **Lee Currie** (Berwick Rangers), **David Anderson** (Queen's Park), **Daniel Moore** (Elgin); **Andrew Little** (Rangers), **Rory McAllister** (Peterhead), **David Templeton** (Rangers).

2012-2013 SFA YOUTH CUP

FIRST ROUND: East Stirling v Civil Service Strollers (walkover for East Stirling), Rangers 2 St Johnstone 1, Clyde 5 Dundee 2.

SECOND ROUND: Arbroath 4 Preston Ath 0, Alloa 2 Queen's Park 7, Rangers 3 Dumbarton 0, Partick Th 3 Spartans 1, Raith Rovers 3 Berwick 0 (aet), Hearts 2 Clyde 1, East Fife 1 Motherwell 0, Cowdenbeath 6 East Stirling 3 (continued/)

2012-2013 SFA YOUTH CUP

Edinburgh City 3 Stirling 2, Huntly 1 Fort William 2, Ross County 6 Clach 0, Brora Rangers 1 Formartine 8, Annan v Threave Rovers (Annan walkover), Stranraer 2 Kilmarnock 6.

THIRD ROUND

Hearts	1	Celtic	2
Hibs	13	Fort William	1
Annan Athletic	w/o	Montrose	..
Edinburgh City	1	Partick Thistle	3
Gala Fairydean	0	Kilmarnock	13
Queen of the South	1	Hamilton	5
Stenhousemuir	1	St Mirren	3
(after extra time)			
Cowdenbeath	2	Airdrie Utd	1
Arbroath	1	Aberdeen	5
Queen's Park	0	Rangers	4
Ross Co	0	Dunfermline	2
Livingston	8	Formartine	0
Dundee Utd	7	Morton	1
Ayr Utd	3	East Fife	0
Raith Rovs	1	Falkirk	3
Fraserburgh	0	Inverness CT	8

FOURTH ROUND

Partick Thistle	0	Inverness CT	6
Dunfermline	10	Montrose	0
Rangers	1	Kilmarnock	5
Aberdeen	4	Hamilton	2
Falkirk	0	St Mirren	0

(after extra time, St Mirren win 5-4 on penalties)

2012-2013 SFA YOUTH CUP

Livingston	2	Cowdenbeath	3
Hibs	2	Celtic	3

(after extra time)

Ayr United	1	Dundee United	2

QUARTER-FINALS

Celtic	2	Aberdeen	0
Dundee United	1	St Mirren	3
Dunfermline	3	Inverness CT	2
Kilmarnock	6	Cowdenbeath	0

SEMI-FINALS

Dunfermline	3	St Mirren	2

(after extra time)

Celtic	1	Kilmarnock	0

FINAL

Celtic	3	Dunfermline	1

SCOTTISH WOMEN'S PREMIER LEAGUE

	P	W	D	L	F	A	Pts
Glasgow City	21	20	0	1	143	10	60
Forfar Farmington	21	14	2	5	50	23	44
Celtic	21	14	1	6	72	19	43
Hibernian	21	14	1	6	80	31	43
Spartans	21	8	2	11	42	49	26
Aberdeen	21	5	1	15	18	94	16
Hamilton	21	10	6	5	74	42	36
Hutchison Vale	21	9	3	9	61	65	30
Rangers	21	7	3	11	37	41	24
Falkirk	21	7	2	12	36	71	23
Inverness City	21	4	3	14	38	87	15
FC Kilmarnock Ladies	21	1	2	18	23	142	5

TOP Division Two scorer Nicky Clark won a move to Rangers as a result of his 32 league strikes

TOP SCORERS – 2012/13

SCOTLAND

Premier League .... Michael Higdon (Motherwell) 26

First Division .... Stevie May (Hamilton) 25

Second Division .... Nicky Clark (Queen of the South) 32

Third Division .... Andy Little (Rangers) 22

ENGLAND

Premier League .... Robin van Persie (Manchester United) 26

Championship .... Glenn Murray (Crystal Palace) 30

League One .... Patrick Madden (Yeovil Town) 23

League Two .... Tom Pope (Port Vale) 31

SPAIN

Primera Liga .... Lionel Messi (Barcelona) 46

ITALY

Serie A .... Edinson Cavani (Napoli) 29

FRANCE

Ligue One .... Zlatan Ibrahimovic (PSG) 29

GERMANY

Bundesliga .... Stefan Kießling (Bayer Leverkusen) 25

CHAMPIONS LEAGUE

Cristiano Ronaldo (Real Madrid) 12

EUROPA LEAGUE

Libor Kozák (Lazio) 10

SCOTLAND MANAGERS

NAME	DATES	P	W	D	L	F	A
Andy Beattie	2/54-6/54	6	2	1	3	6	14
Sir Matt Busby	9/58-12/58	2	1	1	0	5	2
Andy Beattie	3/59-10/60	12	3	3	6	19	23
Ian McColl	11/60-5/65	28	17	3	8	77	52
Jock Stein	5/65-12/65	7	3	1	3	11	11
John Prentice	3/66-9/66	4	0	1	3	4	9
Malcolm McDonald	10/66-11/66	2	1	1	0	3	2
Bobby Brown	2/67-7/71	28	9	8	11	37	35
Tommy Docherty	9/71-12/72	12	7	2	3	17	8
Willie Ormond	1/73-5/77	38	18	8	12	55	38
Ally McLeod	5/77-9/78	17	7	5	5	26	21
Jock Stein	10/78-9/85	61	26	12	23	80	70
Alex Ferguson	10/85-6/86	10	3	4	3	8	5
Andy Roxburgh	7/86-9/93	61	23	19	19	67	60
Craig Brown	11/93-10/01	70	32	18	20	85	60
Berti Vogts	3/02-11/04	31	8	7	16	23	50
Walter Smith	12/04-1/07	16	7	4	5	16	8
Alex McLeish	1/07- 11/07	10	7	0	3	14	9
George Burley	1/08-11/09	14	3	3	8	8	21
Craig Levein	12/09-11/12	24	10	5	9	30	31
Gordon Strachan	01/13-present	4	2	0	2	4	5

RESULTS FOR SEASON 2012/13

(Scotland scores first)

Opponents	Venue	Res	Scorers	Competition
Australia	H	3-1	Rhodes, Davidson (og), McCormack	Friendly
Serbia	H	0-0		World Cup Qualifier
Macedonia	H	1-1	Miller	World Cup Qualifier
Wales	A	1-2	Morrison	World Cup Qualifier
Belgium	A	0-2		World Cup Qualifier
Luxembourg	A	2-1	Rhodes 2	Friendly
Estonia	H	1-0	Mulgrew	Friendly
Wales	H	1-2	Hanley	World Cup Qualifier
Serbia	A	0-2		World Cup Qualifier
Croatia	A	1-0	Snodgrass	World Cup Qualifier

NORWICH ace Robert Snodgrass has progressed from his early days at Livingston to become a full Scotland international and netted the winner against Croatia

ABERDEEN

NICKNAME: The Dons
COLOURS: Red and white
GROUND: Pittodrie
TELEPHONE: 01224 631903
FAX: 01224 644173
WEBSITE: afc.co.uk
CAPACITY: 20,500
RECORD ATT: 45,061 (v Hearts, 1954)
RECORD VICTORY: 13-0 (v Peterhead, 1923)
RECORD DEFEAT: 0-9 (v Celtic, 2010)
MANAGER: Derek McInnes
CHAIRMAN: Stewart Milne
MOST LEAGUE
GOALS (1 SEASON): 38, Benny Yorston, 1929-30
GOALS (OVERALL): 206, Joe Harper

HONOURS

LEAGUE-CHAMPIONSHIP-(4):-Division A -1954-55. Premier Division – 1979-80, 1983-84, 1984-85. SCOTTISH CUP (7): 1947, 1970, 1982, 1983, 1984, 1986, 1990. LEAGUE CUP (5): 1955-56, 1976-77, 1985-86, 1989-90, 1995-96. EUROPEAN CUP-WINNERS' CUP: 1983. EUROPEAN SUPER CUP: 1983-84.

LEAGUE RESULTS 2012-2013

Celtic 1-0 Aberdeen
Aberdeen 0-0 Ross County
St Johnstone 1-2 Aberdeen
Aberdeen 0-0 Hearts
Aberdeen 0-0 St Mirren
Inverness CT 1-1 Aberdeen
Aberdeen 3-3 Motherwell
Aberdeen 2-1 Hibernian
Kilmarnock 1-3 Aberdeen
Dundee Utd 1-1 Aberdeen
Aberdeen 2-0 Dundee
Ross County 2-1 Aberdeen
St Mirren 1-4 Aberdeen
Aberdeen 0-2 Celtic
Hibernian 0-1 Aberdeen
Aberdeen 2-3 Inverness CT
Hearts 2-0 Aberdeen
Aberdeen 0-2 Kilmarnock
Aberdeen 2-0 St Johnstone
Motherwell 4-1 Aberdeen
Dundee 1-3 Aberdeen
Aberdeen 2-2 Dundee Utd
Inverness CT 3-0 Aberdeen
Aberdeen 0-0 Hibernian
St Johnstone 3-1 Aberdeen
Aberdeen 0-0 St Mirren
Aberdeen 1-0 Dundee
Kilmarnock 1-1 Aberdeen
Aberdeen 0-1 Ross County
Aberdeen 0-0 Motherwell
Celtic 4-3 Aberdeen
Aberdeen 2-0 Hearts
Dundee Utd 1-0 Aberdeen
Hibernian 0-0 Aberdeen
Aberdeen 1-0 Kilmarnock
Dundee 1-1 Aberdeen
St Mirren 0-0 Aberdeen
Aberdeen 1-1 Hearts

AIRDRIEONIANS

NICKNAME: The Diamonds
COLOURS: White and red
GROUND: Excelsior Stadium
TELEPHONE No: 07710 230775
FAX No: 0141 221 1497
WEBSITE: airdriefc.com
CAPACITY: 10,170
RECORD ATT: 5924 (v Motherwell, 2007)
RECORD VICTORY: 11-0 (v Gala Fairydean, 2011)
RECORD DEFEAT: 0-7 (v Partick Thistle, 2012)
FOUNDED: 2002
MANAGER: Jimmy Boyle
CHAIRMAN: Jim Ballantyne
MOST LEAGUE GOALS (1 SEASON): 21, Ryan Donnelly, 2011-12

HONOURS

LEAGUE CHAMPIONSHIP: Second Division – 2003-04.
CHALLENGE CUP: 2008-2009.

LEAGUE RESULTS 2012-2013

Airdrie Utd 4-1 Dumbarton
Livingston 0-2 Airdrie Utd
Airdrie Utd 1-2 Dunfermline
Airdrie Utd 0-3 Cowdenbeath
Raith 2-0 Airdrie Utd
Falkirk 1-1 Airdrie Utd
Airdrie Utd 2-3 Morton
Airdrie Utd 0-4 Hamilton
Partick 7-0 Airdrie Utd
Dumbarton 3-4 Airdrie Utd
Airdrie Utd 1-3 Livingston
Cowdenbeath 1-1 Airdrie Utd
Airdrie Utd 0-0 Raith
Morton 2-0 Airdrie Utd
Airdrie Utd 1-4 Falkirk
Hamilton 3-0 Airdrie Utd
Airdrie Utd 1-1 Partick
Airdrie Utd 1-1 Cowdenbeath
Raith 2-0 Airdrie Utd
Dunfermline 1-3 Airdrie Utd
Airdrie Utd 1-2 Dumbarton
Falkirk 4-3 Airdrie Utd
Airdrie Utd 0-4 Morton
Airdrie Utd 2-2 Hamilton
Partick 1-0 Airdrie Utd
Livingston 4-1 Airdrie Utd
Airdrie Utd 3-3 Dunfermline
Cowdenbeath 3-2 Airdrie Utd
Airdrie Utd 1-2 Raith
Airdrie Utd 0-1 Falkirk
Morton 5-2 Airdrie Utd
Hamilton 5-0 Airdrie Utd
Airdrie Utd 1-2 Partick
Dumbarton 4-1 Airdrie Utd
Airdrie Utd 0-2 Livingston
Dunfermline 1-2 Airdrie Utd

ALBION ROVERS

NICKNAME:	Wee Rovers
COLOURS:	Yellow and red
GROUND:	Cliftonhill Stadium
TELEPHONE No:	01236 606334
FAX No:	01236 606334
CAPACITY:	1238
RECORD ATT:	27,381 (v Rangers, 1936)
RECORD VICTORY:	12-0 (v Airdriehill, 1887)
RECORD DEFEAT:	1-11 (v Partick Thistle, 1993)
MANAGER:	James Ward
CHAIRMAN:	Robert Watt
MOST LEAGUE GOALS (1 SEASON):	41, Jim Renwick, 1932-33

HONOURS

LEAGUE CHAMPIONSHIP: Division II – 1933-34. Second Division – 1988-89.

LEAGUE RESULTS 2012-2013

Brechin 1-0 Albion
Albion 0-3 Alloa
Queen of Sth 1-0 Albion
East Fife 1-2 Albion
Albion 2-1 Stranraer
Albion 4-4 Stenh'semuir
Forfar 4-2 Albion
Ayr 2-1 Albion
Albion 4-0 Arbroath
Alloa 5-1 Albion
Albion 0-3 East Fife
Albion 1-2 Brechin
Stranraer 1-1 Albion
Stenh'semuir 1-0 Albion
Albion 2-3 Forfar
Albion 2-0 Ayr
Arbroath 2-1 Albion
Albion 2-3 Stranraer
East Fife 2-0 Albion
Albion 0-3 Queen of Sth
Albion 0-1 Arbroath
Ayr 5-2 Albion
Queen of Sth 3-0 Albion
Forfar 4-2 Albion
Albion 1-5 Alloa
Albion 4-3 Stenh'semuir
Stranraer 3-2 Albion
Albion 1-1 East Fife
Stenh'semuir 0-1 Albion
Albion 1-2 Forfar
Arbroath 2-1 Albion
Albion 1-3 Ayr
Albion 3-1 Brechin
Alloa 4-1 Albion
Brechin 2-0 Albion
Albion 0-1 Queen of Sth

JOHN McGLYNN was sacked as manager of financially-troubled Hearts in season 2012/13

ALLOA

NICKNAME:	The Wasps
COLOURS:	Gold and black
GROUND:	Recreation Park
TELEPHONE No:	01259 722695
FAX No:	01259 210886
WEBSITE:	alloaathletic.co.uk
CAPACITY:	3100
RECORD ATT:	13,000 (v Dunfermline, 1939)
RECORD VICTORY:	9-0 (v Selkirk, 2005)
RECORD DEFEAT:	0-10 (v Dundee, 1937), 0-10 (v Third Lanark, 1953)
MANAGER:	Paul Hartley
CHAIRMAN:	Mike Mulraney
MOST LEAGUE GOALS (1 SEASON):	49, William Crilley, 1921-22

HONOURS

LEAGUE CHAMPIONS: Division II – 1921-22. Third Division – 1997-98, 2011-12. CHALLENGE CUP: 1999-00.

LEAGUE RESULTS 2012-2013

Alloa 1-1 East Fife
Albion 0-3 Alloa
Alloa 2-3 Arbroath
Brechin 1-3 Alloa
Alloa 0-2 Stenh'semuir
Alloa 3-0 Stranraer
Queen of Sth 1-0 Alloa
Forfar 2-3 Alloa
Alloa 1-0 Ayr
Alloa 5-1 Albion
East Fife 0-1 Alloa
Alloa 2-2 Brechin
Stenh'semuir 0-2 Alloa
Alloa 1-0 Queen of Sth
Stranraer 3-2 Alloa
Alloa 2-1 Forfar
Ayr 0-0 Alloa
Alloa 1-0 Stenh'semuir
Brechin 3-2 Alloa
Alloa 1-1 East Fife
Alloa 4-1 Stranraer
Queen of Sth 0-0 Alloa
Alloa 2-2 Ayr
Forfar 0-1 Alloa
Alloa 0-1 Arbroath
Arbroath 1-2 Alloa
Albion 1-5 Alloa
Stenh'semuir 1-1 Alloa
Alloa 0-1 Brechin
Alloa 1-2 Queen of Sth
Stranraer 1-2 Alloa
Ayr 0-2 Alloa
Alloa 1-0 Forfar
East Fife 2-1 Alloa
Alloa 4-1 Albion
Arbroath 0-1 Alloa

ANNAN ATHLETIC

NICKNAME:	Galabankies
COLOURS:	Black and gold
GROUND:	Galabank
TELEPHONE No:	01461 204108
FAX No:	01461 204108
CAPACITY:	3500
RECORD ATT:	2517 (v Rangers, 2012)
RECORD VICTORY:	18-0 (v Newton Stewart, 2004)
RECORD DEFEAT:	2-5 (v Brechin City, 2011)
MANAGER:	Jim Chapman
CHAIRMAN:	Henry McClelland
MOST LEAGUE GOALS (1 SEASON):	15, Mike Jack, 2008-09

LEAGUE RESULTS 2012-2013

Stirling 5-1 Annan
Annan 3-2 Berwick
Montrose 0-0 Annan
Clyde 2-1 Annan
Annan 0-0 Rangers
Annan 2-1 Peterhead
Queen's Park 2-2 Annan
Elgin City 2-2 Annan
Annan 5-2 East Stirling
Annan 5-2 Stirling
Berwick 3-1 Annan
Annan 1-3 Clyde
Annan 2-3 Queen's Park
Peterhead 2-0 Annan
Rangers 3-0 Annan
East Stirling 2-2 Annan
Annan 2-0 Elgin City
Annan 1-3 Rangers
Clyde 2-3 Annan
Annan 2-1 Montrose
Annan 0-0 Peterhead
Queen's Park 2-2 Annan
Elgin City 3-1 Annan
Annan 1-2 East Stirling
Stirling 2-1 Annan
Montrose 5-1 Annan
Annan 2-2 Berwick
Rangers 1-2 Annan
Annan 0-1 Clyde
Peterhead 2-0 Annan
Annan 2-2 Elgin City
Annan 2-0 Queen's Park
East Stirling 1-2 Annan
Annan 0-1 Stirling
Berwick 0-2 Annan
Annan 1-1 Montrose

ARBROATH

NICKNAME:	The Red Lichties
COLOURS:	Maroon and white
GROUND:	Gayfield Park
TELEPHONE No:	01241 872157
FAX No:	01241 431125
WEBSITE:	arbroathfc.co.uk
CAPACITY:	5940
RECORD ATT:	13,510 (v Rangers, 1952)
RECORD VICTORY:	36-0 (v Bon Accord, 1885)
RECORD DEFEAT:	1-9 (v Celtic, 1993)
MANAGER:	Paul Sheerin
CHAIRMAN:	John D Christison
MOST LEAGUE GOALS (1 SEASON):	45, Dave Easson, 1958-59

HONOURS

LEAGUE CHAMPIONS: Third Division – 2010-11

LEAGUE RESULTS 2012-2013

Stranraer 1-1 Arbroath
Arbroath 4-2 Ayr
Alloa 2-3 Arbroath
Queen of Sth 6-0 Arbroath
Arbroath 2-0 East Fife
Arbroath 1-1 Forfar
Stenh'semuir 2-2 Arbroath
Arbroath 3-1 Brechin
Albion 4-0 Arbroath
Ayr 2-0 Arbroath
Arbroath 2-3 Queen of Sth
Arbroath 2-1 Stranraer
East Fife 2-1 Arbroath
Arbroath 2-2 Stenh'semuir
Forfar 1-1 Arbroath
Brechin 3-2 Arbroath
Arbroath 2-1 Albion
Arbroath 1-0 East Fife
Queen of Sth 5-1 Arbroath
Arbroath 3-1 Forfar
Stenh'semuir 1-0 Arbroath
Albion 0-1 Arbroath
Arbroath 0-1 Brechin
Stranraer 2-0 Arbroath
Alloa 0 - 1 Arbroath
Arbroath 1-2 Alloa
Arbroath 1-4 Ayr
East Fife 0-1 Arbroath
Arbroath 1-1 Queen of Sth
Forfar 2-4 Arbroath
Arbroath 0-0 Stenh'semuir
Arbroath 2-1 Albion
Brechin 2-0 Arbroath
Arbroath 1-0 Stranraer
Ayr 0-1 Arbroath
Arbroath 0-1 Alloa

AYR UNITED

NICKNAME: The Honest Men
COLOURS: White and black
GROUND: Somerset Park
TELEPHONE No: 01292 263435
FAX No: 01292 281314
WEBSITE: ayrunitedfc.co.uk
CAPACITY: 10,184
RECORD ATT: 25,225 (v Rangers, 1969)
RECORD VICTORY: 11-1 (v Dumbarton, 1952)
RECORD DEFEAT: 0-9 (v Rangers, 1929; v Hearts, 1931; v Third Lanark, 1954)
MANAGER: Mark Roberts
CHAIRMAN: Lachlan Cameron
MOST LEAGUE GOALS (1 SEASON): 66, Jimmy Smith, 1927-28
GOALS (OVERALL): 213, Peter Price, 1955-61

HONOURS

LEAGUE CHAMPIONS: Division II (6) – 1911-12, 1912-13, 1927-28, 1936-37, 1958-59, 1965-66. Second Division (2) – 1987-88, 1996-97.

LEAGUE RESULTS 2012-2013

Ayr 1-1 Stenh'semuir
Arbroath 4-2 Ayr
Ayr 2-3 Forfar
Stranraer 2-0 Ayr
Ayr 2-4 Queen of Sth
East Fife 2-3 Ayr
Ayr 3-0 Brechin
Ayr 2-1 Albion
Alloa 1-0 Ayr
Ayr 2-0 Arbroath
Stenh'semuir 1-1 Ayr
Ayr 2-1 Stranraer
Queen of Sth 2-0 Ayr
Ayr 2-3 East Fife
Albion 2-0 Ayr
Ayr 0-0 Alloa
Ayr 1-5 Queen of Sth
Stranraer 0-1 Ayr
Forfar 2-1 Ayr
East Fife 3-3 Ayr
Alloa 2-2 Ayr
Ayr 5-2 Albion
Brechin 2-1 Ayr
Ayr 2-1 Forfar
Ayr 1-2 Stenh'semuir
Arbroath 1-4 Ayr
Ayr 1-2 Brechin
Queen of Sth 2-0 Ayr
Ayr 2-1 Stranraer
Brechin 2-1 Ayr
Ayr 2-1 East Fife
Ayr 0-2 Alloa
Albion 1-3 Ayr
Stenh'semuir 4-0 Ayr
Ayr 0-1 Arbroath
Forfar 2-1 Ayr

BERWICK RANGERS

NICKNAME: The Borderers
COLOURS: Black and gold
GROUND: Shielfield Park
TELEPHONE No: 01289 307424
FAX No: 01289 309424
WEBSITE: berwickrangersfc.co.uk
CAPACITY: 4500
RECORD ATT: 13,365 (v Rangers, 1967)
RECORD VICTORY: 8-1 (v Forfar Athletic, 1965; Vale of Leithen, 1966)
RECORD DEFEAT: 1-9 (v Hamilton, 1980)
MANAGER: Ian Little
CHAIRMAN: Brian Porteous
MOST LEAGUE GOALS (1 SEASON): 33, Ken Bowron, 1963-64

HONOURS

LEAGUE CHAMPIONSHIP: Second Division – 1978-79. Third Division – 2006-07.

LEAGUE RESULTS 2012-2013

Berwick 0-0 Elgin City
Annan 3-2 Berwick
Berwick 1-1 Rangers
Berwick 3-0 East Stirling
Montrose 3-1 Berwick
Berwick 4-1 Stirling
Peterhead 1-0 Berwick
Berwick 2-1 Clyde
Queen's Park 1-1 Berwick
Elgin City 3-1 Berwick
Berwick 3-1 Annan
East Stirling 0-1 Berwick
Berwick 1-4 Montrose
Berwick 1-1 Peterhead
Stirling 6-3 Berwick
Clyde 2-1 Berwick
Montrose 1-3 Berwick
Berwick 2-0 East Stirling
Rangers 4-2 Berwick
Peterhead 1-1 Berwick
Berwick 3-3 Clyde
Queen's Park 2-1 Berwick
Berwick 1-3 Rangers
Berwick 2-1 Elgin City
Annan 2-2 Berwick
Berwick 1-0 Stirling
Berwick 4-0 Montrose
Berwick 2-0 Queen's Park
East Stirling 0-3 Berwick
Berwick 0-2 Peterhead
Stirling 1-0 Berwick
Clyde 2-1 Berwick
Berwick 4-1 Queen's Park
Elgin City 1-2 Berwick
Berwick 0-2 Annan
Rangers 1-0 Berwick

BRECHIN CITY

NICKNAME:	The City
COLOURS:	Red and white
GROUND:	Glebe Park
TELEPHONE No:	01356 622856
FAX No:	01356 625667/ 01382 206331
WEBSITE:	brechincity.com
CAPACITY:	3960
RECORD ATT:	8122 (v Aberdeen, 1973)
RECORD VICTORY:	12-1 (v Thornhill, 1926)
RECORD DEFEAT:	0-10 (v Airdrie, Albion Rovers, Cowdenbeath, all 1937-38)
MANAGER:	Ray McKinnon
CHAIRMAN:	Ken Ferguson
MOST LEAGUE GOALS (1 SEASON):	26, W McIntosh, 1959-60

HONOURS

LEAGUE CHAMPIONS: Second Division (3) – 1982-83, 1989-90, 2004-05. Third Division – 2001-02. C Division – 1953-54.

LEAGUE RESULTS 2012-2013

Brechin 1-0 Albion
Stenh'semuir 3-1 Brechin
Brechin 2-1 East Fife
Brechin 1-3 Alloa
Forfar 1-0 Brechin
Brechin 0-3 Queen of Sth
Ayr 3-0 Brechin
Arbroath 3-1 Brechin
Brechin 3-0 Stranraer
Brechin 7-2 Stenh'semuir
Alloa 2-2 Brechin
Albion 1-2 Brechin
Brechin 4-1 Forfar
Queen of Sth 1-0 Brechin
Brechin 3-2 Arbroath
Stranraer 0-2 Brechin
Forfar 1-4 Brechin
Brechin 3-2 Alloa
East Fife 2-2 Brechin
Arbroath 0-1 Brechin
Brechin 2-1 Ayr
Stenh'semuir 3-3 Brechin
Ayr 1-2 Brechin
Alloa 0-1 Brechin
Brechin 2-1 Ayr
Brechin 0-6 Queen of Sth
Queen of Sth 2-1 Brechin
Brechin 6-0 East Fife
Stranraer 3-2 Brechin
Brechin 3-4 Forfar
Brechin 2-0 Arbroath
Albion 3-1 Brechin
Brechin 2-2 Stranraer
Brechin 1-2 Stenh'semuir
Brechin 2-0 Albion
East Fife 0-3 Brechin

CELTIC

NICKNAME: The Bhoys
COLOURS: Green and white
GROUND: Celtic Park
TELEPHONE No: 0871 226 1888
FAX No: 0141 551 4223
WEBSITE: celticfc.net
CAPACITY: 60,506
RECORD ATT: 92,000 (v Rangers, 1938)
RECORD VICTORY: 11-0 (v Dundee, 1895)
RECORD DEFEAT: 0-8 (v Motherwell, 1937)
MANAGER: Neil Lennon
CHIEF EXECUTIVE: Peter Lawwell
MOST LEAGUE
GOALS (1 SEASON): 50, Jimmy McGrory, 1935-36
GOALS (OVERALL): 472, Jimmy McGrory, 1922-37

HONOURS

LEAGUE CHAMPIONS (44): 1892-93, 1893-94, 1895-96, 1897-98, 1904-05, 1905-06, 1906-07, 1907-08, 1908-09, 1909-10, 1913-14, 1914-15, 1915-16, 1916-17, 1918-19, 1921-22, 1925-26, 1935-36, 1937-38, 1953-54, 1965-66, 1966-67, 1967-68, 1968-69, 1969-70, 1970-71, 1971-72, 1972-73, 1973-74, 1976-77, 1978-79, 1980-81, 1981-82, 1985-86, 1987-88, 1997-98, 2000-01, 2001-02, 2003-2004, 2005-2006, 2006-07, 2007-08, 2011-12, 2012-13.

SCOTTISH CUP (36): 1892, 1899, 1900, 1904, 1907, 1908, 1911, 1912, 1914, 1923, 1925, 1927, 1931, 1933, 1937, 1951, 1954, 1965, 1967, 1969, 1971, 1972, 1974, 1975, 1977, 1980, 1985, 1988, 1989, 1995, 2001, 2004, 2005, 2007, 2011, 2013.

LEAGUE CUP (14): 1956-57, 1957-58, 1965-66, 1966-67, 1967-68, 1968-69, 1969-70, 1974-75, 1982-83,1997-98,1999-00, 2000-01, 2005-06, 2008-09.

EUROPEAN CUP: 1966-67.

EFE AMBROSE

KRIS COMMONS

LEAGUE RESULTS 2012-2013

Celtic 1-0 Aberdeen
Ross County 1-1 Celtic
Inverness CT 2-4 Celtic
Celtic 2-2 Hibernian
St Johnstone 2-1 Celtic
Celtic 2-0 Dundee
Motherwell 0-2 Celtic
Celtic 1-0 Hearts
St Mirren 0-5 Celtic
Celtic 0-2 Kilmarnock
Dundee Utd 2-2 Celtic
Celtic 1-1 St Johnstone
Aberdeen 0-2 Celtic
Celtic 0-1 Inverness CT
Hearts 0-4 Celtic
Kilmarnock 1-3 Celtic
Celtic 2-0 St Mirren
Celtic 4-0 Ross County
Dundee 0-2 Celtic
Hibernian 1-0 Celtic
Celtic 1-0 Motherwell
Celtic 4-1 Hearts
Celtic 4-0 Dundee Utd
Celtic 4-1 Kilmarnock
Inverness CT 1-3 Celtic
Celtic 6-2 Dundee Utd
St Johnstone 1-1 Celtic
Celtic 5-0 Dundee
Motherwell 2-1 Celtic
Ross County 3-2 Celtic
Celtic 4-3 Aberdeen
St Mirren 1-1 Celtic
Celtic 3-0 Hibernian
Celtic 4-1 Inverness CT
Motherwell 3-1 Celtic
Ross County 1-1 Celtic
Celtic 4-0 St Johnstone
Dundee Utd 0-4 Celtic

CLYDE

NICKNAME:	The Bully Wee
COLOURS:	White and red
GROUND:	Broadwood Stadium
TELEPHONE No:	01236 451511
FAX No:	01236 733490
WEBSITE:	clydefc.co.uk
CAPACITY:	8029
RECORD ATT:	52,000 (v Rangers, 1908, at Shawfield)
RECORD VICTORY:	11-1 (v Cowdenbeath, 1951)
RECORD DEFEAT:	0-11 (v Dumbarton 1879, Rangers, 1880)
FOUNDED:	1877
MANAGER:	Jim Duffy
CHAIRMAN:	John Alexander
MOST LEAGUE GOALS (1 SEASON):	32, Bill Boyd, 1932-33

HONOURS

LEAGUE CHAMPIONS: Division II (5) – 1904-05, 1951-52, 1956-57, 1961-62, 1972-73. Second Division (4) – 1977-78, 1981-82, 1992-93, 1999-00. SCOTTISH CUP (3): 1939, 1955, 1958.

LEAGUE RESULTS 2012-2013

Montrose 2-3 Clyde
Clyde 0-2 Peterhead
Stirling 0-1 Clyde
Clyde 2-1 Annan
Queen's Park 1-0 Clyde
East Stirling 3-0 Clyde
Clyde 2-2 Elgin City
Berwick 2-1 Clyde
Clyde 0-2 Rangers
Clyde 1-2 Montrose
Peterhead 1-0 Clyde
Annan 1-3 Clyde
Elgin City 2-1 Clyde
Clyde 2-1 East Stirling
Rangers 3-0 Clyde
Clyde 2-1 Berwick
Queen's Park 4-1 Clyde
Clyde 2-3 Annan
Clyde 2-1 Stirling
Montrose 1-1 Clyde
Clyde 1-1 Elgin City
Berwick 3-3 Clyde
Clyde 1-4 Rangers
East Stirling 3-0 Clyde
Stirling 2-0 Clyde
Clyde 0-3 Queen's Park
Clyde 2-0 Peterhead
Clyde 2-3 Queen's Park
Annan 0-1 Clyde
Clyde 2-0 East Stirling
Elgin City 4-2 Clyde
Clyde 2-1 Berwick
Rangers 2-0 Clyde
Clyde 1-0 Montrose
Peterhead 3-0 Clyde
Clyde 1-2 Stirling

COWDENBEATH

NICKNAME:	The Blue Brazil
COLOURS:	Royal blue and white
GROUND:	Central Park
TELEPHONE No:	01383 610166
FAX No:	01383 512132
WEBSITE:	cowdenbeathfc.com
CAPACITY:	4370
RECORD ATT:	25,586 (v Rangers, 1949)
RECORD VICTORY:	12-0 (v Johnstone, 1928)
RECORD DEFEAT:	1-11 (v Clyde, 1951)
FOUNDED:	1881
MANAGER:	Colin Cameron
CHAIRMAN:	Donald Findlay QC
MOST LEAGUE GOALS (1 SEASON):	54, Rab Walls 1938-39
GOALS (OVERALL):	127, Willie Devlin, 1922-26/1929-1930

HONOURS

LEAGUE CHAMPIONSHIP: Division II (3) – 1913-14, 1914-15, 1938-39. Second Division – 2011-12. Third Division – 2005-06.

LEAGUE RESULTS 2012-2013

Cowdenbeath 0-4 Dunfermline
Dumbarton 0-3 Cowdenbeath
Cowdenbeath 1-0 Hamilton
Airdrie Utd 0-3 Cowdenbeath
Cowdenbeath 3-4 Morton
Partick 2-1 Cowdenbeath
Cowdenbeath 1-1 Falkirk
Livingston 1-1 Cowdenbeath
Cowdenbeath 4-4 Raith
Dunfermline 3-0 Cowdenbeath
Cowdenbeath 0-1 Dumbarton
Cowdenbeath 1-1 Airdrie Utd
Morton 1-0 Cowdenbeath
Falkirk 2-0 Cowdenbeath
Cowdenbeath 1-1 Livingston
Raith 2-2 Cowdenbeath
Airdrie Utd 1-1 Cowdenbeath
Cowdenbeath 1-1 Morton
Hamilton 2-1 Cowdenbeath
Partick 2-1 Cowdenbeath
Cowdenbeath 4-1 Falkirk
Cowdenbeath 4-2 Dunfermline
Livingston 3-0 Cowdenbeath
Cowdenbeath 1-1 Raith
Dumbarton 2-2 Cowdenbeath
Cowdenbeath 1-1 Hamilton
Cowdenbeath 3-2 Airdrie Utd
Morton 4-2 Cowdenbeath
Cowdenbeath 0-3 Partick
Cowdenbeath 1-2 Partick
Falkirk 4-0 Cowdenbeath
Cowdenbeath 2-2 Livingston
Raith 0-1 Cowdenbeath
Dunfermline 1-0 Cowdenbeath
Cowdenbeath 2-3 Dumbarton
Hamilton 1-3 Cowdenbeath

DUMBARTON

NICKNAME:	The Sons
COLOURS:	White, gold, and black
GROUND:	The Bet Butler Stadium
TELEPHONE No:	01389 762569
FAX No:	01389 762629
WEBSITE:	dumbartonfootballclub.com
CAPACITY:	2020
RECORD ATT:	18,000 (v Raith Rovers, 1957)
RECORD VICTORY:	13-1 (v Kirkintilloch, 1888)
RECORD DEFEAT:	1-11 (v Albion Rovers, 1926; v Ayr United, 1952)
FOUNDED:	1872
MANAGER:	Ian Murray
CHAIRMAN:	Alan Jardine
GOALS (1 SEASON):	38, Kenny Wilson, 1971-72

HONOURS

LEAGUE CHAMPIONS: Division I (2) – 1890-91 (shared with Rangers), 1891-92. Division II (2) – 1910-11, 1971-72. Second Division – 1991-92. Division 3 – 2008-09. SCOTTISH CUP: 1883.

LEAGUE RESULTS 2012-2013

Airdrie Utd 4-1 Dumbarton
Dumbarton 0-3 Cowdenbeath
Partick 3-0 Dumbarton
Morton 3-0 Dumbarton
Dumbarton 0-2 Dunfermline
Dumbarton 3-3 Hamilton
Livingston 5-0 Dumbarton
Raith 2-2 Dumbarton
Dumbarton 0-2 Falkirk
Dumbarton 3-4 Airdrie Utd
Cowdenbeath 0-1 Dumbarton
Dumbarton 1-5 Morton
Dunfermline 4-0 Dumbarton
Falkirk 3-4 Dumbarton
Morton 0-3 Dumbarton
Dumbarton 0-1 Dunfermline
Dumbarton 2-0 Partick
Airdrie Utd 1-2 Dumbarton
Dumbarton 3-1 Hamilton
Dumbarton 3-4 Livingston
Livingston 2-3 Dumbarton
Raith 3-2 Dumbarton
Dumbarton 0-2 Falkirk
Dumbarton 2-2 Cowdenbeath
Partick 3-0 Dumbarton
Dumbarton 0-3 Morton
Dunfermline 3-4 Dumbarton
Dumbarton 4-2 Raith
Hamilton 2-3 Dumbarton
Hamilton 2-1 Dumbarton
Dumbarton 0-3 Livingston
Dumbarton 1-2 Raith
Falkirk 1-3 Dumbarton
Dumbarton 4-1 Airdrie Utd
Cowdenbeath 2-3 Dumbarton
Dumbarton 0-0 Partick

DUNDEE

NICKNAME:	The Dark Blues
COLOURS:	Dark blue, red and white
GROUND:	Dens Park
TELEPHONE No:	01382 889966
FAX No:	01382 832284
WEBSITE:	dundeefc.co.uk
CAPACITY:	11,200
RECORD ATT:	43,024 (v Rangers, 1953)
RECORD VICTORY:	10-0 (v Alloa, 1957; v Dunfermline, 1957)
RECORD DEFEAT:	0-11 (v Celtic, 1895)
MANAGER:	John Brown
CHIEF EXECUTIVE:	Scot Gardiner
MOST LEAGUE GOALS (1 SEASON):	38, Dave Halliday, 1923-24
GOALS (OVERALL):	113, Alan Gilzean

HONOURS

LEAGUE CHAMPIONS: 1961-62. First Division (3) – 1978-79, 1991-92, 1997-98. Division II – 1946-47. SCOTTISH CUP: 1910. LEAGUE CUP WINNERS (3): 1951-52, 1952-53, 1973-74. CHALLENGE CUP (2): 1990-91, 2009-10.

LEAGUE RESULTS 2012-2013

Kilmarnock 0-0 Dundee
Dundee 0-2 St Mirren
Dundee Utd 3-0 Dundee
Dundee 0-1 Ross County
Hearts 0-1 Dundee
Dundee 1-2 Motherwell
Celtic 2-0 Dundee
Dundee 1-3 St Johnstone
Hibernian 3-0 Dundee
Dundee 1-4 Inverness
Aberdeen 2-0 Dundee
Dundee 1-0 Hearts
Motherwell 1-1 Dundee
Dundee 3-1 Hibernian
St Mirren 3-1 Dundee
Dundee 0-3 Dundee Utd
Ross County 1-1 Dundee
Inverness CT 4-1 Dundee
Dundee 0-2 Celtic
Dundee 1-3 Aberdeen
St Johnstone 1-0 Dundee
Hibernian 1-1 Dundee
Dundee 0-0 Kilmarnock
Hearts 1-0 Dundee
Dundee 0-2 Ross County
Aberdeen 1-0 Dundee
Celtic 5-0 Dundee
Dundee 2-2 St Johnstone
Dundee 2-1 St Mirren
Dundee 1-1 Inverness CT
Dundee Utd 1-1 Dundee
Dundee 0-3 Motherwell
Kilmarnock 1-2 Dundee
St Mirren 1-2 Dundee
Dundee 1-0 Hearts
Dundee 1-1 Aberdeen
Dundee 2-3 Kilmarnock
Hibernian 1-0 Dundee

DUNDEE UNITED

NICKNAME: The Terrors
COLOURS: Tangerine and black
GROUND: Tannadice Park
TELEPHONE No: 01382 833166
FAX No: 01382 889398
WEBSITE: dundeeunitedfc.co.uk
CAPACITY: 14,209
RECORD ATT: 28,000 (v Barcelona, 1966)
RECORD VICTORY: 14-0 (v Nithsdale, 1931)
RECORD DEFEAT: 1-12 (v Motherwell, 1954)
MANAGER: Jackie McNamara
CHAIRMAN: Stephen Thompson
MOST LEAGUE GOALS (1 SEASON): 41, John Coyle, 1955-56
GOALS (OVERALL): 158, Peter Mackay

HONOURS

LEAGUE CHAMPIONS: 1982-83. Division 2 (2) – 1924-25, 1928-29. SCOTTISH CUP (2): 1994, 2010. LEAGUE CUP (2): 1979-80, 1980-81.

LEAGUE RESULTS 2012-2013

Dundee Utd 3-0 Hibernian
Dundee Utd 3-0 Dundee
Kilmarnock 3-1 Dundee Utd
St Johnstone 0-0 Dundee Utd
Dundee Utd 0-0 Ross County
Dundee Utd 0-3 Hearts
Inverness CT 4-0 Dundee Utd
Dundee Utd 1-1 Aberdeen
St Mirren 0-1 Dundee Utd
Dundee Utd 2-2 Celtic
Motherwell 0-1 Dundee Utd
Hibernian 2-1 Dundee Utd
Dundee Utd 3-3 Kilmarnock
Ross County 1-2 Dundee Utd
Dundee Utd 1-2 Motherwell
Dundee 0-3 Dundee Utd
Dundee Utd 4-4 Inverness CT
Hearts 2-1 Dundee Utd
Dundee Utd 1-1 St Johnstone
Dundee Utd 3-4 St Mirren
Aberdeen 2-2 Dundee Utd
Kilmarnock 2-3 Dundee Utd
Celtic 4-0 Dundee Utd
Dundee Utd 1-1 Ross County
Dundee Utd 3-1 Hearts
Celtic 6-2 Dundee Utd
Motherwell 0-1 Dundee Utd
Dundee Utd 2-2 Hibernian
Inverness CT 0-0 Dundee Utd
St Mirren 0-0 Dundee Utd
Dundee Utd 1-1 Dundee
St Johnstone 1-1 Dundee Utd
Dundee Utd 1-0 Aberdeen
Dundee Utd 1-3 Motherwell
Ross County 1-0 Dundee Utd
Dundee Utd 0-1 St Johnstone
Inverness CT 1-2 Dundee Utd
Dundee Utd 0-4 Celtic

DUNFERMLINE

NICKNAME:	The Pars
COLOURS:	Black and white
GROUND:	East End Park
TELEPHONE No:	01383 724295
FAX No:	01383 745949
WEBSITE:	dafc.co.uk
CAPACITY:	11,508
RECORD ATT:	27,816 (v Celtic, 1968)
RECORD VICTORY:	11-2 (v Stenhousemuir, 1930)
RECORD DEFEAT:	0-10 (v Dundee, 1947)
MANAGER:	Jim Jefferies
MOST LEAGUE GOALS (1 SEASON):	53, Bobby Skinner, 1925-26

·D·A·F·C·

HONOURS

LEAGUE CHAMPIONS: Division II – 1925-26. Second Division – 1985-86. First Division (3) – 1988-89, 1995-96, 2010-11. SCOTTISH CUP (2): 1961, 1968.

LEAGUE RESULTS 2012-2013

Cowdenbeath 0-4 Dunfermline
Dunfermline 0-1 Partick
Airdrie Utd 1-2 Dunfermline
Dunfermline 3-1 Raith
Dumbarton 0-2 Dunfermline
Dunfermline 4-0 Livingston
Hamilton 0-3 Dunfermline
Falkirk 2-2 Dunfermline
Dunfermline 2-2 Morton
Dunfermline 3-0 Cowdenbeath
Partick 5-1 Dunfermline
Raith 1-3 Dunfermline
Dunfermline 4-0 Dumbarton
Livingston 2-1 Dunfermline
Dunfermline 1-1 Hamilton
Dunfermline 0-1 Falkirk
Morton 4-2 Dunfermline
Dunfermline 1-0 Raith
Dumbarton 0-1 Dunfermline
Dunfermline 1-3 Airdrie Utd
Dunfermline 0-1 Livingston
Hamilton 1-2 Dunfermline
Cowdenbeath 4-2 Dunfermline
Falkirk 1-0 Dunfermline
Dunfermline 1-4 Morton
Dunfermline 0-4 Partick
Airdrie Utd 3-3 Dunfermline
Raith 1-1 Dunfermline
Dunfermline 3-4 Dumbarton
Dunfermline 0-2 Falkirk
Livingston 2-2 Dunfermline
Dunfermline 2-3 Hamilton
Morton 0-1 Dunfermline
Dunfermline 1-0 Cowdenbeath
Partick 3-3 Dunfermline
Dunfermline 1-2 Airdrie Utd

EAST FIFE

NICKNAME: The Fifers/The Fife
COLOURS: Black and gold
GROUND: Bayview Stadium
TELEPHONE No: 01333 426323
FAX No: 01333 426376
WEBSITE: eastfifefc.com
CAPACITY: 1992
RECORD ATT: 22,515 (v Raith Rovers,1950)
RECORD VICTORY: 13-2 (v Edinburgh City, 1937)
RECORD DEFEAT: 0-9 (v Hearts, 1957)
MANAGER: Willie Aitchison
MANAGING DIRECTOR: Lee Murray
MOST LEAGUE GOALS (1 SEASON): 42, Jock Wood, 1926-27

HONOURS

LEAGUE CHAMPIONSHIP: Division II – 1947-48. Third Division – 2007-08. SCOTTISH CUP: 1938. LEAGUE CUP (3): 1947-48, 1949-50, 1953-54.

LEAGUE RESULTS 2012-2013

Alloa 1-1 East Fife
East Fife 0-0 Queen of Sth
Brechin 2-1 East Fife
East Fife 1-2 Albion
Arbroath 2-0 East Fife
East Fife 2-3 Ayr
Stranraer 2-6 East Fife
Stenh'semuir 3-0 East Fife
East Fife 3-0 Forfar
Queen of Sth 1-0 East Fife
East Fife 0-1 Alloa
Albion 0-3 East Fife
East Fife 2-1 Arbroath
Ayr 2-3 East Fife
East Fife 0-1 Stranraer
East Fife 3-2 Stenh'semuir
Forfar 3-2 East Fife
Arbroath 1-0 East Fife
East Fife 2-0 Albion
East Fife 2-2 Brechin
Alloa 1-1 East Fife
East Fife 3-3 Ayr
Stranraer 3-1 East Fife
East Fife 1-2 Forfar
Stenh'semuir 2-1 East Fife
East Fife 2-3 Queen of Sth
East Fife 0-1 Arbroath
Albion 1-1 East Fife
Ayr 2-1 East Fife
Brechin 6-0 East Fife
Forfar 3-2 East Fife
East Fife 1-1 Stranraer
East Fife 1-2 Stenh'semuir
East Fife 2-1 Alloa
Queen of Sth 2-2 East Fife
East Fife 0-3 Brechin

EAST STIRLINGSHIRE

NICKNAME:	The Shire
COLOURS:	Black and white
GROUND:	Ochilview Park
TELEPHONE No:	01324 629942
FAX No:	01324 629942
WEBSITE:	eaststirlingshirefc.co.uk
CAPACITY:	2654
RECORD ATT:	12,000 (v Partick Thistle, 1921)
RECORD VICTORY:	11-2 (v Vale of Bannock, 1888)
RECORD DEFEAT:	1-12 (v Dundee United, 1936)
MANAGER:	John Coughlin
CHAIRMAN:	Tony Ford
MOST LEAGUE GOALS (1 SEASON):	36, Malcolm Morrison, 1938-39

EAST STIRLINGSHIRE F.C. EST. 1881

HONOURS

LEAGUE CHAMPIONSHIP: Division II – 1931-32. C Division – 1947-48.

LEAGUE RESULTS 2012-2013

East Stirling 0-2 Queen's Park
Rangers 5-1 East Stirling
East Stirling 1-4 Elgin City
Berwick 3-0 East Stirling
East Stirling 3-1 Stirling
East Stirling 3-0 Clyde
Montrose 3-1 East Stirling
East Stirling 2-1 Peterhead
Annan 5-2 East Stirling
Queen's Park 1-2 East Stirling
East Stirling 2-6 Rangers
East Stirling 0-1 Berwick
Clyde 2-1 East Stirling
East Stirling 2-2 Montrose
East Stirling 2-2 Annan
Peterhead 2-0 East Stirling
East Stirling 1-1 Stirling
Berwick 2-0 East Stirling
Elgin City 3-4 East Stirling
East Stirling 0-2 Queen's Park
Montrose 2-2 East Stirling
East Stirling 2-4 Peterhead
Stirling 1-1 East Stirling
Annan 1-2 East Stirling
East Stirling 3-0 Clyde
East Stirling 3-2 Elgin City
Rangers 3-1 East Stirling
Stirling 9-1 East Stirling
East Stirling 0-3 Berwick
East Stirling 1-2 Montrose
Clyde 2-0 East Stirling
Peterhead 6-0 East Stirling
East Stirling 1-2 Annan
Queen's Park 5-1 East Stirling
East Stirling 2-4 Rangers
Elgin City 3-2 East Stirling

ELGIN CITY

NICKNAME:	The City or Black & Whites
COLOURS:	Black and white
GROUND:	Borough Briggs
TELEPHONE No:	01343 551114
FAX No:	01343 547921
WEBSITE:	elgincity.com
CAPACITY:	3716
RECORD ATT:	12,608 (v Arbroath,1968)
RECORD VICTORY:	18-1 (v Brora Rangers, 1960)
RECORD DEFEAT:	1-14 (v Hearts, 1939)
MANAGER:	Ross Jack
CHAIRMAN:	Graham Tatters
MOST LEAGUE GOALS (1 SEASON):	66, Willie Grant, 1960-61

LEAGUE RESULTS 2012-2013

Berwick 0-0 Elgin City
Elgin City 3-1 Stirling
East Stirling 1-4 Elgin City
Rangers 5-1 Elgin City
Elgin City 2-0 Peterhead
Elgin City 0-4 Queen's Park
Elgin City 6-1 Montrose
Clyde 2-2 Elgin City
Elgin City 2-2 Annan
Montrose 2-2 Elgin City
Elgin City 3-1 Berwick
Stirling 1-4 Elgin City
Peterhead 1-1 Elgin City
Elgin City 2-1 Clyde
Queen's Park 1-1 Elgin City
Elgin City 2-6 Rangers
Annan 2-0 Elgin City
Elgin City 0-3 Peterhead
Rangers 1-1 Elgin City
Elgin City 3-4 East Stirling
Clyde 1-1 Elgin City
Elgin City 3-1 Annan
Montrose 4-1 Elgin City
East Stirling 3-2 Elgin City
Berwick 2-1 Elgin City
Elgin City 1-2 Stirling
Elgin City 3-5 Queen's Park
Peterhead 0-1 Elgin City
Elgin City 0-1 Rangers
Queen's Park 0-1 Elgin City
Elgin City 4-2 Clyde
Annan 2-2 Elgin City
Elgin City 3-2 Montrose
Elgin City 1-2 Berwick
Stirling 1-1 Elgin City
Elgin City 3-2 East Stirling

FALKIRK

NICKNAME:	The Bairns
COLOURS:	Navy blue and white
GROUND:	The Falkirk Stadium
TELEPHONE No:	01324 624121
FAX No:	01324 612418
WEBSITE:	falkirkfc.co.uk
CAPACITY:	8750
RECORD ATT:	23,100 (v Celtic, 1953)
RECORD VICTORY:	12-1 (v Laurieston, 1893)
RECORD DEFEAT:	1-11 (v Airdrie, 1951)
MANAGER:	Gary Holt
CHAIRMAN:	Martin Ritchie
MOST LEAGUE GOALS (1 SEASON):	43, Evelyn Morrison, 1928-29
GOALS (OVERALL):	243, Kenny Dawson, 1934-51

Est. 1876

HONOURS

LEAGUE CHAMPIONS: Division II (3) – 1935-36, 1969-70, 1974-75. First Division (4) – 1990-91, 1993-94, 2002-03, 2004-05. Second Division – 1979-80. SCOTTISH CUP (2): 1913, 1957. CHALLENGE CUP (4): 1993-94, 1997-98, 2004-05, 2011-12.

LEAGUE RESULTS 2012-2013

Partick 3-1 Falkirk
Falkirk 0-2 Raith
Morton 1-2 Falkirk
Falkirk 1-2 Livingston
Hamilton 1-1 Falkirk
Falkirk 1-1 Airdrie Utd
Cowdenbeath 1-1 Falkirk
Falkirk 2-2 Dunfermline
Dumbarton 0-2 Falkirk
Falkirk 0-0 Partick
Raith 2-1 Falkirk
Livingston 2-1 Falkirk
Falkirk 2-1 Hamilton
Falkirk 2-0 Cowdenbeath
Airdrie Utd 1-4 Falkirk
Dunfermline 0-1 Falkirk
Falkirk 3-4 Dumbarton
Hamilton 1-1 Falkirk
Falkirk 0-1 Morton
Partick 4-1 Falkirk
Falkirk 4-3 Airdrie Utd
Cowdenbeath 4-1 Falkirk
Falkirk 1-0 Dunfermline
Falkirk 2-0 Livingston
Dumbarton 0-2 Falkirk
Falkirk 1-1 Raith
Morton 2-0 Falkirk
Falkirk 0-2 Hamilton
Dunfermline 0-2 Falkirk
Airdrie Utd 0-1 Falkirk
Livingston 1-2 Falkirk
Falkirk 4-0 Cowdenbeath
Falkirk 1-3 Dumbarton
Falkirk 0-2 Partick
Raith 0-0 Falkirk
Falkirk 4-1 Morton

ALLY McCOIST with ex-Rangers chief executive Charles Green after unveiling a new sponsorship deal

FORFAR ATHLETIC

NICKNAME:	The Loons
COLOURS:	Sky/navy
GROUND:	Station Park
TELEPHONE:	01307 463576
FAX:	01307 466956
WEBSITE:	forfarathletic.co.uk
CAPACITY:	5177
RECORD ATT:	10,780 (v Rangers, 1970)
RECORD VICTORY:	14-1 (v Lindertis, 1888)
RECORD DEFEAT:	2-12 (v King's Park, 1930)
MANAGER:	Dick Campbell
CHAIRMAN:	Alastair Donald
MOST LEAGUE GOALS (1 SEASON):	45, Dave Kilgour, 1929-30

HONOURS

LEAGUE CHAMPIONSHIP: Second Division – 1983-84. Third Division – 1994-95.

LEAGUE RESULTS 2012-2013

Queen of Sth 2-0 Forfar
Forfar 4-0 Stranraer
Ayr 2-3 Forfar
Stenh'semuir 0-4 Forfar
Forfar 1-0 Brechin
Arbroath 1-1 Forfar
Forfar 4-2 Albion
Forfar 2-3 Alloa
East Fife 3-0 Forfar
Stranraer 4-1 Forfar
Forfar 3-2 Stenh'semuir
Forfar 1-5 Queen of Sth
Brechin 4-1 Forfar
Forfar 1-1 Arbroath
Albion 2-3 Forfar
Alloa 2-1 Forfar
Forfar 3-2 East Fife
Forfar 1-4 Brechin
Stenh'semuir 2-0 Forfar
Forfar 2-1 Ayr
Queen of Sth 3-1 Forfar
Arbroath 3-1 Forfar
East Fife 1-2 Forfar
Forfar 0-1 Alloa
Ayr 2-1 Forfar
Forfar 4-2 Albion
Forfar 3-1 Stranraer
Forfar 3-3 Stenh'semuir
Forfar 2-4 Arbroath
Albion 1-2 Forfar
Forfar 3-2 East Fife
Brechin 3-4 Forfar
Alloa 1-0 Forfar
Forfar 0-4 Queen of Sth
Stranraer 0-3 Forfar
Forfar 2-1 Ayr

HAMILTON ACCIES

NICKNAME:	The Accies
COLOURS:	Red and white
GROUND:	New Douglas Park
TELEPHONE No:	01698 368652
FAX No:	01698 285422
WEBSITE:	acciesfc.co.uk
CAPACITY:	6014
RECORD ATT:	28,690 (v Hearts, 1937)
RECORD VICTORY:	11-1 (v Chryston, 1885)
RECORD DEFEAT:	1-11 (v Hibs, 1965)
MANAGER:	Alex Neil
CHAIRMAN:	Les Gray
MOST LEAGUE GOALS (1 SEASON):	35, David Wilson, 1936-37

HAMILTON ACADEMICAL FOOTBALL CLUB 1874

HONOURS

LEAGUE CHAMPIONS (3): First Division: 1985-86, 1987-88, 2007-08. Second Division: 1903-04. Third Division: 2000-01. CHALLENGE CUP (2); 1991-92, 1992-93.

LEAGUE RESULTS 2012-2013

Raith 2-0 Hamilton
Hamilton 1-1 Morton
Cowdenbeath 1-0 Hamilton
Partick 4-0 Hamilton
Hamilton 1-1 Falkirk
Dumbarton 3-3 Hamilton
Hamilton 0-3 Dunfermline
Airdrie Utd 0-4 Hamilton
Hamilton 1-2 Livingston
Hamilton 0-1 Raith
Morton 0-1 Hamilton
Hamilton 1-0 Partick
Falkirk 2-1 Hamilton
Dunfermline 1-1 Hamilton
Hamilton 3-0 Airdrie Utd
Hamilton 1-1 Falkirk
Hamilton 2-1 Cowdenbeath
Raith 0-2 Hamilton
Dumbarton 3-1 Hamilton
Hamilton 1-2 Dunfermline
Airdrie Utd 2-2 Hamilton
Partick 1-0 Hamilton
Hamilton 1-1 Livingston
Hamilton 2-1 Morton
Cowdenbeath 1-1 Hamilton
Hamilton 0-2 Partick
Falkirk 0-2 Hamilton
Hamilton 2-3 Dumbarton
Hamilton 2-1 Dumbarton
Dunfermline 2-3 Hamilton
Hamilton 5-0 Airdrie Utd
Livingston 0-3 Hamilton
Livingston 0-0 Hamilton
Hamilton 2-0 Raith
Morton 0-2 Hamilton
Hamilton 1-3 Cowdenbeath

HEART OF MIDLOTHIAN

NICKNAME: The Jambos
COLOURS: Maroon and white
GROUND: Tynecastle Park
TELEPHONE No: 0871 663 1874
FAX No: 0131 200 7222
WEBSITE: heartsfc.co.uk
CAPACITY: 17,420
RECORD ATT: 53,396 (v Rangers, 1932)
RECORD VICTORY: 21-0 (v Anchor, 1880)
RECORD DEFEAT: 1-8 (v Vale of Leven, 1882)
MANAGER: Gary Locke
CHAIRMAN: Roman Romanov
MOST LEAGUE
GOALS (1 SEASON): 44, Barney Battles
GOALS (OVERALL): 214, John Robertson

HONOURS

LEAGUE CHAMPIONS: Division I (4) – 1894-95, 1896-97, 1957-58, 1959-60. First Division – 1979-80. SCOTTISH CUP (8): 1891, 1896, 1901, 1906, 1956, 1998, 2006, 2012. LEAGUE CUP (4): 1954-55, 1958-59, 1959-60, 1962-63.

LEAGUE RESULTS 2012-2013

Hearts 2-0 St Johnstone
Hibernian 1-1 Hearts
Hearts 2-2 Inverness CT
Aberdeen 0-0 Hearts
Hearts 0-1 Dundee
St Mirren 2-0 Hearts
Dundee Utd 0-3 Hearts
Hearts 1-3 Kilmarnock
Celtic 1-0 Hearts
Hearts 1-0 Motherwell
Hearts 2-2 Ross County
Dundee 1-0 Hearts
Inverness CT 1-1 Hearts
Hearts 1-0 St Mirren
Motherwell 0-0 Hearts
Hearts 0-4 Celtic
Hearts 2-0 Aberdeen
St Johnstone 2-2 Hearts
Hearts 2-1 Dundee Utd
Kilmarnock 1-0 Hearts
Hearts 0-0 Hibernian
Celtic 4-1 Hearts
Hearts 1-0 Dundee
Ross County 2-2 Hearts
Dundee Utd 3-1 Hearts
Hearts 0-3 Kilmarnock
Hearts 2-3 Inverness CT
St Mirren 2-0 Hearts
Hearts 1-2 Motherwell
Hearts 2-0 St Johnstone
Hibernian 0-0 Hearts
Aberdeen 2-0 Hearts
Hearts 4-2 Ross County
Kilmarnock 0-1 Hearts
Dundee 1-0 Hearts
Hearts 3-0 St Mirren
Hearts 1-2 Hibernian
Aberdeen 1-1 Hearts

HIBERNIAN

NICKNAME: The Hibees
COLOURS: Green and white
GROUND: Easter Road
TELEPHONE No: 0131 661 2159
FAX No: 0131 659 6488
WEBSITE: hibernianfc.co.uk
CAPACITY: 20,400
RECORD ATT: 65,860 (v Hearts, 1950)
RECORD VICTORY: 22-1 (v 42nd Highlanders, 1881)
RECORD DEFEAT: 0-10 (v Rangers, 1898)
MANAGER: Pat Fenlon
CHAIRMAN: Rod Petrie
MOST LEAGUE
GOALS (1 SEASON): 42, Joe Baker
GOALS (OVERALL): 364, Gordon Smith

HONOURS

LEAGUE CHAMPIONS: Division I (4) – 1902-03, 1947-48, 1950-51,1951-52. Division II (3) – 1893-94, 1894-94, 1932-33. First Division (2) – 1980-81, 1998-99. SCOTTISH CUP (2): 1887, 1902. LEAGUE CUP (3): 1972-73, 1991-92, 2006-07.

LEAGUE RESULTS 2012-2013

Dundee Utd 3-0 Hibernian
Hibernian 1-1 Hearts
St Mirren 1-2 Hibernian
Hibernian 2-0 St Johnstone
Celtic 2-2 Hibernian
Hibernian 2-1 Kilmarnock
Hibernian 2-2 Inverness CT
Aberdeen 2-1 Hibernian
Hibernian 3-0 Dundee
Ross County 3-2 Hibernian
Motherwell 0-4 Hibernian
Hibernian 2-1 St Mirren
Hibernian 2-1 Dundee Utd
Dundee 3-1 Hibernian
Hibernian 0-1 Aberdeen
St Johnstone 0-1 Hibernian
Inverness CT 3-0 Hibernian
Hibernian 2-3 Motherwell
Kilmarnock 1-1 Hibernian
Hibernian 0-1 Ross County
Hibernian 1-0 Celtic
Hearts 0-0 Hibernian
Hibernian 1-1 Dundee
Aberdeen 0-0 Hibernian
Ross County 1-0 Hibernian
Hibernian 1-3 St Johnstone
St Mirren 0-1 Hibernian
Dundee Utd 2-2 Hibernian
Hibernian 2-2 Kilmarnock
Hibernian 0-0 Hearts
Motherwell 4-1 Hibernian
Hibernian 1-2 Inverness CT
Celtic 3-0 Hibernian
Hibernian 0-0 Aberdeen
Hibernian 3-3 St Mirren
Hearts 1-2 Hibernian
Kilmarnock 1-3 Hibernian
Hibernian 1-0 Dundee

INVERNESS CT

NICKNAME: Caley Thistle
COLOURS: Blue and red
GROUND: Tulloch Caledonian Stadium
TELEPHONE No: 01463 222880
FAX No: 01463 227479
WEBSITE: ictfc.co.uk
CAPACITY: 7812
RECORD ATT: 7753 (v Rangers, 2008)
RECORD VICTORY: 8-1 (v Annan Athletic, 1998)
RECORD DEFEAT: 0-6 (v Airdrie, 2001)
MANAGER: Terry Butcher
CHAIRMAN: Kenny Cameron
MOST LEAGUE GOALS (1 SEASON): 29, Iain Stewart, 1996-97

HONOURS

LEAGUE CHAMPIONS: Third Division - 1996-97. First Division (2) - 2003-04, 2009-10. CHALLENGE CUP - 2003-04.

LEAGUE RESULTS 2012-2013

St Mirren 2-2 Inverness CT
Inverness CT 1-1 Kilmarnock
Hearts 2-2 Inverness CT
Inverness CT 2-4 Celtic
Motherwell 4-1 Inverness CT
Inverness CT 1-1 Aberdeen
Hibernian 2-2 Inverness CT
Inverness CT 4-0 Dundee Utd
Inverness CT 3-1 Ross County
Dundee 1-4 Inverness CT
Inverness CT 1-1 St Johnstone
Kilmarnock 1-2 Inverness CT
Inverness CT 1-1 Hearts
Inverness CT 1-5 Motherwell
Celtic 0-1 Inverness CT
Aberdeen 2-3 Inverness CT
Inverness CT 3-0 Hibernian
Dundee Utd 4-4 Inverness CT
Inverness CT 4-1 Dundee
Inverness CT 2-2 St Mirren
St Johnstone 0-0 Inverness CT
Inverness CT 3-0 Aberdeen
St Mirren 2-1 Inverness CT
Inverness CT 1-3 Celtic
Inverness CT 1-1 Kilmarnock
Motherwell 3-0 Inverness CT
Hearts 2-3 Inverness CT
Inverness CT 0-0 Dundee Utd
Ross County 0-0 Inverness CT
Dundee 1-1 Inverness CT
Inverness CT 2-1 Ross County
Hibernian 1-2 Inverness CT
Inverness CT 0-0 St Johnstone
Celtic 4-1 Inverness CT
St Johnstone 1-0 Inverness CT
Inverness CT 4-3 Motherwell
Inverness CT 1-2 Dundee Utd
Ross County 1-0 Inverness CT

KILMARNOCK

NICKNAME:	Killie
COLOURS:	Blue and white
GROUND:	Rugby Park
TELEPHONE No:	01563 545300
FAX No:	01563 522181
WEBSITE:	kilmarnockfc.co.uk
CAPACITY:	18,128
RECORD ATT:	35,995 (v Rangers, 1962)
RECORD VICTORY:	11-1 (v Paisley Academical, 1930)
RECORD DEFEAT:	1-9 (v Celtic, 1938)
MANAGER:	Vacant
CHAIRMAN:	Michael Johnston
MOST LEAGUE	
GOALS (1 SEASON):	34, Harry Cunningham, 1927-28
GOALS (OVERALL):	148, W Culley, 1912-23

CONFIDEMUS
KILMARNOCK F.C.

HONOURS

LEAGUE CHAMPIONS: Division I – 1964-65. Division II (2) – 1897-98, 1898-99. SCOTTISH CUP (3): 1920, 1929, 1997. LEAGUE CUP: 2011-12.

LEAGUE RESULTS 2012-2013

Kilmarnock 0-0 Dundee
Inverness CT 1-1 Kilmarnock
Kilmarnock 1-2 Motherwell
Kilmarnock 3-1 Dundee Utd
Ross County 0-0 Kilmarnock
Hibernian 2-1 Kilmarnock
Kilmarnock 3-1 St Mirren
Hearts 1-3 Kilmarnock
Kilmarnock 1-3 Aberdeen
St Johnstone 2-1 Kilmarnock
Celtic 0-2 Kilmarnock
Kilmarnock 1-2 Inverness
Kilmarnock 3-0 Ross County
Dundee Utd 3-3 Kilmarnock
Kilmarnock 1-2 St Johnstone
Kilmarnock 1-3 Celtic
Aberdeen 0-2 Kilmarnock
Kilmarnock 1-1 Hibernian
Kilmarnock 1-0 Hearts
Motherwell 2-2 Kilmarnock
St Mirren 1-1 Kilmarnock
Kilmarnock 2-3 Dundee Utd
Dundee 0-0 Kilmarnock
Celtic 4-1 Kilmarnock
Kilmarnock 2-0 Motherwell
Inverness CT 1-1 Kilmarnock
Hearts 0-3 Kilmarnock
Kilmarnock 1-1 Aberdeen
Hibernian 2-2 Kilmarnock
St Johnstone 2-0 Kilmarnock
Ross County 0-1 Kilmarnock
Kilmarnock 1-1 St Mirren
Kilmarnock 1-2 Dundee
Kilmarnock 0-1 Hearts
Aberdeen 1-0 Kilmarnock
Dundee 2-3 Kilmarnock
Kilmarnock 1-3 Hibernian
Kilmarnock 1-3 St Mirren

LIVINGSTON

NICKNAME:	Livi Lions
COLOURS:	Amber and Black
GROUND:	Almondvale Stadium
TELEPHONE No:	01506 417000
FAX No:	01506 429948
WEBSITE:	livingstonfc.co.uk
CAPACITY:	10,122
RECORD ATT:	10,112 (v Rangers, 2001)
RECORD VICTORY:	8-0 (v Stranraer, 2012)
RECORD DEFEAT:	0-8 (v Hamilton Accies, 1974)
MANAGER:	Richie Burke
CHAIRMAN:	Gordon McDougall
MOST LEAGUE GOALS (1 SEASON):	22, Iain Russell, 2010-11

HONOURS

LEAGUE CHAMPIONS: Third Division (2) – 1995-96, 2009-10. Second Division (3) – 1986-87, 1998-99, 2010-11. First Division – 2000-01. LEAGUE CUP: 2003-04.

LEAGUE RESULTS 2012-2013

Morton 2-2 Livingston
Livingston 0-2 Airdrie Utd
Raith 0-0 Livingston
Falkirk 1-2 Livingston
Livingston 1-2 Partick
Dunfermline 4-0 Livingston
Livingston 5-0 Dumbarton
Livingston 1-1 Cowdenbeath
Hamilton 1-2 Livingston
Livingston 2-2 Morton
Airdrie Utd 1-3 Livingston
Livingston 2-1 Falkirk
Partick 2-0 Livingston
Livingston 2-1 Dunfermline
Cowdenbeath 1-1 Livingston
Livingston 2-2 Partick
Livingston 2-1 Raith
Morton 2-1 Livingston
Dunfermline 0-1 Livingston
Dumbarton 3-4 Livingston
Livingston 2-3 Dumbarton
Livingston 3-0 Cowdenbeath
Falkirk 2-0 Livingston
Hamilton 1-1 Livingston
Livingston 4-1 Airdrie Utd
Raith 0-2 Livingston
Partick 6-1 Livingston
Livingston 2-2 Dunfermline
Livingston 1-2 Falkirk
Dumbarton 0-3 Livingston
Cowdenbeath 2-2 Livingston
Livingston 0-3 Hamilton
Livingston 0-0 Hamilton
Livingston 0-2 Morton
Airdrie Utd 0-2 Livingston
Livingston 2-3 Raith

SAINTS captain Jim Goodwin roars with delight as he raises the Scottish Communities League Cup after Danny Lennon's side beat SPL rivals Hearts

MONTROSE

NICKNAME:	The Gable Endies
COLOURS:	Blue and white
GROUND:	Links Park Stadium
TELEPHONE No:	01674 673200
FAX No:	01674 677311
WEBSITE:	montrosefc.co.uk
CAPACITY:	4936
RECORD ATT:	8983 (v Dundee, 1973)
RECORD VICTORY:	12-0 (v Vale of Leithen, 1975)
RECORD DEFEAT:	0-13 (v Aberdeen, 1951)
MANAGER:	Stuart Garden
CHAIRMAN:	Derek Sim
MOST LEAGUE GOALS (1 SEASON):	28, Brian Third, 1972-73

HONOURS

LEAGUE CHAMPIONSHIP: Second Division – 1984-85

LEAGUE RESULTS 2012-2013

Montrose 2-3 Clyde
Queen's Park 2-2 Montrose
Montrose 0-0 Annan
Peterhead 2-0 Montrose
Montrose 3-1 Berwick
Rangers 4-1 Montrose
Montrose 3-1 East Stirling
Elgin City 6-1 Montrose
Stirling 1-3 Montrose
Montrose 2-2 Elgin City
Clyde 1-2 Montrose
Montrose 1-1 Queen's Park
Montrose 2-0 Peterhead
Berwick 1-4 Montrose
Montrose 2-4 Rangers
East Stirling 2-2 Montrose
Montrose 3-2 Stirling
Montrose 1-3 Berwick
Peterhead 0-1 Montrose
Annan 2-1 Montrose
Montrose 1-1 Clyde
Rangers 1-1 Montrose
Montrose 2-2 East Stirling
Stirling 3-1 Montrose
Montrose 4-1 Elgin City
Montrose 5-1 Annan
Queen's Park 1-2 Montrose
Berwick 4-0 Montrose
Montrose 0-6 Peterhead
East Stirling 1-2 Montrose
Montrose 0-0 Rangers
Montrose 2-2 Stirling
Elgin City 3-2 Montrose
Clyde 1-0 Montrose
Montrose 1-2 Queen's Park
Annan 1-1 Montrose

CELTIC manager Neil Lennon led the team to a league and cup double in 2012/13

MORTON

NICKNAME: The Ton
COLOURS: Blue and white
GROUND: Cappielow Park
TELEPHONE No: 01475 723571
FAX No: 01475 781084
WEBSITE: gmfc.net
CAPACITY: 11,841
RECORD ATT: 23,500 (v Celtic, 1922)
RECORD VICTORY: 11-0 (v Carfin Shamrock, 1886)
RECORD DEFEAT: 1-10 (v Port Glasgow Athletic, 1894; v St Bernard's, 1933)
MANAGER: Allan Moore
CHAIRMAN: Douglas Rae
MOST LEAGUE GOALS (1 SEASON): 58, Allan McGraw, 1963-64

HONOURS

LEAGUE CHAMPIONS: First Division (3) – 1977-78, 1983-84, 1986-87. Division II (3) – 1949-50, 1963-64, 1966-67. Second Division (2)– 1994-95, 2006-07. Third Division – 2002-03. SCOTTISH CUP: 1922.

LEAGUE RESULTS 2012-2013

Morton 2-2 Livingston
Hamilton 1-1 Morton
Morton 1-2 Falkirk
Morton 3-0 Dumbarton
Cowdenbeath 3-4 Morton
Morton 1-0 Raith
Airdrie Utd 2-3 Morton
Morton 3-1 Partick
Dunfermline 2-2 Morton
Livingston 2-2 Morton
Morton 0-1 Hamilton
Dumbarton 1-5 Morton
Morton 1-0 Cowdenbeath
Raith 3-3 Morton
Morton 2-0 Airdrie Utd
Partick 1-2 Morton
Morton 4-2 Dunfermline
Morton 0-3 Dumbarton
Cowdenbeath 1-1 Morton
Falkirk 0-1 Morton
Morton 2-1 Livingston
Morton 1-0 Raith
Airdrie Utd 0-4 Morton
Morton 2-2 Partick
Dunfermline 1-4 Morton
Hamilton 2-1 Morton
Morton 2-0 Falkirk
Dumbarton 0-3 Morton
Morton 4-2 Cowdenbeath
Raith 2-1 Morton
Morton 5-2 Airdrie Utd
Partick 1-0 Morton
Morton 0-1 Dunfermline
Livingston 0-2 Morton
Morton 0-2 Hamilton
Falkirk 4-1 Morton

MOTHERWELL

NICKNAME: The Well
COLOURS: Claret and amber
GROUND: Fir Park
TELEPHONE No: 01698 333333
FAX No: 01698 338001
WEBSITE: motherwellfc.co.uk
CAPACITY: 13,742
RECORD ATT: 35,632 (v Rangers, 1952)
RECORD VICTORY: 12-1 (v Dundee United, 1954)
RECORD DEFEAT: 0-8 (v Aberdeen, 1979)
MANAGER: Stuart McCall
VICE-*CHAIRMAN:* Derek Weir
MOST LEAGUE
GOALS (1 SEASON): 52, William McFadyen, 1931-32
GOALS (OVERALL): 283, Hugh Ferguson, 1916-25

HONOURS

LEAGUE CHAMPIONSHIP: Division I – 1931-32. Division II (2) – 1953-54, 1968-69. First Division (2) – 1981-82, 1984-85. SCOTTISH CUP: (2) 1952, 1991. LEAGUE CUP: 1950-51.

LEAGUE RESULTS 2012-2013

Ross County 0-0 Motherwell
Motherwell 1-1 St Johnstone
Kilmarnock 1-2 Motherwell
Motherwell 1-1 St Mirren
Motherwell 4-1 Inverness CT
Dundee 1-2 Motherwell
Aberdeen 3-3 Motherwell
Motherwell 0-2 Celtic
Hearts 1-0 Motherwell
Motherwell 0-4 Hibernian
St Johnstone 1-3 Motherwell
Motherwell 0-1 Dundee Utd
Motherwell 1-1 Dundee
Inverness CT 1-5 Motherwell
Motherwell 0-0 Hearts
Dundee Utd 1-2 Motherwell
Motherwell 3-2 Ross County
Hibernian 2-3 Motherwell
St Mirren 2-1 Motherwell
Motherwell 4-1 Aberdeen
Motherwell 2-2 Kilmarnock
Celtic 1-0 Motherwell
Motherwell 3-2 St Johnstone
Kilmarnock 2-0 Motherwell
Motherwell 3-0 Inverness CT
Motherwell 0-1 Dundee Utd
Ross County 3-0 Motherwell
Motherwell 2-1 Celtic
Hearts 1-2 Motherwell
Aberdeen 0-0 Motherwell
Motherwell 4-1 Hibernian
Dundee 0-3 Motherwell
Motherwell 2-2 St Mirren
Dundee Utd 1-3 Motherwell
Motherwell 3-1 Celtic
Inverness CT 4-3 Motherwell
Motherwell 2-0 Ross County
St Johnstone 2-0 Motherwell

PARTICK THISTLE

NICKNAME: The Jags
COLOURS: Red and yellow
GROUND: Firhill Stadium
TELEPHONE No: 0141 579 1971
FAX No: 0141 945 1525
WEBSITE: ptfc.co.uk
CAPACITY: 10,921
RECORD ATT: 49,838 (v Rangers, 1922)
RECORD VICTORY: 16-0 (v Royal Albert, 1931)
RECORD DEFEAT: 0-10 (v Queen's Park, 1881)
MANAGER: Alan Archibald
CHAIRMAN: David Beattie
MOST LEAGUE GOALS (1 SEASON): 41, Alex Hair, 1926-27

HONOURS

LEAGUE CHAMPIONS: Division II (3) – 1896-97, 1899-1900, 1970-71. First Division (3) – 1975-76, 2001-2002, 2012-13. Second Division – 2000-01. SCOTTISH CUP: 1921. LEAGUE CUP: 1971-72.

LEAGUE RESULTS 2012-2013

Partick 3-1 Falkirk
Dunfermline 0-1 Partick
Partick 3-0 Dumbarton
Partick 4-0 Hamilton
Livingston 1-2 Partick
Partick 2-1 Cowdenbeath
Raith 1-1 Partick
Morton 3-1 Partick
Partick 7-0 Airdrie Utd
Falkirk 0-0 Partick
Partick 5-1 Dunfermline
Hamilton 1-0 Partick
Partick 2-0 Livingston
Partick 3-2 Raith
Partick 1-2 Morton
Airdrie Utd 1-1 Partick
Livingston 2-2 Partick
Dumbarton 2-0 Partick
Partick 4-1 Falkirk
Partick 2-1 Cowdenbeath
Morton 2-2 Partick
Partick 1-0 Hamilton
Partick 1-0 Airdrie Utd
Dunfermline 0-4 Partick
Partick 3-0 Dumbarton
Hamilton 0-2 Partick
Partick 6-1 Livingston
Cowdenbeath 0-3 Partick
Cowdenbeath 1-2 Partick
Raith 0-0 Partick
Partick 1-0 Morton
Airdrie Utd 1-2 Partick
Partick 0-0 Raith
Falkirk 0-2 Partick
Partick 3-3 Dunfermline
Dumbarton 0-0 Partick

PETERHEAD

NICKNAME:	The Blue Toon
COLOURS:	Blue and white
GROUND:	Balmoor Stadium
TELEPHONE:	01779 478256
FAX:	01779 490682
WEBSITE:	peterheadfc.co.uk
CAPACITY:	4500
RECORD ATT:	8643 (v Raith Rovers, 1987)
RECORD VICTORY:	17-1 (v Fort William, 1998)
RECORD DEFEAT:	0-13 (v Aberdeen, 1923-24)
MANAGER:	Jim McInally
CHAIRMAN:	Rodger Morrison
MOST LEAGUE GOALS (1 SEASON):	21, Iain Stewart, 2002-03

LEAGUE RESULTS 2012-2013

Peterhead 2-2 Rangers
Clyde 0-2 Peterhead
Peterhead 1-0 Queen's Park
Peterhead 2-0 Montrose
Elgin City 2-0 Peterhead
Annan 2-1 Peterhead
Peterhead 1-0 Berwick
East Stirling 2-1 Peterhead
Peterhead 2-2 Stirling
Rangers 2-0 Peterhead
Peterhead 1-0 Clyde
Montrose 2-0 Peterhead
Peterhead 1-1 Elgin City
Berwick 1-1 Peterhead
Peterhead 2-0 Annan
Stirling 1-0 Peterhead
Peterhead 2-0 East Stirling
Elgin City 0-3 Peterhead
Peterhead 0-1 Montrose
Queen's Park 0-0 Peterhead
Peterhead 0-1 Rangers
Annan 0-0 Peterhead
Peterhead 1-1 Berwick
East Stirling 2-4 Peterhead
Peterhead 0-0 Stirling
Peterhead 0-2 Queen's Park
Clyde 2-0 Peterhead
Peterhead 0-1 Elgin City
Montrose 0-6 Peterhead
Berwick 0-2 Peterhead
Peterhead 2-0 Annan
Peterhead 6-0 East Stirling
Stirling 0-1 Peterhead
Rangers 1-2 Peterhead
Peterhead 3-0 Clyde
Queen's Park 0-3 Peterhead

QUEEN OF THE SOUTH

NICKNAME:	The Doonhamers
COLOURS:	Royal blue
GROUND:	Palmerston Park
TELEPHONE No:	01387 254853
FAX No:	01387 240470
WEBSITE:	qosfc.com
CAPACITY:	6412
RECORD ATT:	26,552 (v Hearts, 1952)
RECORD VICTORY:	11-1 (v Stranraer, 1932)
RECORD DEFEAT:	2-10 (v Dundee, 1962)
MANAGER:	Allan Johnston
CHAIRMAN:	Billy Hewitson
MOST LEAGUE GOALS (1 SEASON):	41, Jimmy Rutherford, 1931-32

HONOURS

LEAGUE CHAMPIONS: Division II – 1950-51. Second Division (2) – 2001-02, 2012-13. CHALLENGE CUP (2): 2002-03, 2012-13.

LEAGUE RESULTS 2012-2013

Queen of Sth 2-0 Forfar
East Fife 0-0 Queen of Sth
Queen of Sth 1-0 Albion
Queen of Sth 6-0 Arbroath
Ayr 2-4 Queen of Sth
Brechin 0-3 Queen of Sth
Queen of Sth 1-0 Alloa
Stranraer 0-2 Queen of Sth
Queen of Sth 2-2 Stenh'semuir
Queen of Sth 1-0 East Fife
Arbroath 2-3 Queen of Sth
Forfar 1-5 Queen of Sth
Queen of Sth 2-0 Ayr 2
Alloa 1-0 Queen of Sth
Queen of Sth 1-0 Brechin
Queen of Sth 4-1 Stranraer
Stenh'semuir 1-3 Queen of Sth
Ayr 1-5 Queen of Sth
Queen of Sth 5-1 Arbroath
Albion 0-3 Queen of Sth
Queen of Sth 3-1 Forfar
Queen of Sth 0-0 Alloa
Queen of Sth 2-1 Stenh'semuir
Stranraer 0-5 Queen of Sth
Queen of Sth 3-0 Albion
East Fife 2-3 Queen of Sth
Queen of Sth 2-0 Ayr
Arbroath 1-1 Queen of Sth
Alloa 1-2 Queen of Sth
Brechin 0-6 Queen of Sth
Queen of Sth 2-1 Brechin
Queen of Sth 2-0 Stranraer
Stenh'semuir 2-1 Queen of Sth
Forfar 0-4 Queen of Sth
Queen of Sth 2-2 East Fife
Albion 0-1 Queen of Sth

QUEEN'S PARK

NICKNAME:	The Spiders
COLOURS:	White and black
GROUND:	Hampden Park
TELEPHONE No:	0141 632 1275
FAX No:	0141 636 1612
WEBSITE:	queensparkfc.co.uk
CAPACITY:	52,046
RECORD ATT:	95,772 (v Rangers, 1930). 149,547 (for ground Scotland v England, 1937)
RECORD VICTORY:	16-0 (v St Peter's, 1885)
RECORD DEFEAT:	0-9 (v Motherwell, 1930)
MANAGER:	Gardner Speirs
PRESIDENT:	Ross Caven
MOST LEAGUE GOALS (1 SEASON):	30, William Martin, 1937-38

HONOURS

LEAGUE CHAMPIONSHIP: Division II – 1922-23. B Division – 1955-56. Second Division – 1980-81. Third Division – 1999-00. SCOTTISH CUP (10): 1874, 1875, 1876, 1880, 1881, 1882, 1884, 1886, 1890, 1893.

LEAGUE RESULTS 2012-2013

East Stirling 0-2 Queen's Park
Queen's Park 2-2 Montrose
Peterhead 1-0 Queen's Park
Stirling 1-2 Queen's Park
Queen's Park 1-0 Clyde
Elgin City 0-4 Queen's Park
Queen's Park 2-2 Annan
Rangers 2-0 Queen's Park
Queen's Park 1-1 Berwick
Queen's Park 1-2 East Stirling
Montrose 1-1 Queen's Park
Queen's Park 2-1 Stirling
Annan 2-3 Queen's Park
Queen's Park 1-1 Elgin City
Queen's Park 0-1 Rangers
Queen's Park 4-1 Clyde
Stirling 2-3 Queen's Park
Queen's Park 0-0 Peterhead
East Stirling 0-2 Queen's Park
Queen's Park 2-2 Annan
Rangers 4-0 Queen's Park
Queen's Park 2-1 Berwick
Peterhead 0-2 Queen's Park
Clyde 0-3 Queen's Park
Queen's Park 1-2 Montrose
Elgin City 3-5 Queen's Park
Clyde 2-3 Queen's Park
Berwick 2-0 Queen's Park
Queen's Park 0-1 Elgin City
Queen's Park 2-2 Stirling
Queen's Park 1-4 Rangers
Annan 2-0 Queen's Park
Berwick 4-1 Queen's Park
Queen's Park 5-1 East Stirling
Montrose 1-2 Queen's Park
Queen's Park 0-3 Peterhead

RAITH ROVERS

NICKNAME: The Rovers
COLOURS: White and navy blue
GROUND: Stark's Park
TELEPHONE No: 01592 263514
FAX No: 01592 642833
WEBSITE: raithrovers.net
CAPACITY: 8475
RECORD ATT: 31,306 (v Hearts, 1953)
RECORD VICTORY: 10-1 (v Coldstream, 1954)
RECORD DEFEAT: 2-11 (v Morton, 1936)
MANAGER: Grant Murray
CHAIRMAN: Turnbull Hutton
MOST LEAGUE GOALS (1 SEASON): 42, Norman Haywood, 1937-38

R.R.F.C

HONOURS

LEAGUE CHAMPIONS: First Division (2) - 1992-93, 1994-95. Second Division - 2002-03, 2008-09. Division II (4) - 1907-08, 1909-10 (shared), 1937-38, 1948-49. LEAGUE CUP - 1994-95.

LEAGUE RESULTS 2012-2013

Raith 2-0 Hamilton
Falkirk 0-2 Raith
Raith 0-0 Livingston
Dunfermline 3-1 Raith
Raith 2-0 Airdrie Utd
Morton 1-0 Raith
Raith 1-1 Partick
Raith 2-2 Dumbarton
Cowdenbeath 4-4 Raith
Hamilton 0-1 Raith
Raith 2-1 Falkirk
Raith 1-3 Dunfermline
Airdrie Utd 0-0 Raith
Raith 3-3 Morton
Partick 3-2 Raith
Raith 2-2 Cowdenbeath
Dunfermline 1-0 Raith
Raith 2-0 Airdrie Utd
Livingston 2-1 Raith
Raith 0-2 Hamilton
Morton 1-0 Raith
Raith 3-2 Dumbarton
Cowdenbeath 1-1 Raith
Falkirk 1-1 Raith
Raith 0-2 Livingston
Raith 1-1 Dunfermline
Airdrie Utd 1-2 Raith
Dumbarton 4-2 Raith
Raith 2-1 Morton
Raith 0-0 Partick
Dumbarton 1-2 Raith
Raith 0-1 Cowdenbeath
Partick 0-0 Raith
Hamilton 2-0 Raith
Raith 0-0 Falkirk
Livingston 2-3 Raith

RANGERS

NICKNAME: The Gers
COLOURS: Blue, red and white
GROUND: Ibrox Stadium
TELEPHONE No: 0871 702 1972
FAX No: 0870 600 1978
WEBSITE: rangers.co.uk
CAPACITY: 51,082
RECORD ATT: 118,567 (v Celtic, 1939)
RECORD VICTORY: 14-2 (v Blairgowrie, 1934)
RECORD DEFEAT: 2-10 (v Airdrie, 1886)
MANAGER: Ally McCoist
CHAIRMAN: Walter Smith
MOST LEAGUE GOALS (1 SEASON): 44, Sam English, 1931-32
GOALS (OVERALL): 355, Ally McCoist

HONOURS

LEAGUE CHAMPIONSHIP (54): 1890-91 (shared), 1898-99, 1899-1900, 1900-01, 1901-02, 1910-11, 1911-12, 1912-13, 1917-18, 1919-20, 1920-21, 1922-23, 1923-24, 1924-25, 1926-27, 1927-28, 1928-29, 1929-30, 1930-31, 1932-33, 1933-34, 1934-35, 1936-37, 1938-39, 1946-47, 1948-49, 1949-50, 1952-53, 1955-56, 1956-57, 1958-59, 1960-61, 1962-63, 1963-64, 1974-75, 1975-76, 1977-78, 1986-87, 1988-89, 1989-90, 1990-91, 1991-92, 1992-93, 1993-94, 1994-95, 1995-96, 1996-97, 1998-99, 1999-00, 2002-03, 2004-05, 2008-09, 2009-10, 2010-11.
THIRD DIVISION: 2012-2013.

SCOTTISH CUP (33): 1894, 1897, 1898, 1903, 1928, 1930, 1932, 1934, 1935, 1936, 1948, 1949, 1950, 1953, 1960, 1962, 1963, 1964, 1966, 1973, 1976, 1978, 1979, 1981, 1992, 1993, 1996, 1999, 2000, 2002, 2003, 2008, 2009.

LEAGUE CUP (27): 1946-47, 1948-49, 1960-61, 1961-62, 1963-64, 1964-65, 1970-71, 1975-76, 1977-78, 1978-79, 1981-82, 1983-84, 1984-85, 1986-87, 1987-88, 1988-89, 1990-91, 1992-93, 1993-94, 1996-97, 1998-99, 2001-02, 2002-03, 2004-05, 2007-08, 2009-10, 2010-11.

EUROPEAN CUP-WINNERS' CUP: 1971-72.

ANDREW LITTLE

FRASER AIRD

LEAGUE RESULTS 2012-2013

Peterhead 2-2 Rangers
Rangers 5-1 East Stirling
Berwick 1-1 Rangers
Rangers 5-1 Elgin City
Annan 0-0 Rangers
Rangers 4-1 Montrose
Stirling 1-0 Rangers
Rangers 2-0 Queen's Park
Clyde 0-2 Rangers
Rangers 2-0 Peterhead
East Stirling 2-6 Rangers
Rangers 2-0 Stirling
Montrose 2-4 Rangers
Rangers 3-0 Annan
Elgin City 2-6 Rangers
Rangers 3-0 Clyde
Queen's Park 0-1 Rangers
Annan 1-3 Rangers
Rangers 1-1 Elgin City
Rangers 4-2 Berwick
Peterhead 0-1 Rangers
Rangers 1-1 Montrose
Rangers 4-0 Queen's Park
Clyde 1-4 Rangers
Berwick 1-3 Rangers
Stirling 1-1 Rangers
Rangers 3-1 East Stirling
Rangers 1-2 Annan
Elgin City 0-1 Rangers
Rangers 0-0 Stirling
Montrose 0-0 Rangers
Queen's Park 1-4 Rangers
Rangers 2-0 Clyde
Rangers 1-2 Peterhead
East Stirling 2-4 Rangers
Rangers 1-0 Berwick

ROSS COUNTY

NICKNAME:	The Staggies
COLOURS:	Navy blue, white and red
GROUND:	The Global Energy Stadium
TELEPHONE No:	01349 860860
FAX No:	01349 866277
WEBSITE:	rosscountyfootball club.co.uk
CAPACITY:	6000
RECORD ATT:	8000 (v Rangers, 1966)
RECORD VICTORY:	11-0 (v St Cuthbert's Wanderers, 1993)
RECORD DEFEAT:	1-10 (v Inverness Thistle)
MANAGER:	Derek Adams
CHAIRMAN:	Roy MacGregor
MOST LEAGUE GOALS (1 SEASON):	24, Andy Barrowman, 2007-08

HONOURS

LEAGUE CHAMPIONSHIP: First Division – 2011-12. Second Division – 2007-08. Third Division – 1998-99.
CHALLENGE CUP (2): 2006-07, 2010-11.

LEAGUE RESULTS 2012-2013

Ross County 0-0 Motherwell
Aberdeen 0-0 Ross County
Ross County 1-1 Celtic
Dundee 0-1 Ross County
Ross County 0-0 Kilmarnock
Dundee Utd 0-0 Ross County
Ross County 1-2 St Johnstone
St Mirren 5-4 Ross County
Inverness CT 3-1 Ross County
Ross County 3-2 Hibernian
Hearts 2-2 Ross County
Ross County 2-1 Aberdeen
Kilmarnock 3-0 Ross County
St Johnstone 1-1 Ross County
Ross County 1-2 Dundee Utd
Ross County 0-0 St Mirren
Motherwell 3-2 Ross County
Ross County 1-1 Dundee
Celtic 4-0 Ross County
Hibernian 0-1 Ross County
St Mirren 1-4 Ross County
Dundee Utd 1-1 Ross County
Ross County 1-0 Hibernian
Ross County 2-2 Hearts
Dundee 0-2 Ross County
Ross County 1-0 St Johnstone
Ross County 3-0 Motherwell
Aberdeen 0-1 Ross County
Ross County 0-0 Inverness CT
Ross County 3-2 Celtic
Inverness CT 2-1 Ross County
Ross County 0-1 Kilmarnock
Hearts 4-2 Ross County
St Johnstone 2-2 Ross County
Ross County 1-0 Dundee Utd
Ross County 1-1 Celtic
Motherwell 2-0 Ross County
Ross County 1- 0 Inverness CT

ST JOHNSTONE

NICKNAME:	The Saints
COLOURS:	Blue and white
GROUND:	McDiarmid Park
TELEPHONE No:	01738 459090
FAX No:	01738 625771
WEBSITE:	perthstjohnstonefc.co.uk
CAPACITY:	10,673
RECORD ATT:	10,545 (v Dundee, 1999)
RECORD VICTORY:	9-0 (v Albion Rovers, 1946)
RECORD DEFEAT:	1-10 (v Third Lanark, 1903)
MANAGER:	Tommy Wright
CHAIRMAN:	Steve Brown
MOST LEAGUE GOALS (1 SEASON):	36, Jimmy Benson, 1931-32
GOALS (OVERALL):	140, John Brogan, 1977-83

HONOURS

LEAGUE CHAMPIONSHIP: First Division (4) – 1982-83, 1989-90, 1996-97, 2008-09. Division II (3) – 1923-24, 1959-60, 1962-63. CHALLENGE CUP: 2007-08.

LEAGUE RESULTS 2012-2013

Hearts 2-0 St Johnstone
Motherwell 1-1 St Johnstone
St Johnstone 1-2 Aberdeen
Hibernian 2-0 St Johnstone
St Johnstone 0-0 Dundee Utd
St Johnstone 2-1 Celtic
Ross County 1-2 St Johnstone
Dundee 1-3 St Johnstone
St Johnstone 2-1 St Mirren
St Johnstone 2-1 Kilmarnock
Inverness CT 1-1 St Johnstone
St Johnstone 1-3 Motherwell
Celtic 1-1 St Johnstone
St Johnstone 1-1 Ross County
Kilmarnock 1-2 St Johnstone
St Johnstone 0-1 Hibernian
St Mirren 1-1 St Johnstone
St Johnstone 2-2 Hearts
Aberdeen 2-0 St Johnstone
Dundee Utd 1-1 St Johnstone
St Johnstone 0-0 Inverness CT
St Johnstone 1-0 Dundee
Motherwell 3-2 St Johnstone
St Johnstone 3-1 Aberdeen
Hibernian 1-3 St Johnstone
Ross County 1-0 St Johnstone
St Johnstone 1-1 Celtic
St Johnstone 1-0 St Mirren
Dundee 2-2 St Johnstone
Hearts 2-0 St Johnstone
St Johnstone 2-0 Kilmarnock
St Johnstone 1-1 Dundee Utd
Inverness CT 0-0 St Johnstone
St Johnstone 2-2 Ross County
St Johnstone 1-0 Inverness CT
Dundee Utd 0-1 St Johnstone
Celtic 4-0 St Johnstone
St Johnstone 2-0 Motherwell

ST MIRREN

NICKNAME: The Buddies
COLOURS: Black and white
GROUND: St Mirren Park
TELEPHONE No: 0141 889 2558
FAX No: 0141 848 6444
WEBSITE: saintmirren.net
CAPACITY: 8023
RECORD ATT: 47,438 (v Celtic, 1949)
RECORD VICTORY: 15-0 (v Glasgow University, 1960)
RECORD DEFEAT 0-9 (v Rangers, 1897)
MANAGER: Danny Lennon
CHAIRMAN: Stewart Gilmour
MOST LEAGUE
GOALS (1 SEASON): 45, Dunky Walker, 1921-22
GOALS (OVERALL): 251, David McCrae

HONOURS

LEAGUE CHAMPIONS: First Division (3) – 1976-77, 1999-00, 2005-06. Division II – 1967-68. SCOTTISH CUP (3): 1926, 1959, 1987. LEAGUE CUP: 2012-2013. CHALLENGE CUP – 2005-06.

LEAGUE RESULTS 2012-2013

St Mirren 2-2 Inverness CT
Dundee 0-2 St Mirren
St Mirren 1-2 Hibernian
Motherwell 1-1 St Mirren
Aberdeen 0-0 St Mirren
St Mirren 2-0 Hearts
Kilmarnock 3-1 St Mirren
St Mirren 5-4 Ross County
St Johnstone 2-1 St Mirren
St Mirren 0-5 Celtic
St Mirren 0-1 Dundee Utd
Hibernian 2-1 St Mirren
St Mirren 1-4 Aberdeen
Hearts 1-0 St Mirren
St Mirren 3-1 Dundee
Ross County 0-0 St Mirren
St Mirren 1-1 St Johnstone
Celtic 2-0 St Mirren
St Mirren 2-1 Motherwell
Inverness CT 2-2 St Mirren
Dundee Utd 3-4 St Mirren
St Mirren 1-1 Kilmarnock
St Mirren 1-4 Ross County
St Mirren 2-1 Inverness CT
Aberdeen 0-0 St Mirren
St Mirren 0-1 Hibernian
St Johnstone 1-0 St Mirren
St Mirren 2-0 Hearts
Dundee 2-1 St Mirren
St Mirren 0-0 Dundee Utd
St Mirren 1-1 Celtic
Kilmarnock 1-1 St Mirren
Motherwell 2-2 St Mirren
St Mirren 1-2 Dundee
Hibernian 3-3 St Mirren
Hearts 3-0 St Mirren
St Mirren 0-0 Aberdeen
Kilmarnock 1-3 St Mirren

STENHOUSEMUIR

NICKNAME:	The Warriors
COLOURS:	Maroon and white
GROUND:	Ochilview Park
TELEPHONE No:	01324 562992
FAX No:	01324 562980
WEBSITE:	stenhousemuirfc.com
CAPACITY:	3096
RECORD ATT:	12,500 (v East Fife, 1950)
RECORD VICTORY:	9-2 (v Dundee United, 1937)
RECORD DEFEAT:	2-11 (v Dunfermline, 1930)
MANAGER:	Martyn Corrigan
CHAIRMAN:	Bill Darroch
MOST LEAGUE GOALS (1 SEASON):	32, Robert Taylor, 1995-96

HONOURS

CHALLENGE CUP: 1995-96.

LEAGUE RESULTS 2012-2013

Ayr 1-1 Stenh'semuir
Stenh'semuir 3-1 Brechin
Stranraer 1-1 Stenh'semuir
Stenh'semuir 0-4 Forfar
Alloa 0-2 Stenh'semuir
Albion 4-4 Stenh'semuir
Stenh'semuir 2-2 Arbroath
Stenh'semuir 3-0 East Fife
Queen of Sth 2-2 Stenh'semuir
Brechin 7-2 Stenh'semuir
Stenh'semuir 1-1 Ayr
Forfar 3-2 Stenh'semuir
Stenh'semuir 0-2 Alloa
Arbroath 2-2 Stenh'semuir
Stenh'semuir 1-0 Albion
East Fife 3-2 Stenh'semuir
Stenh'semuir 1-3 Queen of Sth
Alloa 1-0 Stenh'semuir
Stenh'semuir 2-0 Forfar
Stenh'semuir 0-0 Stranraer
Stenh'semuir 1-0 Arbroath
Queen of Sth 2-1 Stenh'semuir
Stenh'semuir 2-1 East Fife
Stranraer 1-1 Stenh'semuir
Ayr 1-2 Stenh'semuir
Stenh'semuir 3-3 Brechin
Albion 4-3 Stenh'semuir
Stenh'semuir 1-1 Alloa
Forfar 3-3 Stenh'semuir
Stenh'semuir 0-1 Albion
Arbroath 0-0 Stenh'semuir
East Fife 1-2 Stenh'semuir
Stenh'semuir 2-1 Queen of Sth
Stenh'semuir 4-0 Ayr
Brechin 1-2 Stenh'semuir
Stenh'semuir 1-2 Stranraer

STIRLING ALBION

NICKNAME: The Binos
COLOURS: Red and white
GROUND: Doubletree Dunblane Stadium
TELEPHONE No: 01786 450399
FAX No: 01786 448592
WEBSITE: stirlingalbionfc.co.uk
CAPACITY: 3808
RECORD ATT: 26,400 (v Celtic, 1959, at Annfield)
RECORD VICTORY: 20-0 (v Selkirk, 1984)
RECORD DEFEAT: 0-9 (v Dundee United, 1967; v Ross County, 2010)
MANAGER: Greig McDonald
TRUST BOARD CHAIRMAN: Eddie Docherty
MOST LEAGUE GOALS (1 SEASON:) 27, Joe Hughes, 1969-70

HONOURS

LEAGUE CHAMPIONS: Division II (4) – 1952-53, 1957-58, 1960-61, 1964-65. Second Division (4) – 1976-77, 1990-91, 1995-96, 2009-10.

LEAGUE RESULTS 2012-2013

Stirling 5-1 Annan
Elgin City 3-1 Stirling
Stirling 0-1 Clyde
Stirling 1-2 Queen's Park
East Stirling 3-1 Stirling
Berwick 4-1 Stirling
Stirling 1-0 Rangers
Stirling 1-3 Montrose
Peterhead 2-2 Stirling
Annan 5-2 Stirling
Stirling 1-4 Elgin City
Queen's Park 2-1 Stirling
Rangers 2-0 Stirling
Stirling 6-3 Berwick
Stirling 1-0 Peterhead
Montrose 3-2 Stirling
East Stirling 1-1 Stirling
Stirling 2-3 Queen's Park
Clyde 2-1 Stirling
Stirling 3-1 Montrose
Stirling 1-1 East Stirling
Peterhead 0-0 Stirling
Stirling 2-1 Annan
Stirling 2-0 Clyde
Stirling 1-1 Rangers
Elgin City 1-2 Stirling
Berwick 1-0 Stirling
Stirling 9-1 East Stirling
Rangers 0-0 Stirling
Stirling 1-0 Berwick
Queen's Park 2-2 Stirling
Montrose 2-2 Stirling
Stirling 0-1 Peterhead
Annan 0-1 Stirling
Stirling 1-1 Elgin City
Clyde 1-2 Stirling

STRANRAER

NICKNAME:	The Blues
COLOURS:	Blue and white
GROUND:	Stair Park
TELEPHONE No:	01776 703271
E-MAIL ADDRESS:	secretary@ stranraerfc.org
WEBSITE:	stranraerfc.org
CAPACITY:	6100
RECORD ATT:	6500 (v Rangers, 1948)
RECORD VICTORY:	9-0 (v St Cuthbert Wanderers, 2011)
RECORD DEFEAT:	1-11 (v Queen of the South, 1932)
MANAGER:	Stephen Aitken
CHAIRMAN:	Robert Rice
MOST LEAGUE GOALS (1 SEASON):	27, Derek Frye, 1997-98

STRANRAER F.C. 1870

HONOURS

LEAGUE CHAMPIONS: Second Division (2) – 1993-94, 1997-98. Third Division – 2003-04. CHALLENGE CUP: 1996-97.

LEAGUE RESULTS 2012-2013

Stranraer 1-1 Arbroath
Forfar 4-0 Stranraer
Stranraer 1-1 Stenh'semuir
Stranraer 2-0 Ayr
Albion 2-1 Stranraer
Alloa 3-0 Stranraer
Stranraer 2-6 East Fife
Stranraer 0-2 Queen of Sth
Brechin 3-0 Stranraer
Stranraer 4-1 Forfar
Ayr 2-1 Stranraer
Arbroath 2-1 Stranraer
Stranraer 1-1 Albion
Stranraer 3-2 Alloa
East Fife 0-1 Stranraer
Queen of Sth 4-1 Stranraer
Stranraer 0-2 Brechin
Albion 2-3 Stranraer
Stranraer 0-1 Ayr
Stenh'semuir 0-0 Stranraer
Alloa 4-1 Stranraer
Stranraer 3-1 East Fife
Stranraer 0-5 Queen of Sth
Stranraer 2-0 Arbroath
Stranraer 1-1 Stenh'semuir
Forfar 3-1 Stranraer
Stranraer 3-2 Albion
Ayr 2-1 Stranraer
Stranraer 1-2 Alloa
Stranraer 3-2 Brechin
East Fife 1-1 Stranraer
Queen of Sth 2-0 Stranraer
Arbroath 1-0 Stranraer
Brechin 2-2 Stranraer
Stranraer 0-3 Forfar
Stenh'semuir 1-2 Stranraer

LEAGUE CHAMPIONS

YEAR	WINNERS
1890-91	RANGERS/ DUMBARTON
1891-92	DUMBARTON
1892-93	CELTIC
1893-94	CELTIC
1894-95	HEARTS
1895-96	CELTIC
1896-97	HEARTS
1897-98	CELTIC
1898-99	RANGERS
1899-1900	RANGERS
1900-01	RANGERS
1901-02	RANGERS
1902-03	HIBERNIAN
1903-04	THIRD LANARK
1904-05	CELTIC
1905-06	CELTIC
1906-07	CELTIC
1907-08	CELTIC
1908-09	CELTIC
1909-10	CELTIC
1910-11	RANGERS
1911-12	RANGERS
1912-13	RANGERS
1913-14	CELTIC
1914-15	CELTIC
1915-16	CELTIC
1916-17	CELTIC
1917-18	RANGERS
1918-19	CELTIC
1919-20	RANGERS
1920-21	RANGERS
1921-22	CELTIC
1922-23	RANGERS
1923-24	RANGERS
1924-25	RANGERS
1925-26	CELTIC
1926-27	RANGERS
1927-28	RANGERS
1928-29	RANGERS
1929-30	RANGERS

YEAR	WINNERS
1930-31	RANGERS
1931-32	MOTHERWELL
1932-33	RANGERS
1933-34	RANGERS
1934-35	RANGERS
1935-36	CELTIC
1936-37	RANGERS
1937-38	CELTIC
1938-39	RANGERS
NO CHAMPIONSHIP	
1946-47	RANGERS
1947-48	HIBERNIAN
1948-49	RANGERS
1949-50	RANGERS
1950-51	HIBERNIAN
1951-52	HIBERNIAN
1952-53	RANGERS
1953-54	CELTIC
1954-55	ABERDEEN
1955-56	RANGERS
1956-57	RANGERS
1957-58	HEARTS
1958-59	RANGERS
1959-60	HEARTS
1960-61	RANGERS
1961-62	DUNDEE
1962-63	RANGERS
1963-64	RANGERS
1964-65	KILMARNOCK
1965-66	CELTIC
1966-67	CELTIC
1967-68	CELTIC
1968-69	CELTIC
1969-70	CELTIC
1970-71	CELTIC
1971-72	CELTIC
1972-73	CELTIC
1973-74	CELTIC
1974-75	RANGERS
1975-76	RANGERS

PREMIER DIVISION

YEAR	WINNERS
1976-77	CELTIC
1977-78	RANGERS
1978-79	CELTIC
1979-80	ABERDEEN
1980-81	CELTIC
1981-82	CELTIC
1982-83	DUNDEE UNITED
1983-84	ABERDEEN
1984-85	ABERDEEN
1985-86	CELTIC
1986-87	RANGERS
1987-88	CELTIC
1988-89	RANGERS
1989-90	RANGERS
1990-91	RANGERS
1991-92	RANGERS
1992-93	RANGERS
1993-94	RANGERS

YEAR	WINNERS
1994-95	RANGERS
1995-96	RANGERS
1996-97	RANGERS
1997-98	CELTIC
1998-99	RANGERS
1999-00	RANGERS
2000-01	CELTIC
2001-02	CELTIC
2002-03	RANGERS
2003-04	CELTIC
2004-05	RANGERS
2005-06	CELTIC
2006-07	CELTIC
2007-08	CELTIC
2008-09	RANGERS
2009-10	RANGERS
2010-11	RANGERS
2011-12	CELTIC
2012-13	CELTIC

NEIL LENNON celebrates with his team after Celtic clinched the 2012/13 SPL title

PROMOTION/RELEGATION

1921-1922	**Promoted**	Alloa
	Relegated	Dumbarton, Queen's Park, Clydebank
1922-23	**Promoted**	Queen's Park, Clydebank
	Relegated	Albion Rovers, Alloa
1923-24	**Promoted**	St Johnstone, Cowdenbeath
	Relegated	Clyde, Clydebank
1924-25	**Promoted**	Dundee Utd, Clydebank
	Relegated	Ayr United, Third Lanark
1925-26	**Promoted**	Dunfermline, Clyde
	Relegated	Raith Rovers, Clydebank
1926-27	**Promoted**	Bo'ness, Raith Rovers
	Relegated	Morton, Dundee United
1927-28	**Promoted**	Ayr United, Third Lanark
	Relegated	Bo'ness, Dunfermline
1928-29	**Promoted**	Dundee United, Morton
	Relegated	Third Lanark, Raith Rovers
1929-30	**Promoted**	Leith Ath, East Fife
	Relegated	Dundee United, St Johnstone
1930-31	**Promoted**	Third Lanark, Dundee United
	Relegated	Hibernian, East Fife
1931-32	**Promoted**	East Stirling, St Johnstone
	Relegated	Dundee United, Leith Ath
1932-33	**Promoted**	Hibernian, Queen of the South
	Relegated	Morton, East Stirling
1933-34	**Promoted**	Albion Rovers, Dunfermline
	Relegated	Third Lanark, Cowdenbeath
1934-35	**Promoted**	Third Lanark, Arbroath
	Relegated	St Mirren, Falkirk
1935-36	**Promoted**	Falkirk, St Mirren
	Relegated	Airdrie, Ayr United
1936-37	**Promoted**	Ayr United, Morton
	Relegated	Dunfermline, Albion Rovers
1937-38	**Promoted**	Raith Rovers, Albion Rovers
	Relegated	Dundee, Morton
1938-39	**Promoted**	Cowdenbeath, Alloa
	Relegated	Queen's Park, Raith Rovers
1946-47	**Promoted**	Dundee, Airdrie
	Relegated	Kilmarnock, Hamilton
1947-48	**Promoted**	East Fife, Albion Rovers
	Relegated	Airdrie, Queen's Park
1948-49	**Promoted**	Raith Rovers, Stirling Albion
	Relegated	Morton, Albion Rovers
1949-50	**Promoted**	Morton, Airdrie
	Relegated	Queen of the South, Stirling Alb
1950-51	**Promoted**	Queen of the South, Stirling Alb
	Relegated	Clyde, Falkirk
1951-52	**Promoted**	Clyde, Falkirk
	Relegated	Morton, Stirling Albion
1952-53	**Promoted**	Stirling Albion, Hamilton Accies
	Relegated	Motherwell, Third Lanark
1953-54	**Promoted**	Motherwell, Kilmarnock
	Relegated	Airdrie, Hamilton Accies
1954-55	**Promoted**	Airdrie, Dunfermline
	Relegated	Motherwell, Stirling Albion
1955-56	**Promoted**	Queen's Park, Ayr United
	Relegated	Clyde, Stirling Albion

1956-57	**Promoted**	Clyde, Third Lanark
	Relegated	Dunfermline, Ayr United
1957-58	**Promoted**	Stirling Albion, Dunfermline
	Relegated	East Fife, Queen's Park
1958-59	**Promoted**	Ayr United, Arbroath
	Relegated	Falkirk, Queen of the South
1959-60	**Promoted**	St Johnstone, Dundee United
	Relegated	Stirling Albion, Arbroath
1960-61	**Promoted**	Stirling Albion, Falkirk
	Relegated	Clyde, Ayr United
1961-62	**Promoted**	Clyde, Queen of the South
	Relegated	St Johnstone, Stirling Albion
1962-63	**Promoted**	St Johnstone, East Stirling
	Relegated	Clyde, Raith Rovers
1963-64	**Promoted**	Morton, Clyde
	Relegated	Queen of the South, East Stirling
1964-65	**Promoted**	Stirling Albion, Hamilton Accies
	Relegated	Airdrie, Third Lanark
1965-66	**Promoted**	Ayr United, Airdrie
	Relegated	Morton, Hamilton Accies
1966-67	**Promoted**	Morton, Raith Rovers
	Relegated	St Mirren, Ayr United
1967-68	**Promoted**	St Mirren, Arbroath
	Relegated	Motherwell, Stirling Albion
1968-69	**Promoted**	Motherwell, Ayr United
	Relegated	Falkirk, Arbroath
1969-70	**Promoted**	Falkirk, Cowdenbeath
	Relegated	Raith Rovers, Partick Thistle
1970-71	**Promoted**	Partick Thistle, East Fife
	Relegated	St Mirren, Cowdenbeath
1971-72	**Promoted**	Dumbarton, Arbroath
	Relegated	Clyde, Dunfermline
1972-73	**Promoted**	Clyde, Dunfermline
	Relegated	Kilmarnock, Airdrie
1973-74	**Promoted**	Airdrie, Kilmarnock
	Relegated	East Fife, Falkirk

1974-75 Leagues reformed into Premier, First and Second Divisions

1975-76 **Promoted to Premier** – Kilmarnock, Partick Th
Relegated to First – Dundee, St Johnstone
Promoted to First – Clydebank, Raith Rovers
Relegated to Second – Clyde, Dunfermline

1976-77 **Promoted to Premier** – St Mirren, Clydebank
Relegated to First – Hearts, Kilmarnock
Promoted to First – Alloa, Stirling Albion
Relegated to Second – Falkirk, Raith Rovers

1977-78 **Promoted to Premier** – Morton, Hearts
Relegated to First – Ayr United, Clydebank
Promoted to First – Clyde, Raith Rovers
Relegated to Second – Alloa Athletic, East Fife

1978-79 **Promoted to Premier** – Dundee, Kilmarnock
Relegated to First – Hearts, Motherwell
Promoted to First – Berwick Ran, Dunfermline
Relegated to Second – Montrose, QOS

1979-80 **Promoted to Premier** – Hearts, Airdrie
Relegated to First – Dundee, Hibernian
Promoted to First – East Stirling, Falkirk
Relegated to Second – Arbroath, Clyde

1980-81 **Promoted to Premier** – Dundee, Hibernian
Relegated to First – Hearts, Kilmarnock
Promoted to First – Queen's Park, QOS
Relegated to Second – Berwick R, Stirling Alb

1981-82 **Promoted to Premier** – Motherwell, Kilmarnock
Relegated to First – Airdrie, Partick Thistle
Promoted to First – Clyde, Alloa Athletic
Relegated to Second – QOS, East Stirling

1982-83 **Promoted to Premier** – St Johnstone, Hearts
Relegated to First – Kilmarnock, Morton
Promoted to First – Brechin, Meadowbank
Relegated to Second – Queen's Pk, Dunf'line

1983-84 **Promoted to Premier** — Dumbarton, Morton
Relegated to First — Motherwell, St Johnstone
Promoted to First — East Fife, Forfar
Relegated to Second — Alloa, Raith Rovers

1984-85 **Promoted to Premier** — Motherwell, Clydebank
Relegated to First — Dumbarton, Morton
Promoted to First — Montrose, Alloa Athletic
Relegated to Second — M'dowbank, St Johnstone

1985-86 **Promoted to Premier** – Hamilton Accies, Falkirk
No relegation to First – league reorganisation
Promoted to First – Dunfermline, QOS
Relegated to Second – Ayr United, Alloa

1986-87 **Promoted to Premier** – Morton, Dunfermline Ath
Relegated to First – Clydebank, Hamilton Accies
Promoted to First – Meadowbank Th, Raith Rovers
Relegated to Second – Brechin, Montrose

1987-88 **Promoted to Premier** – Hamilton Accies
Relegated to First – Falkirk, Dunfermline, Morton
Promoted to First – Ayr United, St Johnstone
Relegated to Second – East Fife, Dumbarton

1988-89 **Promoted to Premier** – Dunfermline Ath
Relegated to First – Hamilton Accies
Promoted to First – Albion Rovers, Alloa Ath
Relegated to Second – QOS, Kilmarnock

1989-90 **Promoted to Premier** – St Johnstone
Relegated to First – Dundee
Promoted to First – Brechin, Kilmarnock
Relegated to Second – Alloa Ath, Albion Rovers

1990-91 **Promoted to Premier** – Falkirk, Airdrie
No relegation to First
Promoted to First – Stirling Albion, Montrose
Relegated to Second – Brechin, Clyde

1991-92 **Promoted to Premier** – Dundee, Partick Thistle
Relegated to First – Dunfermline Ath, St Mirren
Promoted to First – Dumbarton, Cowdenbeath
Relegated to Second – Montrose, Forfar

1992-93 **Promoted to Premier** – Raith Rov, Kilmarnock
Relegated to First – Airdrie, Falkirk
Promoted to First – Clyde, Brechin
Relegated to Second – Cowdenbeath, Meadowb'k

1993-94 **Promoted to Premier** – Falkirk
Relegated to First – St Johnstone, Raith Rovers, Dundee

Promoted to First – Stranraer
Relegated to Second – Dumbarton, Stirling Alb, Clyde, Morton, Brechin
Relegated to Third – Alloa, Forfar
East Stirling, Montrose, Queen's Park, Arbroath
Albion Rovers, Cowdenbeath

Leagues reformed into Premier, First, Second and Third Divisions

1994-95 **Promoted to Premier** — Raith Rovers
Relegated to First — Dundee United
Promoted to First — Morton, Dumbarton
Relegated to Second — Ayr United, Stranraer
Relegated to Third — Meadowbank, Brechin City

1995-96 **Promoted to Premier** — Dunfermline, Dundee Utd
Relegated to First — Falkirk, Partick Thistle
Promoted to First — Stirling Albion, East Fife
Relegated to Second — Dumbarton, Hamilton
Promoted to Second — Livingston, Brechin C
Relegated to Third — Forfar, Montrose

1996-97 **Promoted to Premier** – St Johnstone
Relegated to First – Raith Rovers
Promoted to First – Ayr United, Hamilton Accies
Relegated to Second – Clydebank, East Fife
Promoted to Second – Inverness CT, Forfar
Relegated to Third – Dumbarton, Berwick Rangers

1997-98 **Promoted to Premier** – Dundee
Relegated to First – Hibs
Promoted to First – Stranraer, Clydebank
Relegated to Second – Partick Thistle, Stirling Alb
Promoted to Second – Alloa, Arbroath
Relegated to Third – Stenhousemuir, Brechin

1998-99 **Promoted to Premier** – Hibs
Relegated to First – Dunfermline
Promoted to First – Livingston, Inverness CT
Relegated to Second – Hamilton, Stranraer
Promoted to Second – Ross Co, Stenhousemuir
Relegated to Third – East Fife, Forfar Athletic

1999-00 **Promoted to Premier** – St Mirren, Dunfermline
Relegated to First – No relegation
Promoted to First – Clyde, Alloa, Ross County
Relegated to Second – Clydebank
Promoted to Second – Queen's Pk, Berwick Forfar
Relegated to Third – Hamilton Accies
New league entrants – Elgin City, Peterhead
Relegated to Second – Clydebank
New league entrants – Elgin City, Peterhead

2000-01 **Promoted to Premier** – Livingston
Relegated to First – St Mirren
Promoted to First – Partick Thistle, Arbroath
Relegated to Second – Morton, Alloa
Promoted to Second – Hamilton, Cowdenbeath
Relegated to Third – Queen's Park, Stirling Albion

2001-02 **Promoted to Premier** – Partick Thistle
Relegated to First – St Johnstone
Promoted to First – Queen of the South, Alloa
Relegated to Second – Raith Rovers
Promoted to Second – Brechin, Dumbarton
Relegated to Third – Morton

2002-03 **Promoted to Premier** – No promotion
Relegated to First – No relegation
Promoted to First – Raith Rovers, Brechin City
Relegated to Second – Alloa, Arbroath

	Promoted to Second – Morton, East Fife
	Relegated to Third – Stranraer, Cowdenbeath
2003-04	**Promoted to Premier** – Inverness Caley Thistle
	Relegated to First – Partick Thistle
	Promoted to First – Airdrie United, Hamilton Accies
	Relegated to Second – Brechin City, Ayr United
	Promoted to Second – Stranraer, Stirling Albion
	Relegated to Third – Stenhousemuir, East Fife
2004-05	**Promoted to Premier** – Falkirk
	Relegated to First – Dundee
	Promoted to First – Brechin, Stranraer
	Relegated to Second – Partick, Raith Rovers
	Promoted to Second – Gretna, Peterhead
	Relegated to Third – Arbroath, Berwick Rangers
2005-06	**Promoted to Premier** – St Mirren
	Relegated to First – Livingston
	Promoted to First – Gretna, Partick Thistle (play-off)
	Relegated to Second – Stranraer (play-off), Brechin
	Promoted to Second – Cowdenbeath
	Relegated to Third – Dumbarton
2006-07	**Promoted to Premier** – Gretna
	Relegated to First – Dunfermline
	Promoted to First – Morton, Stirling (play-off)
	Relegated to Second – Ross Co, Airdrie (play-off)
	Promoted to Second – Berwick, Q Park (play-off)
	Relegated to Third – Forfar, Stranraer (play-off)
2007-08	**Promoted to Premier** – Hamilton
	Relegated to First – Gretna
	Promoted to First – Ross County
	Relegated to Second – Stirling
	Promoted to Second – East Fife, Arbroath (play-off)
	Relegated to Third – Berwick, Cowdenbeath (play-off)
2008-09	**Promoted to Premier** – St Johnstone
	Relegated to First – Inverness CT
	Promoted to First – Raith Rovers, Ayr Utd (play-off)
	Relegated to Second – Clyde, Airdrie Utd (play-off)
	Promoted to Second – Dumbarton, Stenh'semuir (play-off)
	Relegated to Third – Stranraer, Queen's Pk (play-off)
2009-10	**Promoted to Premier** – Inverness CT
	Relegated to First – Falkirk
	Promoted to First – Stirling, Cowdenbeath (play-off)
	Relegated to Second – Ayr United, Airdrie United (play-off)
	Promoted to Second – Livingston, Forfar Athletic (play-off)
	Relegated to Third – Clyde, Arbroath (play-off)
2010-11	**Promoted to Premier** – Dunfermline Athletic
	Relegated to First – Hamilton Accies
	Promoted to First – Livingston, Ayr (play-off)
	Relegated to Second – Stirling, Cowdenbeath (play-off)
	Promoted to Second – Arbroath, Albion Rovers (play-off)
	Relegated to Third – Peterhead, Alloa (play-off)
2011-12	**Promoted to Premier** – Ross County
	Relegated to First – Dunfermline Athletic
	Promoted to First – Cowdenbeath, Dumbarton (play-off)
	Relegated to Second – Queen of Sth, Ayr United (play-off)
	Promoted to Second – Alloa
	Relegated to Third – Stirling
2012-13	**Promoted to Premier** – Partick Thistle
	Relegated to First – Dundee
	Promoted to First – Queen of South, Alloa
	Relegated to Second – Airdrie United, Dunfermline
	Promoted to Second – Rangers
	Relegated to Third – Albion Rovers

SCOTTISH COMMUNITIES LEAGUE CUP 2012-2013

FIRST ROUND: Rangers 4 East Fife 0, East Stirlingshire 1 Morton 5, Arbroath 1 Stirling Albion 1 (aet, Arbroath win 3-2 on pens), Ayr United 6 Clyde 1, Dumbarton 2 Albion Rovers 0, Falkirk 2 Elgin City 0, Forfar Athletic 0 Partick Thistle 2, Hamilton 2 Annan Ath 0, Montrose 2 Cowdenbeath 1, Queen of the South 5 Alloa 2, Queen's Park 3 Airdrie United 2 (aet, after 2-2 draw), Raith Rovers 4 Berwick Rangers 3, Stenhousemuir 4 Brechin City 0, Stranraer 0 Livingston 8, Peterhead 0 Dundee 0 (aet, Dundee win 3-1 on pens).

SECOND ROUND

Rangers	3	Falkirk	0
Arbroath	0	Inverness CT	2
Queen's Park	2	Dundee	1
St Mirren	5	Ayr United	1
Dunfermline	3	Montrose	0
Hamilton	1	Partick Thistle	0
(after extra time)			
Kilmarnock	1	Stenhousemuir	2
Livingston	3	Dumbarton	2
(after extra time)			
Queen of the South	2	Hibernian	0
Ross County	1	Raith Rovers	4
Morton	0	Aberdeen	2
(after extra time)			

THIRD ROUND

Dunfermline	0	Aberdeen	1
Rangers	2	Motherwell	0
Celtic	4	Raith Rovers	1
Hearts	3	Livingston	1
Queen of the South	0	Dundee United	1
St Johnstone	4	Queen's Park	1
St Mirren	1	Hamilton	0
Stenhousemuir	1	Inverness CT	1
(aet, Inverness win 6-5 on pens)			

QUARTER-FINALS

Dundee United	1	Hearts	1
(aet, Hearts win 5-4 on pens)			
Rangers	0	Inverness CT	3
Aberdeen	2	St Mirren	2
(aet, St Mirren win 4-2 on pens)			
Celtic	5	St Johnstone	0

SEMI-FINALS

Inverness	1	Hearts	1
(aet, Hearts win 5-4 on pens)			
St Mirren	3	Celtic	2

FINAL

ST MIRREN	3	Hearts	2

LEAGUE CUP WINNERS

Season	Winner	Score	Runner-up	Score
1946-47	RANGERS	4	Aberdeen	0
1947-48	EAST FIFE	4	Falkirk	1
	(after 0-0 draw)			
1948-49	RANGERS	2	Raith Rovers	0
1949-50	EAST FIFE	3	Dunfermline	0
1950-51	MOTHERWELL	3	Hibernian	0
1951-52	DUNDEE	3	Rangers	2
1952-53	DUNDEE	2	Kilmarnock	0
1953-54	EAST FIFE	3	Partick Thistle	2
1954-55	HEARTS	4	Motherwell	2
1955-56	ABERDEEN	2	St Mirren	1
1956-57	CELTIC	3	Partick Thistle	0
1957-58	CELTIC	7	Rangers	1
1958-59	HEARTS	5	Partick Thistle	1
1959-60	HEARTS	2	Third Lanark	1
1960-61	RANGERS	2	Kilmarnock	0
1961-62	RANGERS	3	Hearts	1
	(after 1-1 draw)			
1962-63	HEARTS	1	Kilmarnock	0
1963-64	RANGERS	5	Morton	0
1964-65	RANGERS	2	Celtic	1
1965-66	CELTIC	2	Rangers	1
1966-67	CELTIC	1	Rangers	0
1967-68	CELTIC	5	Dundee	3
1968-69	CELTIC	6	Hibs	2
1969-70	CELTIC	1	St Johnstone	0
1970-71	RANGERS	1	Celtic	0
1971-72	PARTICK THISTLE	4	Celtic	1
1972-73	HIBS	2	Celtic	1
1973-74	DUNDEE	1	Celtic	0
1974-75	CELTIC	6	Hibs	3
1975-76	RANGERS	1	Celtic	0
1976-77	ABERDEEN	2	Celtic	1
	(after extra time)			
1977-78	RANGERS	2	Celtic	1
	(after extra time)			
1978-79	RANGERS	2	Aberdeen	1
1979-80	DUNDEE UNITED	3	Aberdeen	0
	(after 0-0 draw)			
1980-81	DUNDEE UNITED	3	Dundee	0
1981-82	RANGERS	2	Dundee United	1
1982-83	CELTIC	2	Rangers	1
1983-84	RANGERS	3	Celtic	2
	(after extra time)			
1984-85	RANGERS	1	Dundee United	0
1985-86	ABERDEEN	3	Hibernian	0
1986-87	RANGERS	2	Celtic	1
1987-88	RANGERS	3	Aberdeen	3
	(after extra time, Rangers won 5-3 on penalties)			
1988-89	RANGERS	3	Aberdeen	2
1989-90	ABERDEEN	2	Rangers	1
	(after extra time)			
1990-91	RANGERS	2	Celtic	1
	(after extra time)			
1991-92	HIBERNIAN	2	Dunfermline	0

1992-93	RANGERS	2	Aberdeen	1
		(after extra time)		
1993-94	RANGERS	2	Hibernian	1
1994-95	RAITH ROVERS	2	Celtic	2
	(after extra time, Raith Rovers won 6-5 on penalties)			
1995-96	ABERDEEN	2	Dundee	0
1996-97	RANGERS	4	Hearts	3
1997-98	CELTIC	3	Dundee United	0
1998-99	RANGERS	2	St Johnstone	1
1999-00	CELTIC	2	Aberdeen	0
2000-01	CELTIC	3	Kilmarnock	0
2001-02	RANGERS	4	Ayr United	0
2002-03	RANGERS	2	Celtic	1
2003-04	LIVINGSTON	2	Hibernian	0
2004-05	RANGERS	5	Motherwell	1
2005-06	CELTIC	3	Dunfermline	0
2006-07	HIBERNIAN	5	Kilmarnock	1
2007-08	RANGERS	2	Dundee United	2
	(after extra time, Rangers won 3-2 on penalties)			
2008-09	CELTIC	0	Rangers	0
	(after extra time, Celtic won 2-0)			
2009-10	RANGERS	1	St Mirren	0
2010-11	RANGERS	2	Celtic	1
		(after extra time)		
2011-12	KILMARNOCK	1	Celtic	0
2012-13	ST MIRREN	3	Hearts	2

SFL PLAY-OFFS

FIRST DIVISION SEMI-FINAL FIRST LEGS

Forfar .... 3 Dunfermline 1
Brechin .... 0 Alloa 2

FIRST DIVISION SEMI-FINAL SECOND LEGS

Dunfermline .... 6 Forfar 1
(Dunfermline win 7-4 on aggregate after extra time)
Alloa .... 2 Brechin 3
(Alloa win 4-3 on aggregate)

FIRST DIVISION PLAY-OFF FINAL FIRST LEG

Alloa .... 3 Dunfermline 0

FIRST DIVISION PLAY-OFF FINAL SECOND LEG

Dunfermline .... 1 Alloa 0
(Alloa win 3-1 on aggregate and are promoted to Division 1 with Dunfermline relegated to Division 2)

SECOND DIVISION SEMI-FINAL FIRST LEGS

Berwick .... 1 East Fife 1
Queen's Park .... 0 Peterhead 1

SECOND DIVISION SEMI-FINAL SECOND LEGS

East Fife .... 2 Berwick 1
(East Fife win 3-2 on aggregate after extra time)
Peterhead .... 3 Queen's Park 1
(Peterhead win 4-1 on aggregate)

SECOND DIVISION PLAY-OFF FINAL FIRST LEG

East Fife .... 0 Peterhead 0

SECOND DIVISION PLAY-OFF FINAL SECOND LEG

Peterhead .... 0 East Fife 1
(East Fife win 1-0 on aggregate to avoid dropping out of Division 2 and Peterhead remain in Division 3)

RAMSDENS CUP 2012-2013

FIRST ROUND NORTH-EAST

Brechin City	1	Rangers	2

(after extra time)

Falkirk	3	Stirling Albion	0
Montrose	4	Inverurie Loco Works	2
Peterhead	1	East Fife	2
Elgin City	5	Arbroath	7
Forfar Athletic	3	Dunfermline	2
Wick Academy	2	Raith Rovers	4
Cowdenbeath	1	Alloa Athletic	1

(aet, Cowdenbeath win 3-1 on pens)

FIRST ROUND SOUTH-WEST

East Stirlingshire	3	Ayr United	1
Morton	2	Albion Rovers	0
Berwick Rangers	2	Queen's Park	2

(aet, Queen's Park win 3-2 on pens)

Dumbarton	0	Queen of the South	1
Hamilton	0	Airdrie United	1
Stranraer	1	Stenhousemuir	2
Annan Athletic	1	Livingston	0
Clyde	0	Partick Thistle	1

SECOND ROUND NORTH-EAST

Cowdenbeath	3	East Fife	0
Raith Rovers	5	Montrose	2
Arbroath	3	Forfar Athletic	2
Falkirk	0	Rangers	1

SECOND ROUND SOUTH-WEST

Annan Athletic	0	Stenhousemuir	3
Queen's Park	4	Partick Thistle	5
Morton	1	Queen of the South	2

(after extra time)

East Stirlingshire	3	Airdrie United	0

QUARTER-FINALS

Arbroath	1	Stenhousemuir	0
East Stirlingshire	1	Cowdenbeath	2
Partick Thistle	3	Queen of Raith Rovers	0
Rangers	2	Queen of the South	2

(aet, Queen of the South win 4-3 on pens)

SEMI-FINALS

Cowdenbeath	0	Partick Thistle	1
Queen of the South	2	Arbroath	1

(after extra time)

FINAL

Queen of the South	1	Partick Thistle	1

(aet, Queen of the South win 6-5 on pens)

WILLIAM HILL SCOTTISH CUP 2012-2013

FIRST ROUND: Threave Rovers 0 Vale of Leithen 1, Bonnyrigg Rose Athletic 2 Girvan 1, Huntly 2 Wigtown & Bladnoch 0 (after 2-2 draw), Edinburgh City 4 Shotts Bon Accord 1 (after 1-1 draw), Irvine Meadow 4 Gala Fairydean 0, Edinburgh University 1 St Cuthbert Wanderers 2, Formartine United 3 Brora Rangers 2, Civil Service Strollers 4 Newton Stewart 0, Spartans 0 Wick Academy 2, Glasgow University 0 Selkirk 2, Clachnacuddin 2 Lossiemouth 1, Hawick Royal Albert 1 Golspie Sutherland 4, Fraserburgh 4 Coldstream 0, Whitehill Welfare 2 Inverurie Loco Works 4, Rothes 0 Buckie Thistle 4 (after 0-0 draw), Hermes 1 Deveronvale 4, Preston Athletic 0 Nairn County 2, Turriff United 6 Burntisland Shipyard 1.

SECOND ROUND: Cove Rangers 7 Golspie Sutherland 0, Fraserburgh 1 East Stirlingshire 2, Forres Mechanics 0 Rangers 1, Clachnacuddin 4 Formartine United 2, Civil Service Strollers 1 Turriff United 2, Montrose 1 Edinburgh City 3, Annan Athletic 1 Buckie Thistle 2, (after 0-0 draw), Berwick Rangers 1 Wick Academy 0, Vale of Leithen 5 Selkirk 1 (after 1-1 draw), Inverurie Loco Works 4 Huntly 3, Deveronvale 3 Peterhead 2, Elgin City 3 St Cuthbert Wanderers 1, Dalbeattie Star 0 Stirling Albion 5, Queen's Park 3 Irvine Meadow 0, Stirling University 0 Bonnyrigg Rose Athletic 1, Nairn County 3 Clyde 2 (after 3-3 draw).

THIRD ROUND: Rangers 7 Alloa Athletic 0, Elgin City 5 East Fife 1, Buckie Thistle 0 Turriff United 1, Dumbarton 4 East Stirlingshire 1, Raith Rovers 4 Airdrie United 3 (aet, after 2-2 draw), Queen's Park 0 Stranraer 4 (after 1-1 draw), Partick Thistle 2 Cove Rangers 1, Nairn County 2 Forfar Athletic 3 (after 3-3 draw), Morton 3 Albion Rovers 0 (after 1-1 draw), Cowdenbeath 8 Vale of Leithen 1, Edinburgh City 0 Queen of the South 2, Stirling Albion 0 Deveronvale 1, Arbroath 3 Inverurie Loco Works 1 (after 3-3 draw), Ayr United 2 Clachnacuddin 1, Berwick Rangers 2 Stenhousemuir 5 (after 1-1 draw), Bonnyrigg Rose Athletic 0 Brechin City 6 (after 2-2 draw).

FOURTH ROUND: Inverness CT 2 Ross County 1 (after 3-3 draw), Motherwell 1 Aberdeen 2 (after 1-1 draw), Partick Thistle 0 Dunfermline 1, Kilmarnock 2 Queen of the South 1, Raith Rovers 2 Deveronvale 1, Morton 6 Turriff United 0 (after 1-1 draw), Livingston 0 Dundee 2, Forfar Athletic 2 Ayr United 1, Arbroath 1 Celtic 0 (after 1-1 draw), Stranraer 0 Dundee United 5, Stenhousemuir 0 Falkirk 1, St Mirren 2 Brechin City 0, Rangers 3 Elgin City 0, Hibernian 1 Hearts 0, Dumbarton 1 Hamilton 3, Cowdenbeath 0 St Johnstone 3.

FIFTH ROUND: Dundee United 3 Rangers 0, St Mirren 2 St Johnstone 0, Dunfermline 0 Hamilton 2, Falkirk 4 Forfar Athletic 1, Kilmarnock 2 Inverness CT 0, Raith Rovers 0 Celtic 3, Dundee 5 Morton 1, Hibernian 1 Aberdeen 0.

QUARTER-FINALS

St Mirren	1	Celtic	2
Hamilton	1	Falkirk	2
Dundee	1	Dundee United	2
Kilmarnock	2	Hibernian	4

SEMI-FINALS

Hibernian	4	Falkirk	3
	(after extra time)		
Dundee United	3	Celtic	4
	(after extra time)		

FINAL

Hibernian	0	CELTIC	3

PREVIOUS WINNERS

1873-74 QUEEN'S PARK......2 Clydesdale..........................0
1874-75 QUEEN'S PARK......3 Renton..................................0
1875-76 QUEEN'S PARK......2 3rd Lanark Rifles 0
(after 1-1 draw)
1876-77 VALE OF LEVEN.....3 Rangers...............................2
(After two replays 0-0, 1-1)
1877-78 VALE OF LEVEN.....1 3rd Lanark Rifles.................0
1878-79 VALE OF LEVEN.....1 Rangers...............................1
(Vale of Leven awarded cup, Rangers failed to appear)
1879-80 QUEEN'S PARK......3 Thornliebank.........................0
1880-81 QUEEN'S PARK......3 Dumbarton 1
(after Dumbarton protested first game)
1881-82 QUEEN'S PARK......4 Dumbarton 1
(after 2-2 draw)
1882-83 DUMBARTON.........2 Vale of Leven........................1
(after 2-2 draw)
1883-84 QUEEN'S PARK...wo Vale of Leven........................
(Queen's Park awarded cup, Vale of Leven failed to appear.)
884-85 RENTON.................3 Vale of Leven........................1
(after 0-0 draw)
1885-86 QUEEN'S PARK......3 Renton..................................1
1886-87 HIBERNIAN.............2 Dumbarton 1
1887-88 RENTON.................6 Cambuslang 1
1888-89 THIRD LANARK......2 Celtic 1
(after replay by order of Scottish FA because of playing conditions in first match)
1889-90 QUEEN'S PARK......2 Vale of Leven........................1
(after 1-1 draw)
1890-91 HEARTS..................1 Dumbarton 0
1891-92 CELTIC....................5 Queen's Park........................1
(after mutually-protested first game)
1892-93 QUEEN'S PARK......2 Celtic 1
(after 0-0 draw)
1893-94 RANGERS...............3 Celtic 1
1894-95 ST BERNARD'S......2 Renton..................................1
1895-96 HEARTS..................3 Hibernian..............................1
1896-97 RANGERS...............5 Dumbarton 1
1897-98 RANGERS...............2 Kilmarnock 0
1898-99 CELTIC....................2 Rangers...............................0
1899-00 CELTIC....................4 Queen's Park........................3
1900-01 HEARTS..................4 Celtic 3
1901-02 HIBS ....1 CELTIC 0
1902-03 RANGERS...............2 Hearts..................................0
(after two replays, 1-1, 0-0)

1903-04	CELTIC	3	Rangers	2
1904-05	THIRD LANARK	3	Rangers	1
	(after 0-0 draw)			
1905-06	HEARTS	1	Third Lanark	0
1906-07	CELTIC	3	Hearts	0
1907-08	CELTIC	5	St Mirren	1
1908-09	Celtic	–	Rangers	–
	(owing to riot, cup was withheld after two drawn games)			
1909-10	DUNDEE	2	Clyde	1
	(after two draws, 2-2, 0-0)			
1910-11	CELTIC	2	Hamilton Accies	0
	(after 0-0 draw)			
1911-12	CELTIC	2	Clyde	0
1912-13	FALKIRK	2	Raith Rovers	0
1913-14	CELTIC	4	HIBS	1
	(after 0-0 draw)			
1919-20	KILMARNOCK	3	Albion Rovers	2
1920-21	PARTICK THISTLE	1	Rangers	0
1921-22	MORTON	1	Rangers	0
1922-23	CELTIC	1	Hibernian	0
1923-24	AIRDRIE	2	Hibernian	0
1924-25	CELTIC	2	Dundee	1
1925-26	ST MIRREN	2	Celtic	0
1926-27	CELTIC	3	East Fife	1
1927-28	RANGERS	4	Celtic	0
1928-29	KILMARNOCK	2	Rangers	0
1929-30	RANGERS	2	Partick Thistle	1
	(after 0-0 draw)			
1930-31	CELTIC	4	Motherwell	2
	(after 2-2 draw)			
1931-32	RANGERS	3	Kilmarnock	0
	(after 1-1 draw)			
1932-33	CELTIC	1	Motherwell	0
1933-34	RANGERS	5	St Mirren	0
1934-35	RANGERS	2	Hamilton Accies	1
1935-36	RANGERS	1	Third Lanark	0
1936-37	CELTIC	2	Aberdeen	1
1937-38	EAST FIFE	4	Kilmarnock	2
	(after 1-1 draw)			
1938-39	CLYDE	4	Motherwell	0
1946-47	ABERDEEN	2	Hibernian	1
1947-48	RANGERS	1	Morton	0
	(after extra time; after 1-1 draw)			
1948-49	RANGERS	4	Clyde	1
1949-50	RANGERS	3	East Fife	0

Season	Winner	Score	Runner-up	Score
1950-51	CELTIC	1	Motherwell	0
1951-52	MOTHERWELL	4	Dundee	0
1952-53	RANGERS	1	Aberdeen	0
	(after 1-1 draw)			
1953-54	CELTIC	2	Aberdeen	1
1954-55	CLYDE	1	Celtic	0
	(after 1-1 draw)			
1955-56	HEARTS	3	Celtic	1
1956-57	FALKIRK	2	Kilmarnock	1
	(after extra time; after 1-1 draw)			
1957-58	CLYDE	1	Hibernian	0
1958-59	ST MIRREN	3	Aberdeen	1
1959-60	RANGERS	2	Kilmarnock	0
1960-61	DUNFERMLINE	2	Celtic	0
	(after 0-0 draw)			
1961-62	RANGERS	2	St Mirren	0
1962-63	RANGERS	3	Celtic	0
	(after 1-1 draw)			
1963-64	RANGERS	3	Dundee	1
1964-65	CELTIC	3	Dunfermline Athletic	2
1965-66	RANGERS	1	Celtic	0
	(after 0-0 draw)			
1966-67	CELTIC	2	Aberdeen	0
1967-68	DUNFERMLINE	3	Hearts	1
1968-69	CELTIC	4	Rangers	0
1969-70	ABERDEEN	3	Celtic	1
1970-71	CELTIC	2	Rangers	1
	(after 1-1 draw)			
1971-72	CELTIC	6	Hibernian	1
1972-73	RANGERS	3	Celtic	2
1973-74	CELTIC	3	Dundee United	0
1974-75	CELTIC	3	Airdrie	1
1975-76	RANGERS	3	Hearts	1
1976-77	CELTIC	1	Rangers	0
1977-78	RANGERS	2	Aberdeen	1
1978-79	RANGERS	3	Hibernian	2
	(after two 0-0 draws, and extra time)			
1979-80	CELTIC	1	Rangers	0
	(after extra time)			
1980-81	RANGERS	4	Dundee United	1
	(after 0-0 draw)			
1981-82	ABERDEEN	4	Rangers	1
	(after extra time)			
1982-83	ABERDEEN	1	Rangers	0
	(after extra time)			

1983-84	ABERDEEN	2	Celtic	1
		(after extra time)		
1984-85	CELTIC	2	Dundee United	1
1985-86	ABERDEEN	3	Hearts	0
1986-87	ST MIRREN	1	Dundee United	0
		(after extra time)		
1987-88	CELTIC	2	Dundee United	1
1988-89	CELTIC	1	Rangers	0
1989-90	ABERDEEN	0	Celtic	0
		(after extra time, Aberdeen won 9-8 on penalties)		
1990-91	MOTHERWELL	4	Dundee United	3
		(after extra time)		
1991-92	RANGERS	2	Airdrie	1
1992-93	RANGERS	2	Aberdeen	1
1993-94	DUNDEE UTD	1	Rangers	0
1994-95	CELTIC	1	Airdrie	0
1995-96	RANGERS	5	Hearts	1
1996-97	KILMARNOCK	1	Falkirk	0
1997-98	HEARTS	2	Rangers	1
1998-99	RANGERS	1	Celtic	0
1999-00	RANGERS	4	Aberdeen	0
2000-01	CELTIC	3	Hibernian	0
2001-02	RANGERS	3	Celtic	2
2002-03	RANGERS	1	Dundee	0
2003-04	CELTIC	3	Dunfermline	1
2004-05	CELTIC	1	Dundee United	0
2005-06	HEARTS	1	Gretna	1
		(after extra time, Hearts win 4-2 on penalties)		
2006-07	CELTIC	1	Dunfermline	0
2007-08	RANGERS	3	Queen of the South	2
2008-09	RANGERS	1	Falkirk	0
2009-10	DUNDEE UNITED	3	Ross County	0
2010-11	CELTIC	3	Motherwell	0
2011-12	HEARTS	5	Hibs	1
2012-13	CELTIC	3	Hibs	0

CELTIC celebrate 2013 Scottish Cup success

SCOTTISH CUP-WINNING TEAMS

1976-77 – CELTIC: Latchford, McGrain, Lynch, Stanton, McDonald, Aitken, Dalglish, Edvaldsson, Craig, Conn, Wilson.
1977-78 – RANGERS: McCloy, Jardine, Greig, Forsyth, Jackson, MacDonald, McLean, Russell, Johnstone, Smith, Cooper.
1978-79 – RANGERS: McCloy, Jardine, Dawson, Johnstone, Jackson, Watson, McLean, Russell, Parlane, McDonald, Cooper.
1979-80 – CELTIC: Latchford, Sneddon, McGrain, Aitken, Conroy, MacLeod, Provan, Doyle, McCluskey, Burns, McGarvey.
1980-81 – RANGERS: Stewart, Jardine, Dawson, Stevens, Forsyth, Bett, Cooper, Russell, D. Johnstone, Redford, MacDonald.
1981-82 – ABERDEEN: Leighton, Kennedy, Rougvie, McMaster, McLeish, Miller, Strachan, Cooper, McGhee, Simpson, Hewitt.
1982-83 – ABERDEEN: Leighton, Rougvie, McMaster, Cooper, McLeish, Miller, Strachan, Simpson, McGhee, Black, Weir.
1983-84 – ABERDEEN: Leighton, McKimmie, Rougvie, Cooper, McLeish, Miller, Strachan, Simpson, McGhee, Black, Weir.
1984-85 – CELTIC: Bonner, W. McStay, McGrain, Aitken, McAdam, MacLeod, Provan, P. McStay, Johnston, Burns, McGarvey.
1985-86 – ABERDEEN: Leighton, McKimmie, McQueen, McMaster, McLeish, Miller, Hewitt, Cooper, McDougall, Bett, Weir.
1986-87 – ST MIRREN: Money, Wilson, D. Hamilton, Abercromby, Winnie, Cooper, Ferguson, McGarvey, McDowall, B. Hamilton, Lambert.
1987-88 – CELTIC: McKnight, Morris, Rogan, Aitken, McCarthy, Whyte, Miller, McStay, McAvennie, Walker, Burns.
1988-89 – CELTIC: Bonner, Morris, Rogan, Aitken, McCarthy, Whyte, Grant, McStay, Miller, McGhee, Burns.
1989-90 – ABERDEEN: Snelders, McKimmie, Robertson, Grant, McLeish, Irvine, Nicholas, Bett, Mason, Connor, Gillhaus.
1990-91 – MOTHERWELL: Maxwell, Nijholt, Boyd, Griffin, Paterson, McCart, Arnott, Angus, Ferguson (Kirk), O'Donnell, Cooper (O'Neill).
1991-92 – RANGERS: Goram, Stevens, Robertson, Gough, Spackman, Brown, McCall, McCoist, Hateley, Mikhailitchenko, Durrant. Subs: Gordon, Rideout.
1992-93 – RANGERS: Goram, McPherson, Gough, Brown, Robertson, Murray, Ferguson, McCall, Durrant, Hateley, Huistra. Subs: Pressley, McSwegan.
1993-94 – DUNDEE UNITED: Van De Kamp, Cleland, Malpas, McInally, Petric, Welsh, Bowman, Hannah, McLaren, Brewster, Dailly. Subs: Nixon, Bollan.
1994-95 – CELTIC: Bonner, Boyd, McKinlay, Vata, McNally, Grant, McLaughlin, McStay, Van Hooijdonk (Falconer), Donnelly (O'Donnell), Collins. **CONTINUED ON PAGE 117**

CELTIC youngster Tony Watt nets the winner against Barcelona in the Champions League group stage on a famous night for the Parkhead club

ST MIRREN won their first major trophy since 1987 when they beat Hearts 3-2 in the League Cup final at Hampden Park

CELTIC skipper Scott Brown returned from injury late in the season to lift the Scottish Cup

IT'S HISTORY IN THE MAKING...
THE HAMPDEN EXPERIENCE
...IT'S WHO WE ARE
SCOTTISH FOOTBALL HAMPDEN MUSEUM
THE STADIUM TOUR
HALL OF FAME
HAMPDEN HOTSHOTS
Bring your Wee Red Book and get 50% Off Entry
Scottish TOURIST BOARD ★★★★★ MUSEUM

print management. simple.

RANGERS manager Ally McCoist celebrates the Third Division title with son Arran

"Touched By Suicide" Scotland

Meeting Venue's

Glasgow West	**102 Kingsway, Scotstoun, Glasgow, 614 9YS** 3rd Monday of the month 7pm to 9pm
Glasgow East	**East Bank Health Promotion Centre** **Academy Street Shettleston 632** 1st Thursday of the Month March 12 5.45pm -7.45pm
Whitburn	**Whitburn Community Centre West Lothian** Last Tuesday of the month 7pm - 9pm
Kilmarnock	**Daniel Coffey Suite, North West Area Centre, Western Road, KA3 1NQ** Last Thursday of the month 7pm to 9pm
Kilbirnie	**Radio City 1a Bridgend Kilbirnie** 2nd Wednesday of the month 7-9pm
Ayr	**John Pollock Centre Mainholm Road KA8 0QD** 1st Tuesday of the month 6.45 pm - 8.45pm
Largs	**The Woodhouse Hotel, 2 Barr Crescent, KA30 8PX** 2nd Monday of the month 7pm - 9pm
Girvan	**Carrick Opportunity Centre Henrietta St KA26 9AL** Last Wednesday of the month 7pm - 9pm

Telephone Helpline Contact: Linda 01294 216895

CELTIC pair Victor Wanyama and Scott Brown revel in the moment after the Parkhead club clinched the SPL title against Inverness

SCOTTISH CUP-WINNING TEAMS (cont'd)

1995-96 – RANGERS: Goram, Cleland, Robertson, Gough, McLaren, Brown, Durie, Gascoigne, Ferguson (Durrant), McCall, Laudrup.
1996-97 – KILMARNOCK: Lekovic, MacPherson, Kerr, Montgomerie, McGowne, Reilly, Bagan (Mitchell), Holt, Wright (Henry), McIntyre (Brown), Burke.
1997-98 – HEARTS: Rousett, McPherson, Naysmith, Weir, Salvatore, Ritchie, McCann, Fulton, Adam (Hamilton), Cameron, Flogel.
1998-99 – RANGERS: Klos, Porrini (Kanchelskis), Vidmar, Amoruso, Hendry, McCann (I Ferguson), McInnes, Wallace, van Bronckhorst, Amato (Wilson), Albertz.
1999-00 – RANGERS: Klos, Reyna, Moore (Porrini), Vidmar, Numan, Kanchelskis, Ferguson, Albertz, van Bronckhorst (Tugay), Wallace (McCann), Dodds.
2000-01 – CELTIC: Douglas, Mjallby, Vega, Valgaeren, Agathe, Lennon, Lambert (Boyd) Moravcik (McNamara) Thompson (Johnson), Larsson, Sutton.
2001-02 – RANGERS: Klos, Ross, Moore, Amoruso, Numan, Ricksen, de Boer, Ferguson, Lovenkrands, McCann, Caniggia (Arveladze).
2002-03 – RANGERS: Klos, Malcolm, Moore, Amoruso, Numan (Muscat), Ricksen, Ferguson, de Boer, McCann, Arveladze (Thompson), Mols (Ross).
2003-04 – CELTIC: Marshall, Varga, Balde, McNamara, Agathe, Lennon, Petrov, Pearson (Wallace), Thompson, Larsson, Sutton.
2004-05 – CELTIC: Douglas, Agathe, Balde, Varga, McNamara, Petrov, Lennon, Sutton, Thompson (McGeady), Hartson (Valgaeren), Bellamy.
2005-06 – HEARTS: Gordon, Neilson, Pressley, Tall, Fyssas, Cesnauskis (Mikoliunas), Aguiar (Brellier), Hartley, Skacel, Bednar (Pospisil), Jankauskas.
2006-07 – CELTIC: Boruc, Doumbe, McManus, Pressley, Naylor, Nakamura, Lennon (Caldwell), Hartley, McGeady, Miller (Beattie), Vennegoor of Hesselink.
2007-08 – RANGERS: Alexander, Whittaker, Cuellar, Weir, Papac, McCulloch, Ferguson, Thomson, Beasley (Davis), Boyd, Darcheville (Fleck).
2008-09 – RANGERS: Alexander, Whittaker, Bougherra, Weir, Papac, Davis, Ferguson, McCulloch, Lafferty (Dailly), Boyd (Novo), Miller (Naismith).
2009-10 – DUNDEE UNITED: Pernis, Kovacevic (Watson), Webster, Kenneth, Dillon, Swanson (Scott Robertson), Buaben, Gomis, Conway, Daly, Goodwillie (David Robertson).
2010-11 – CELTIC: Forster, Izaguirre, Majstorovic, Wilson, Mulgrew, Loovens, Brown, Ki, Samaras (Stokes), Commons (Forrest), Hooper (McCourt).
2011-12 – HEARTS: MacDonald, McGowan, Webster, Zaliukas, Grainger, Black (Robinson), Barr, Santana (Beattie), Skacel, Driver (Taouil), Elliott.
2012-13 – CELTIC: Forster, Izaguirre, Wilson, Mulgrew, Lustig, Brown (Ambrose), Commons (Samaras), Ledley, Forrest (McCourt), Stokes, Hooper.

PLAYER OF THE YEAR

AWARDED BY THE SCOTTISH FOOTBALL WRITERS' ASSOCIATION.

1965........BILLY McNEILL (Celtic)
1966........JOHN GREIG (Rangers)
1967........RONNIE SIMPSON (Celtic)
1968........GORDON WALLACE (Raith Rovers)
1969........BOBBY MURDOCH (Celtic)
1970........PAT STANTON (Hibernian)
1971........MARTIN BUCHAN (Aberdeen)
1972........DAVE SMITH (Rangers)
1973........GEORGE CONNELLY (Celtic)
1974........WORLD CUP SQUAD
1975........SANDY JARDINE (Rangers)
1976........JOHN GREIG (Rangers)
1977........DANNY McGRAIN (Celtic)
1978........DEREK JOHNSTONE (Rangers)
1979........ANDY RITCHIE (Morton)
1980........GORDON STRACHAN (Aberdeen)
1981........ALAN ROUGH (Partick Thistle)
1982........PAUL STURROCK (Dundee United)
1983........CHARLIE NICHOLAS (Celtic)
1984........WILLIE MILLER (Aberdeen)
1985........HAMISH McALPINE (Dundee United)
1986........SANDY JARDINE (Hearts)
1987........BRIAN McCLAIR (Celtic)
1988........PAUL McSTAY (Celtic)
1989........RICHARD GOUGH (Rangers)
1990........ALEX McLEISH (Aberdeen)
1991........MAURICE MALPAS (Dundee United)
1992........ALLY McCOIST (Rangers)
1993........ANDY GORAM (Rangers)
1994........MARK HATELEY (Rangers)
1995........BRIAN LAUDRUP (Rangers)
1996........PAUL GASCOIGNE (Rangers)
1997........BRIAN LAUDRUP (Rangers)
1998........CRAIG BURLEY (Celtic)
1999........HENRIK LARSSON (Celtic)
2000........BARRY FERGUSON (Rangers)
2001........HENRIK LARSSON (Celtic)
2002........PAUL LAMBERT (Celtic)
2003........BARRY FERGUSON (Rangers)
2004........JACKIE McNAMARA (Celtic)
2005........JOHN HARTSON (Celtic)
2006........CRAIG GORDON (Hearts)
2007........SHUNSUKE NAKAMURA (Celtic)
2008........CARLOS CUELLAR (Rangers)
2009........GARY CALDWELL (Celtic)
2010........DAVID WEIR (Rangers)
2011........EMILIO IZAGUIRRE (Celtic
2012........CHARLIE MULGREW (Celtic)
2013........LEIGH GRIFFITHS (Hibernian)

SPFA PLAYER OF THE YEAR

1977-78

Premier Division.. Derek Johnstone (Rangers)
First Division..Billy Pirie (Dundee)
Second Division.......................................Dave Smith (Berwick Rangers)
Young Player ....Graeme Payne (Dundee United)

1978-79

Premier Division... Paul Hegarty (Dundee United)
First Division...Brian McLaughlin (Ayr United)
Second Division............................... Michael Leonard (Dunfermline Ath)
Young Player ....Raymond Stewart (Dundee United)

1979-80

Premier Division...Davie Provan (Celtic)
First Division...Sandy Clark (Airdrie)
Second Division...Paul Leetion (Falkirk)
Young Player .... John MacDonald (Rangers)

1980-81

Premier Division..Mark McGhee (Aberdeen)
First Division...Eric Sinclair (Dundee)
Second Division........................ Jimmy Robertson (Queen of the South)
Young Player ....Charlie Nicholas (Celtic)

1981-82

Premier Division ....Sandy Clark (Airdrie)
First Division.. Brian McLaughlin (Motherwell)
Second Division..Pat Nevin (Clyde)
Young Player .... Frank McAvennie (St Mirren)

1982-83

Premier Division..Charlie Nicholas (Celtic)
First Division... Gerry McCabe (Clydebank)
Second Division................................... John Colquhoun (Stirling Albion)
Young Player .... Paul McStay (Celtic)

1983-84

Premier Division... Willie Miller (Aberdeen)
First Division.. Gerry McCabe (Clydebank)
Second Division...Jim Liddle (Forfar Athletic)
Young Player ....John Robertson (Hearts)

1984-85

Premier Division.. Jim Duffy (Morton)
First Division... Gerry McCabe (Clydebank)
Second Division.. Bernie Slaven (Albion Rovers)
Young Player .... Craig Levein (Hearts)

1985-86

Premier Division...................................Richard Gough (Dundee United)
First Division...John Brogan (Hamilton)
Second Division..Mark Smith (Queen's Park)
Young Player .... Craig Levein (Hearts)

1986-87

Premier Division...Brian McClair (Celtic)
First Division... Jim Holmes (Morton)
Second Division...John Sludden (Ayr United)
Young Player .... Robert Fleck (Rangers)

1987-88

Premier Division... Paul McStay (Celtic)
First Division..Alex Taylor (Hamilton)
Second Division.......................................Henry Templeton (Ayr United)
Young Player ....John Collins (Hibernian)

1988-89

Premier Division.. Theo Snelders (Aberdeen)
First Division...Ross Jack (Dunfermline)
Second Division..Paul Hunter (East Fife)
Young Player .... Billy McKinlay (Dundee United)

1989-90

Premier Division....................Jim Bett (Aberdeen)
First Division....................Ken Eadie (Clydebank)
Second Division....................Willie Watters (Kilmarnock)
Young Player....................Scott Crabbe (Hearts)

1990-91

Premier Division....................Paul Elliott (Celtic)
First Division....................Simon Stainrod (Falkirk)
Second Division....................Kevin Todd (Berwick Rangers)
Young Player....................Eoin Jess (Aberdeen)

1991-92

Premier Division....................Ally McCoist (Rangers)
First Division....................Gordon Dalziel (Raith Rovers)
Second Division....................Andy Thomson (Queen of the South)
Young Player....................Phil O'Donnell (Motherwell)

1992-93

Premier Division....................Andy Goram (Rangers)
First Division....................Gordon Dalziel (Raith Rovers)
Second Division....................Sandy Ross (Brechin City)
Young Player....................Eoin Jess (Aberdeen)

1993-94

Premier Division....................Mark Hateley (Rangers)
First Division....................Richard Cadette (Falkirk)
Second Division....................Andy Thomson (Queen of the South)
Young Player....................Phil O'Donnell (Motherwell)

1994-95

Premier Division....................Brian Laudrup (Rangers)
First Division....................Stephen Crawford (Raith Rovers)
Second Division....................Derek McInnes (Morton)
Third Division....................David Bingham (Forfar Ath.)
Young Player....................Charlie Miller (Rangers)

1995-96

Premier Division....................Paul Gascoigne (Rangers)
First Division....................George O'Boyle (St Johnstone)
Second Division....................Steven McCormick (Stirling A.)
Third Division....................Jason Young (Livingston)
Young Player....................Jackie McNamara (Celtic)

1996-97

Premier Division....................Paolo di Canio (Celtic)
First Division....................Roddy Grant (St Johnstone)
Second Division....................Paul Ritchie (Hamilton)
Third Division....................Ian Stewart (Inverness CT)
Young Player....................Robbie Winters (Dundee United)

1997-98

Premier Division....................Jackie McNamara (Celtic)
First Division....................James Grady (Dundee)
Second Division....................Paul Lovering (Clydebank)
Third Division....................Willie Irvine (Alloa)
Young Player....................Gary Naysmith (Hearts)

1998-99

Premier Division....................Henrik Larsson (Celtic)
First Division....................Russell Latapy (Hibs)
Second Division....................David Bingham (Livingston)
Third Division....................Neil Tarrant (Ross County)
Young Player....................Barry Ferguson (Rangers)

1999-2000

Premier Division....................Mark Viduka (Celtic)
First Division....................Stevie Crawford (Dunfermline)
Second Division....................Brian Carrigan (Clyde)
Third Division....................Stevie Milne (Forfar)
Young Player....................Kenny Miller (Hibs)

2000-2001

Premier Division....................Henrik Larsson (Celtic)
First Division....................David Bingham (Livingston)

Second Division....Scott McLean (Partick Thistle)
Third Division.... Steve Hislop (East Stirling)
Young Player ....Stilian Petrov (Celtic)

2001-2002

Premier Division.... Lorenzo Amoruso (Rangers)
First Division.... Owen Coyle (Airdrie)
Second Division....John O'Neill (Queen of the South)
Third Division....Paul McManus (East Fife)
Young Player ....Kevin McNaughton (Aberdeen)

2002-2003

Premier Division.... Barry Ferguson (Rangers)
First Division.... Dennis Wyness (Inverness Caley Thistle)
Second Division....Chris Templeman (Brechin)
Third Division.... Alex Williams (Morton)
Young Player .... James McFadden (Motherwell)

2003-2004

Premier Division....Chris Sutton (Celtic)
First Division.... Ian Harty (Clyde)
Second Division.... Paul Tosh (Forfar)
Third Division.... Michael Moore (Stranraer)
Young Player .... Stephen Pearson (Celtic)

2004-2005

Premier Division ....John Hartson (Celtic)/Fernando Ricksen (Rangers)
First Division....Russell Latapy (Falkirk)
Second Division.... Steven Hampshire (Brechin)
Third Division....David Bingham (Gretna)
Young Player ....Derek Riordan (Hibs)

2005-2006

Premier Division .... Shaun Maloney (Celtic)
First Division.... John Rankin (Ross County)
Second Division....James Grady (Gretna)
Third Division....Markus Paatelainen (Cowdenbeath)
Young Player ....Shaun Maloney (Celtic)

2006-2007

Premier Division ....Shunsuke Nakamura (Celtic)
First Division....Colin McMenamin (Gretna)
Second Division.... Iain Russell (Brechin City)
Third Division....Scott Chaplain (Albion Rovers)
Young Player ....Steven Naismith (Kilmarnock)

2007-2008

Premier Division ....Aiden McGeady (Celtic)
First Division....Graham Dorrans (Livingston)
Second Division....Allan Russell (Airdrie United)
Third Division.... Jonathan Smart (East Fife)
Young Player .... Aiden McGeady (Celtic)

2008-2009

Premier Division ....Scott Brown (Celtic)
First Division ....Leigh Griffiths (Livingston)
Second Division....Bryan Prunty (Ayr United)
Third Division ....Bobby Barr (Albion Rovers)
Young Player....James McCarthy (Hamilton)

2009-2010

Premier Division .... Steven Davis (Rangers)
First Division ....Adam Rooney (Inverness CT)
Second Division.... Rory McAllister (Brechin City))
Third Division .... Robbie Winters (Livingston)
Young Player.... Danny Wilson (Rangers)

2010-2011

Premier Division .... Emilio Izaguirre (Celtic)
First Division .... John Baird (Raith Rovers)
Second Division.... Rory McAllister (Brechin City)
Third Division ....Gavin Swankie (Arbroath)
Young Player....David Goodwillie (Dundee United)

SPFA PLAYER OF THE YEAR/cont...

2011-2012

Premier Division .... Charlie Mulgrew (Celtic)
First Division .... Farid El Alagui (Falkirk)
Second Division........ John Robertson (Cowdenbeath)
Third Division .... Steven May (Alloa)
Young Player........ James Forrest (Celtic)

2012-2013

Premier Division .... Michael Higdon (Motherwell)
First Division .... Lyle Taylor (Falkirk)
Second Division........ Nicky Clark (Queen of the South)
Third Division .... Lee Wallace (Rangers)
Young Player........ Leigh Griffiths (Hibernian)

ENGLISH PLAYER OF THE YEAR

AWARDED BY THE ENGLISH FOOTBALL WRITERS' ASSOCIATION

1948 **Stanley Matthews** (Blackpool)
1949 **Johnny Carey** (Man U)
1950 **Joe Mercer** (Arsenal)
1951 **Harry Johnston** (Blackpool)
1952 **Billy Wright** (Wolves)
1953 **Nat Lofthouse** (Bolton W.)
1954 **Tom Finney** (Preston NE)
1955 **Don Revie** (Man City)
1956 **Bert Trautmann** (Man City)
1957 **Tom Finney** (Preston NE)
1958 **Danny Blanchflower** (Spurs)
1959 **Syd Owen** (Luton Town)
1960 **Bill Slater** (Wolves)
1961 **Danny Blanchflower** (Spurs)
1962 **Jimmy Adamson** (Burnley)
1963 **Stanley Matthews** (Stoke C)
1964 **Bobby Moore** (West Ham)
1965 **Bobby Collins** (Leeds U)
1966 **Bobby Charlton** (Man U)
1967 **Jackie Charlton** (Leeds U)
1968 **George Best** (Man U)
1969 **Dave Mackay** (Derby)/ **Tony Book** (Man City)
1970 **Billy Bremner** (Leeds U)
1971 **Frank McLintock** (Arsenal)
1972 **Gordon Banks** (Stoke City)
1973 **Pat Jennings** (Spurs)
1974 **Ian Callaghan** (Liverpool)
1975 **Alan Mullery** (Fulham)
1976 **Kevin Keegan** (Liverpool)
1977 **Emlyn Hughes** (Liverpool)
1978 **Kenny Burns** (Notts Forest)
1979 **Kenny Dalglish** (Liverpool)
1980 **Terry McDermott** (Liverpool)
1981 **Frans Thijssen** (Ipswich T)
1982 **Steve Perryman** (Spurs)
1983 **Kenny Dalglish** Liverpool)
1984 **Ian Rush** (Liverpool)
1985 **Neville Southall** (Everton)
1986 **Gary Lineker** (Everton)
1987 **Clive Allen** (Tottenham H.)
1988 **John Barnes** (Liverpool)
1989 **Steve Nicol** (Liverpool)
1990 **John Barnes** (Liverpool)
1991 **Gordon Strachan** (Leeds U)
1992 **Gary Lineker** (Spurs)
1993 **Chris Waddle** (Sheffield W)
1994 **Alan Shearer** (Blackburn R)
1995 **Jurgen Klinsmann** (Spurs)
1996 **Eric Cantona** (Man U)
1997 **Gianfranco Zola** (Chelsea)
1998 **Dennis Bergkamp** (Arsenal)
1999 **David Ginola** (Spurs)
2000 **Roy Keane** (Man U)
2001 **Teddy Sheringham** (Man U)
2002 **Robert Pires** (Arsenal)
2003 **Thierry Henry** (Arsenal)
2004 **Thierry Henry** (Arsenal)
2005 **Frank Lampard** (Chelsea)
2006 **Thierry Henry** (Arsenal)
2007 **Cristiano Ronaldo** (Man U)
2008 **Cristiano Ronaldo** (Man U)
2009 **Steven Gerrard** (Liverpool)
2010 **Wayne Rooney** (Man U)
2011 **Scott Parker** (West Ham)
2012 **Robin van Persie** (Arsenal)
2013 **Gareth Bale** (Tottenham)

FIFA BALLON D'OR

(formerly Fifa World Player of the Year/Ballon d'Or)

1956.......STANLEY MATTHEWS (Blackpool)
1957.......ALFREDO DI STEFANO (Real Madrid)
1958.......RAYMOND KOPA (Real Madrid)
1959.......ALFREDO DI STEFANO (Real Madrid)
1960.......LUIS SUAREZ (Barcelona)
1961.......OMAR SIVORI (Juventus)
1962.......JOSEF MASOPUST (Dukla Prague)
1963.......LEV YASHIN (Moscow Dynamo)
1964.......DENIS LAW (Manchester United)
1965.......EUSEBIO (Benfica)
1966.......BOBBY CHARLTON (Manchester United)
1967.......FLORIAN ALBERT (Ferencvaros)
1968.......GEORGE BEST (Manchester United)
1969.......GIANNI RIVERA (AC Milan)
1970.......GERD MULLER (Bayern Munich)
1971.......JOHAN CRUYFF (Ajax Amsterdam)
1972.......FRANZ BECKENBAUER (Bayern Munich)
1973.......JOHAN CRUYFF (Barcelona)
1974.......JOHAN CRUYFF (Barcelona)
1975.......OLEG BLOKHIN (Dynamo Kiev)
1976.......FRANZ BECKENBAUER (Bayern Munich)
1977.......ALLAN SIMONSEN (Borussia Moenchengladbach)
1978.......KEVIN KEEGAN (SV Hamburg)
1979.......KEVIN KEEGAN (SV Hamburg)
1980.......KARL-HEINZ RUMMENIGGE (Bayern Munich)
1981.......KARL-HEINZ RUMMENIGGE (Bayern Munich)
1982.......PAOLO ROSSI (Juventus)
1983.......MICHEL PLATINI (Juventus)
1984.......MICHEL PLATINI (Juventus)
1985.......MICHEL PLATINI (Juventus)
1986.......IGOR BELANOV (Dynamo Kiev)
1987.......RUUD GULLIT (AC Milan)
1988.......MARCO VAN BASTEN (AC Milan)
1989.......MARCO VAN BASTEN (AC Milan)
1990.......LOTHAR MATTHAUS (West Germany)
1991.......JEAN-PIERRE PAPIN (Marseilles)
1992.......MARCO VAN BASTEN (AC Milan)
1993.......ROBERTO BAGGIO (Juventus)
1994.......HIRSTO STOICHKOV (Barcelona)
1995.......GEORGE WEAH (AC Milan)
1996.......MATTHIAS SAMMER (Borussia Dortmund)
1997.......RONALDO (Inter Milan)
1998.......ZINEDINE ZIDANE (Juventus)
1999.......RIVALDO (Barcelona)
2000.......LUIS FIGO (Real Madrid)
2001.......MICHAEL OWEN (Liverpool)
2002.......RONALDO (Real Madrid)
2003.......PAVEL NEDVED (Juventus)
2004.......ANDRIY SHEVCHENKO (AC Milan)
2005.......RONALDINHO (Barcelona)
2006.......FABIO CANNAVARO (Italy)
2007.......KAKA (AC Milan)
2008.......CRISTIANO RONALD0 (Manchester United)
2009.......LIONEL MESSI (Barcelona)
2010.......LIONEL MESSI (Barcelona)
2011.......LIONEL MESSI (Barcelona)
2012.......LIONEL MESSI (Barcelona)

SCOTLAND'S INTERNATIONAL RECORD

v ENGLAND (Scotland scores first)

The year refers to the season, i.e. 1873 is season 1872-73

Year	Score	Venue
1873	0-0	Partick
1873	2-4	The Oval
1874	2-1	Partick
1875	2-2	The Oval
1876	3-0	Partick
1877	3-1	The Oval
1878	7-2	Hampden
1879	4-5	The Oval
1880	5-4	Hampden
1881	6-1	The Oval
1882	5-1	Hampden
1883	3-2	Sheffield
1884	1-0	Cathkin
1885	1-1	The Oval
1886	1-1	Hampden
1887	3-2	Blackburn
1888	0-5	Hampden
1889	3-2	The Oval
1890	1-1	Hampden
1891	1-2	Blackburn
1892	1-4	Ibrox
1893	2-5	Richmond
1894	2-2	Celtic Park
1895	0-3	Everton
1896	2-1	Celtic Park
1897	2-1	Crystal Pal
1898	1-3	Celtic Park
1899	1-2	Birmingham
1900	4-1	Celtic Park
1901	2-2	Crystal Pal
1902	2-2	Birmingham
1903	2-1	Sheffield
1904	0-1	Celtic Park
1905	0-1	Crystal Pal
1906	2-1	Hampden
1907	1-1	Newcastle
1908	1-1	Hampden
1909	0-2	Crystal Pal
1910	2-0	Hampden
1911	1-1	Liverpool
1912	1-1	Hampden
1913	0-1	Chelsea
1914	3-1	Hampden
1920	4-5	Sheffield
1921	3-0	Hampden
1922	1-0	Aston Villa
1923	2-2	Hampden
1924	1-1	Wembley
1925	2-0	Hampden
1926	1-0	Manchester
1927	1-2	Hampden
1928	5-1	Wembley
1929	1-0	Hampden
1930	2-5	Wembley
1931	2-0	Hampden
1932	0-3	Wembley
1933	2-1	Hampden
1934	0-3	Wembley
1935	2-0	Hampden
1936	1-1	Wembley
1937	3-1	Hampden
1938	1-0	Wembley
1939	1-2	Hampden
1947	1-1	Wembley
1948	0-2	Hampden
1949	3-1	Wembley
1950	0-1	Hampden
1951	3-2	Wembley
1952	1-2	Hampden
1953	2-2	Wembley
1954	2-4	Hampden
1955	2-7	Wembley
1956	1-1	Hampden
1957	1-2	Wembley
1958	0-4	Hampden
1959	0-1	Wembley
1960	1-1	Hampden
1961	3-9	Wembley
1962	2-0	Hampden
1963	2-1	Wembley
1964	1-0	Hampden
1965	2-2	Wembley

1966 3-4 .... Hampden
1967 3-2 .... Wembley
1968 1-1 .... Hampden
1969 1-4 .... Wembley
1970 0-0 .... Hampden
1971 1-3 .... Wembley
1972 0-1 .... Hampden
1973 0-5 .... Hampden
1973 0-1 .... Wembley
1974 2-0 .... Hampden
1975 1-5 .... Wembley
1976 2-1 .... Hampden
1977 2-1 .... Wembley
1978 0-1 .... Hampden
1979 1-3 .... Wembley
1980 0-2 .... Hampden
1981 1-0 .... Wembley
1982 0-1 .... Hampden
1983 0-2 .... Wembley
1984 1-1 .... Hampden

SIR STANLEY ROUS CUP

1985 1-0 .... Hampden
1986 1-2 .... Wembley

BECAME A THREE-NATION COMPETITION

1987 0-0 .... Hampden

(Scotland 0 Brazil 2. England 1 Brazil 1; Winners – Brazil)

1988 0-1 .... Wembley

(Scotland 0 Colombia 0; England 1 Colombia 1. Winners: England)

1989 0-2 .... Hampden

(Scotland 2 Chile 0; England 0 Chile 0. Winners – England)

1996 0-2 .... Wembley
1999 0-2 .... Hampden
1999 1-0 .... Wembley

RAY STEWART celebrates with John Robertson after his winning penalty against England at Wembley in May 1981

v NORTHERN IRELAND

(Scotland scores first)

Year	Score	Venue
1884	5-0	Belfast
1885	8-2	Glasgow
1886	7-2	Belfast
1887	4-1	Glasgow
1888	10-2	Belfast
1889	7-0	Glasgow
1890	4-1	Belfast
1891	2-1	Glasgow
1892	3-2	Belfast
1893	6-1	Glasgow
1894	2-1	Belfast
1895	3-1	Glasgow
1896	3-3	Belfast
1897	5-1	Glasgow
1898	3-0	Belfast
1899	9-1	Glasgow
1900	3-0	Belfast
1901	11-0	Glasgow
1902	5-1	Belfast
1903	0-2	Glasgow
1904	1-1	Dublin
1905	4-0	Glasgow
1906	1-0	Dublin
1907	3-0	Glasgow
1908	5-0	Dublin
1909	5-0	Glasgow
1910	0-1	Belfast
1911	2-0	Glasgow
1912	4-1	Belfast
1913	2-1	Dublin
1914	1-1	Belfast
1920	3-0	Glasgow
1921	2-0	Belfast
1922	2-1	Glasgow
1923	1-0	Belfast
1924	2-0	Glasgow
1925	3-0	Belfast
1926	4-0	Glasgow
1927	2-0	Belfast
1928	0-1	Glasgow
1929	7-3	Belfast
1930	3-1	Glasgow
1931	0-0	Belfast
1932	3-1	Glasgow
1933	4-0	Belfast
1934	1-2	Glasgow
1935	1-2	Belfast
1936	2-1	Edinburgh
1937	3-1	Belfast
1938	1-1	Aberdeen
1939	2-0	Belfast
1947	0-0	Glasgow
1948	0-2	Belfast
1949	3-2	Glasgow
1950	8-2	Belfast
1951	6-1	Glasgow
1952	3-0	Belfast
1953	1-1	Glasgow
1954	3-1	Belfast
1955	2-2	Glasgow
1956	1-2	Belfast
1957	1-0	Glasgow
1958	1-1	Belfast
1959	2-2	Glasgow
1960	4-0	Belfast
1961	5-2	Glasgow
1962	6-1	Belfast
1963	5-1	Glasgow
1964	1-2	Belfast
1965	3-2	Glasgow
1966	2-3	Belfast
1967	2-1	Glasgow
1968	0-1	Belfast
1969	1-1	Glasgow
1970	1-0	Belfast
1971	0-1	Glasgow
1972	2-0	Glasgow
1973	1-2	Glasgow
1974	0-1	Glasgow
1975	3-0	Glasgow
1976	3-0	Glasgow
1977	3-0	Glasgow
1978	1-1	Glasgow
1979	1-0	Glasgow
1980	0-1	Belfast
1981	1-1	Glasgow
1981	2-0	Glasgow

1982 0-0 .... Belfast
1982 1-1 .... Belfast
1983 0-0 .... Glasgow
1984 0-2 .... Belfast
1992 1-0 .... Glasgow
2008 0-0 .... Glasgow
2011 3-0 .... Dublin

v WALES

(Scotland scores first)

1876 4-0 .... Glasgow
1877 2-0 .... Wrexham
1878 9-0 .... Glasgow
1879 3-0 .... Wrexham
1880 5-1 .... Glasgow
1881 5-1 .... Wrexham
1882 5-0 .... Glasgow
1883 4-1 .... Wrexham
1884 4-1 .... Glasgow
1885 8-1 .... Wrexham
1886 4-1 .... Glasgow
1887 2-0 .... Wrexham
1888 5-1 .... Edinburgh
1889 0-0 .... Wrexham
1890 5-0 .... Paisley
1891 4-3 .... Wrexham
1892 6-1 .... Edinburgh
1893 8-0 .... Wrexham
1894 5-2 .... Kilmarnock
1895 2-2 .... Wrexham
1896 4-0 .... Dundee
1897 2-2 .... Wrexham
1898 5-2 .... Motherwell
1899 6-0 .... Wrexham
1900 5-2 .... Aberdeen
1901 1-1 .... Wrexham
1902 5-1 .... Greenock
1903 1-0 .... Cardiff
1904 1-1 .... Dundee
1905 1-3 .... Wrexham
1906 0-2 .... Edinburgh
1907 0-1 .... Wrexham
1908 2-1 .... Dundee
1909 2-3 .... Wrexham
1910 1-0 .... Kilmarnock
1911 2-2 .... Cardiff
1912 1-0 .... Edinburgh
1913 0-0 .... Wrexham
1914 0-0 .... Glasgow
1920 1-1 .... Cardiff
1921 2-1 .... Aberdeen
1922 1-2 .... Wrexham
1923 2-0 .... Paisley
1924 0-2 .... Cardiff
1925 3-1 .... Edinburgh
1926 3-0 .... Cardiff
1927 3-0 .... Glasgow
1928 2-2 .... Wrexham
1929 4-2 .... Glasgow
1930 4-2 .... Cardiff
1931 1-1 .... Glasgow
1932 3-2 .... Wrexham
1933 2-5 .... Edinburgh
1934 2-3 .... Cardiff
1935 3-2 .... Aberdeen
1936 1-1 .... Cardiff
1937 1-2 .... Dundee
1938 1-2 .... Cardiff
1939 3-2 .... Edinburgh
1946 1-3 .... Wrexham
1947 1-2 .... Glasgow
1948 3-1 .... Cardiff
1949 2-0 .... Glasgow
1950 3-1 .... Cardiff
1951 0-1 .... Glasgow
1952 2-1 .... Cardiff
1953 3-3 .... Glasgow
1954 1-0 .... Cardiff
1955 2-0 .... Glasgow
1956 2-2 .... Cardiff
1957 1-1 .... Glasgow
1958 3-0 .... Cardiff
1959 1-1 .... Glasgow
1960 0-2 .... Cardiff
1961 2-0 .... Glasgow
1962 3-2 .... Cardiff

Year	Score	Venue
1963	2-1	Glasgow
1964	2-3	Cardiff
1965	4-1	Glasgow
1966	1-1	Cardiff
1967	3-2	Glasgow
1969	5-3	Wrexham
1970	0-0	Glasgow
1971	0-0	Cardiff
1972	1-0	Glasgow
1973	2-0	Wrexham
1974	2-0	Glasgow
1975	2-2	Cardiff
1976	3-1	Glasgow
1977	1-0	Glasgow
1977	0-0	Wrexham
1978	2-0	Liverpool

(Wales' home game in World Cup qualifier)

Year	Score	Venue
1978	1-1	Glasgow
1979	0-3	Cardiff
1980	1-0	Glasgow
1981	0-2	Swansea
1982	1-0	Glasgow
1983	2-0	Cardiff
1984	2-1	Glasgow
1985	0-1	Glasgow
1986	1-1	Cardiff
1997	0-1	Kilmarnock
2004	0-4	Cardiff
2009	0-3	Cardiff
2011	3-1	Dublin
2013	1-2	Cardiff
2013	1-2	Glasgow

CHARLIE ADAM with Jonathan Williams of Wales as Scotland lose 2-1 in the Hampden snow in March 2013

ARGENTINA

(Scotland scores first)

1977 1-1 .... Buenos Aires
1979 1-3 .... Glasgow
1990 1-0 .... Glasgow
2008 0-1 .... Glasgow

AUSTRALIA

(Scotland scores first)

1986 2-0 .... Glasgow
1986 0-0 .... Melbourne
1996 1-0 .... Glasgow
2000 0-2 .... Glasgow
2013 3-1 .... Edinburgh

AUSTRIA

(Scotland scores first)

1931 0-5 .... Vienna
1934 2-2 .... Glasgow
1937 1-1 .... Vienna
1951 0-1 .... Glasgow
1951 0-4 .... Vienna
1954 0-1 .... Zurich
1955 4-1 .... Vienna
1956 1-1 .... Glasgow
1960 1-4 .... Vienna
1963 4-1 .... Glasgow
(Referee abandoned match after 79 minutes)
1969 2-1 .... Glasgow
1970 0-2 .... Vienna
1979 2-3 .... Vienna
1980 1-1 .... Glasgow
1994 2-1 .... Vienna
1996 0-0 .... Vienna
1997 2-0 .... Glasgow
2003 0-2 .... Glasgow
2006 2-2 .... Graz
2007 1-0 .... Vienna

BELARUS

(Scotland scores first)

1997 1-0 .... Minsk
1998 4-1 .... Aberdeen
2005 0-0 .... Minsk
2006 0-1 .... Glasgow

BELGIUM

(Scotland scores first)

1946 2-2 .... Glasgow
1947 1-2 .... Brussels
1948 2-0 .... Glasgow
1951 5-0 .... Brussels
1971 0-3 .... Liege
1972 1-0 .... Aberdeen
1974 1-2 .... Brussels
1980 0-2 .... Brussels
1983 2-3 .... Brussels
1984 1-1 .... Glasgow
1987 1-4 .... Brussels
1988 2-0 .... Glasgow
2001 2-2 .... Glasgow
2001 0-2 .... Brussels
2013 0-2 .... Brussels

BOSNIA

(Scotland scores first)

1999 2-1 .... Sarajevo
1999 1-0 .... Glasgow

BRAZIL

(Scotland scores first)

1966 1-1 .... Glasgow
1972 0-1 .... Rio
1973 0-1 .... Glasgow
1974 0-0 .... Frankfurt
1977 0-2 .... Rio
1982 1-4 .... Seville
1987 0-2 .... Glasgow
1990 0-1 .... Turin
1998 1-2 .... Paris
2011 0-2 .... London

BULGARIA

(Scotland scores first)

1978 2-1 .... Glasgow
1987 0-0 .... Glasgow
1988 1-0 .... Sofia
1991 1-1 .... Sofia
1991 1-1 .... Glasgow
2006 5-1 .... Kobe

CANADA

(Scotland scores first)

1983 2-0 .... Vancouver
1983 3-0 .... Edmonton
1983 2-0 .... Toronto
1992 3-1 .... Toronto
2003 3-1 .... Edinburgh

CHILE

(Scotland scores first)

1977 4-2 .... Santiago
1989 2-0 .... Glasgow

CIS

(Scotland score first)

1992 3-0 .... Sweden

COLOMBIA

(Scotland scores first)

1988 0-0 .... Glasgow
1996 0-1 .... Miami
1998 2-2 .... New Jersey

COSTA RICA
(Scotland score first)

1990 0-1 .... Genoa

CROATIA
(Scotland scores first)

2001 1-1 .... Zagreb
2002 0-0 .... Glasgow
2008 1-1 .... Glasgow
2013 1-0 .... Zagreb

CYPRUS
(Scotland scores first)

1969 5-0 .... Nicosia
1969 8-0 .... Glasgow
1989 3-2 .... Limassol
1989 2-1 .... Glasgow
2011 2-2 .... Larnaca

CZECHOSLOVAKIA
(Scotland scores first)

1937 3-1 .... Prague
1938 5-0 .... Glasgow
1961 0-4 .... Bratislava
1962 3-2 .... Glasgow
1962 2-4 .... Brussels
1972 0-0 .... Porto Alegre
1974 2-1 .... Glasgow
1974 0-1 .... Bratislava
1977 0-2 .... Prague
1978 3-1 .... Glasgow

CZECH REPUBLIC
(Scotland scores first)

1999 1-2 .... Glasgow
1999 2-3 .... Prague
2008 1-3 .... Prague
2010 1-0 .... Glasgow
2011 0-1 .... Prague
2012 2-2 .... Glasgow

DENMARK
(Scotland scores first)

1951 3-1 .... Glasgow
1952 2-1 .... Copenhagen
1969 1-0 .... Copenhagen
1971 1-0 .... Glasgow
1971 0-1 .... Copenhagen
1973 4-1 .... Copenhagen
1973 2-0 .... Glasgow
1976 1-0 .... Copenhagen
1976 3-1 .... Glasgow
1986 0-1 .... Neza
1996 0-2 .... Copenhagen
1998 0-1 .... Glasgow
2003 0-1 .... Glasgow
2004 0-1 .... Copenhagen
2012 2-1 .... Glasgow

EAST GERMANY
(Scotland scores first)

1975 3-0 .... Glasgow
1978 0-1 .... East Berlin
1983 2-0 .... Glasgow
1984 1-2 .... Halle
1986 0-0 .... Glasgow
1990 0-1 .... Glasgow

ECUADOR

(Scotland score first)

1995 2-1 .... Toyama

EGYPT

(Scotland score first)

1990 1-3............. Aberdeen

ESTONIA

(Scotland scores first)

1993 3-0........................ Tallinn
1993 3-1 .... Aberdeen
1997 0-0....................... Tallinn
(abandoned after 3 seconds, replay ordered in Monaco)
1997 0-0..................... Monaco
1997 2-0............... Kilmarnock
1998 3-2................ Tynecastle
1999 0-0........................ Tallinn
2004 1-0........................ Tallinn
2013 1-0................. Aberdeen

FAROE ISLANDS

(Scotland scores first)

1995 5-1 .... Glasgow
1995 2-0................. Torshavn
1998 2-1 .... Aberdeen
1999 1-1 .... Toftir
2003 2-2......................... Toftir
2004 3-1 .... Glasgow
2007 6-0................... Glasgow
2007 2-0.......................... Toftir
2011 3-0................ Aberdeen

FINLAND

(Scotland scores first)

1954 2-1 .... Helsinki
1965 3-1 .... Glasgow
1965 2-1 .... Helsinki
1977 6-0................... Glasgow
1992 1-1 .... Glasgow
1995 2-0..................... Helsinki
1996 1-0................... Glasgow
1998 1-1 .... Edinburgh

FRANCE

(Scotland scores first)

1930 2-0......................... Paris
1932 3-1 .... Paris
1948 0-3......................... Paris
1949 2-0................. Glasgow
1950 1-0......................... Paris
1951 1-0................. Glasgow
1958 1-2..................... Obrero
1984 0-2................ Marseilles
1989 2-0.................. Glasgow
1990 0-3......................... Paris
1998 1-2................ St Etienne
2000 0-2.................. Glasgow
2002 0-5......................... Paris
2007 1-0.................. Glasgow
2008 1-0......................... Paris

GEORGIA

(Scotland scores first)

2007 2-1 .... Glasgow
2008 0-2....................... Tbilisi

GERMANY
(Scotland scores first)

1929 1-1 .... Berlin
1937 2-0 .... Glasgow
1992 0-2 .... Sweden
1993 0-1 .... Glasgow
1999 1-0 .... Bremen
2003 1-1 .... Glasgow
2004 1-2 .... Dortmund

GREECE
(Scotland scores first)

1995 0-1 .... Athens
1996 1-0 ....Glasgow

HOLLAND
(Scotland scores first)

1929 2-0 .... Amsterdam
1938 3-1 .... Amsterdam
1959 2-1 .... Amsterdam
1966 0-3 ....Glasgow
1968 0-0 .... Amsterdam
1972 1-2 .... Amsterdam
1978 3-2 .... Argentina
1982 2-1 ....Glasgow
1986 0-0 ....Eindhoven
1992 0-1 ....Sweden
1994 0-1 ....Glasgow
1994 1-3 ....Utrecht
1996 0-0 .... Birmingham
2000 0-0 .... Arnhem
2004 1-0 ....Glasgow
2004 0-6 .... Amsterdam
2009 0-3 .... Amsterdam
2010 0-1 ....Glasgow

HONG KONG
(Scotland score first)

2002 4-0 .... Hong Kong

HUNGARY
(Scotland scores first)

1939 3-1 ....Glasgow
1955 2-4 ....Glasgow
1955 1-3 .... Budapest
1958 1-1 ....Glasgow
1960 3-3 .... Budapest
1980 1-3 .... Budapest
1988 2-0 ....Glasgow
2004 0-3 ....Glasgow

ICELAND
(Scotland scores first)

1985 3-0 ....Glasgow
1985 1-0 .... Reykjavik
2003 2-0 .... Reykjavik
2003 2-1 ....Glasgow
2008 2-1 .... Reykjavik
2009 2-1 ....Glasgow

IRAN
(Scotland score first)

1978 1-1 ....Cordoba

ISRAEL

(Scotland scores first)

1981 1-0 .... Tel Aviv
1981 3-1 .... Glasgow
1986 1-0 .... Tel Aviv

ITALY

(Scotland scores first)

1931 0-3 .... Rome
1965 1-0 .... Glasgow
1965 0-3 .... Naples
1989 0-2 .... Perugia
1993 0-0 .... Ibrox
1994 1-3 .... Rome
2005 0-2 .... Milan
2006 1-1 .... Glasgow
2007 0-2 .... Bari
2008 1-2 .... Glasgow

JAPAN

(Scotland scores first)

1995 0-0 .... Hiroshima
2006 0-0 .... Saitama
2010 0-2 .... Yokohama

LATVIA

(Scotland scores first)

1997 2-0 .... Riga
1998 2-0 .... Celtic Park
2000 1-0 .... Riga
2001 2-1 .... Glasgow

LIECHTENSTEIN

(Scotland scores first)

2011 2-1 .... Glasgow
2012 1-0 .... Vaduz

LITHUANIA

(Scotland scores first)

1998 0-0 .... Vilnius
1999 3-0 .... Glasgow
2003 0-1 .... Kaunas
2004 1-0 .... Glasgow
2007 2-1 .... Kaunas
2008 3-1 .... Glasgow
2011 0-0 .... Kaunas
2012 1-0 .... Glasgow

LUXEMBOURG

(Scotland scores first)

1947 6-0 .... Luxembourg
1987 3-0 .... Glasgow
1988 0-0 .... Luxembourg
2013 2-1 .... Luxembourg

MACEDONIA

(Scotland scores first)

2008 0-1 .... Skopje
2010 2-0 .... Glasgow
2013 1-1 .... Glasgow

MALTA

(Scotland scores first)

1988 1-1 .... Valetta
1990 2-1 .... Valetta
1993 3-0 .... Glasgow
1994 2-0 .... Valetta
1997 3-2 .... Valetta

MOLDOVA
(Scotland scores first)

2005 1-1 .... Chisinau
2005 2-0 .... Glasgow

MOROCCO
(Scotland score first)

1998 0-3 .... St Etienne

NEW ZEALAND
(Scotland scores first)

1982 5-2 .... Malaga
2003 1-1 .... Edinburgh

NIGERIA
(Scotland score first)

2002 1-2 .... Aberdeen

NORWAY
(Scotland scores first)

1929 7-3 .... Bergen
1954 1-0 .... Glasgow
1954 1-1 .... Oslo
1963 3-4 .... Bergen
1964 6-1 .... Glasgow
1974 2-1 .... Oslo
1979 3-2 .... Glasgow
1979 4-0 .... Oslo
1989 2-1 .... Oslo
1990 1-1 .... Glasgow
1992 0-0 .... Oslo
1998 1-1 .... Bordeaux
2004 0-0 .... Oslo
2005 0-1 .... Glasgow
2006 2-1 .... Oslo
2008 0-0 .... Glasgow
2010 0-4 .... Oslo

PARAGUAY
(Scotland score first)

1958 2-3 .... Norrkoping

PERU
(Scotland scores first)

1972 2-0 .... Glasgow
1978 1-3 .... Cordoba
1980 1-1 .... Glasgow

POLAND
(Scotland scores first)

1958 2-1 .... Warsaw
1960 2-3 .... Glasgow
1965 1-1 .... Chorzow
1966 1-2 .... Glasgow
1980 0-1 .... Poznan
1990 1-1 .... Glasgow
2001 1-1 .... Bydgoszcz

ASTON VILLA star Barry Bannan has made his mark in Scotland's midfield since his debut against the Faroe Islands in 2010

PORTUGAL

(Scotland scores first)

1950 2-2 .... Lisbon
1955 3-0 .... Glasgow
1959 0-1 .... Lisbon
1966 0-1 .... Glasgow
1971 0-2 .... Lisbon
1972 2-1 .... Glasgow
1975 1-0 .... Glasgow
1979 1-0 .... Lisbon
1980 4-1 .... Glasgow
1981 0-0 .... Glasgow
1982 1-2 .... Lisbon
1993 0-0 .... Glasgow
1993 0-5 .... Lisbon
2003 0-2 .... Braga

REPUBLIC OF IRELAND

(Scotland scores first)

1961 4-1 .... Glasgow
1961 3-0 .... Dublin
1963 0-1 .... Dublin
1970 1-1 .... Dublin
1987 0-0 .... Dublin
1987 0-1 .... Glasgow
2000 2-1 .... Dublin
2003 0-2 .... Glasgow
2011 0-1 .... Dublin

ROMANIA

(Scotland scores first)

1975 1-1 .... Bucharest
1976 1-1 .... Glasgow
1986 3-0 .... Glasgow
1991 2-1 .... Glasgow
1992 0-1 .... Bucharest
2004 1-2 .... Glasgow

RUSSIA

(Scotland scores first)

1995 1-1 .... Glasgow
1995 0-0 .... Moscow

SAN MARINO

(Scotland scores first)

1991 2-0 .... Serravalle
1992 4-0 .... Glasgow
1995 2-0 .... Serravalle
1996 5-0 .... Glasgow
2000 2-0 .... Serravalle
2001 4-0 .... Glasgow

SAUDI ARABIA

(Scotland score first)

1988 2-2 .... Riyadh

SERBIA

(Scotland score first)

2013 0-0 .... Glasgow
2013 0-2 .... Novi Sad

SLOVENIA

(Scotland scores first)

2005 0-0 .... Glasgow
2006 3-0 .... Celje
2012 1-1 .... Koper

SOUTH AFRICA
(Scotland scores first)

2002 0-2..............Hong Kong
2008 1-0.................Aberdeen

SOUTH KOREA
(Scotland score first)

2002 1-4.......................Busan

SOVIET UNION
(Scotland scores first)

1967 0-2...................Glasgow
1971 0-1...................Moscow
1982 2-2......................Malaga
1991 0-1...................Glasgow

SPAIN
(Scotland scores first)

1957 4-2..................Glasgow
1957 1-4......................Madrid
1963 6-2......................Madrid
1965 0-0..................Glasgow
1975 1-2..................Glasgow
1975 1-1..................Valencia
1982 0-3..................Valencia
1985 3-1..................Glasgow
1985 0-1......................Seville
1988 0-0......................Madrid
2005 1-1..................Valencia
2011 2-3..................Glasgow
2012 1-3....................Alicante

SWEDEN
(Scotland scores first)

1952 1-3...............Stockholm
1953 1-2..................Glasgow
1975 1-1.............Gothenburg
1977 3-1..................Glasgow
1981 1-0...............Stockholm
1982 2-0..................Glasgow
1990 2-1........................Genoa
1996 0-2...............Stockholm
1997 1-0..................Glasgow
1997 1-2.............Gothenburg
2005 1-4................Edinburgh
2011 0-3........................Solna

SWITZERLAND
(Scotland scores first)

1931 3-2......................Geneva
1946 3-1...................Glasgow
1948 1-2........................Berne
1950 3-1...................Glasgow
1957 2-1........................Basel
1958 3-2...................Glasgow
1973 0-1........................Berne
1976 1-0...................Glasgow
1983 0-2........................Berne
1983 2-2...................Glasgow
1991 2-1...................Glasgow
1992 2-2........................Berne
1993 1-3........................Berne
1994 1-1.................Aberdeen
1996 1-0.............Birmingham
2006 1-3...................Glasgow

TRINIDAD & TOBAGO
(Scotland score first)

2004 4-1 ....Edinburgh

TURKEY
(Scotland score first)

1960 2-4 ....Ankara

UKRAINE
(Scotland scores first)

2007 0-2 ....Kiev
2008 3-1 ....Glasgow

URUGUAY
(Scotland scores first)

1954 0-7 .... Switzerland
1962 2-3 ....Glasgow
1984 2-0 ....Glasgow
1986 0-0 ....Neza

USA
(Scotland scores first)

1952 6-0 ....Glasgow
1992 1-0 .... Denver
1996 1-2 .... Hartford
1998 0-0 ....Washington
2006 1-1 ....Glasgow
2012 1-5 ....Florida

WEST GERMANY
(Scotland scores first)

1957 3-1 ....Stuttgart
1959 3-2 ....Glasgow
1964 2-2 .... Hanover
1969 1-1 ....Glasgow
1970 2-3 ....Hamburg
1974 1-1 ....Glasgow
1974 1-2 .... Frankfurt
1986 1-2 ....Queretaro

YUGOSLAVIA
(Scotland scores first)

1955 2-2 .... Belgrade
1957 2-0 ....Glasgow
1958 1-1 .... Vaasteras
1972 2-2 .... Belo Horizonte
1974 1-1 .... Frankfurt
1985 6-1 ....Glasgow
1989 1-1 ....Glasgow
1990 1-3 .... Zagreb

ZAIRE
(Scotland score first)

1974 2-0 ....Dortmund

GARY CALDWELL has experienced the full range of emotions as a Scotland stalwart

LIST OF PLAYERS HONOURED

This is a list of full international appearances by Scots in matches against the Home Countries and against foreign nations.

The code for countries is as follows

A, Austria; Arg, Argentina; Aus, Australia; Bel, Belgium; Blr, Belarus; Bos, Bosnia; Br, Brazil; Bul, Bulgaria; Ca, Canada; Ch, Chile; CIS, Commeonwealth of Independent Staes; Co, Colombia; Cr, Costa Rica; Cro, Croatia; Cy, Cyprus; Cz, Czechoslovakia; CzR, Czech Republic; D, Denmark; E, England; Ec, Ecuador; EG, East Germany; Eg, Egypt; Est, Estonia; Fr, France; Fin, Finland; Fi, Faroes Islands; G, Germany; Geo, Georgia; Gr, Greece; H, Hungary; Holl, Holland; HK, Hong Kong; I, Italy; Ice, Iceland; Ir, Iran; Is, Israel; J, Japan; L, Luxembourg; La, Latvia; Li, Liechtenstein; Lth, Lithuania; M, Morocco; Ma, Malta; Mac, Macedonia; Mo, Moldova; Nig, Nigeria; N, Norway; Ni, Northern Ireland; Nz, New Zealand; Por, Portugal; Pe, Peru; Pol, Poland; Ei, Republic of Ireland; R, Romania; Ru, Russia; SAr, Saudi Arabia; Se, Sweden; Sm, San Marino; Ser, Serbia; Slo, Slovenia; SA, South Africa; Skor, South Korea; Sp, Spain; Sw, Switzerland; Trin, Trinidad & Tobago; T, Turkey; U, Uruguay; Uk, Ukraine; US, United States of America; USSR, Soviet Union; W, Wales; WG, West Germany; Y, Yugoslavia; Z, Zaire.

The year refers to the season. For example, 2013 is the 2012-13 season.

ADAM, C. (Rangers, Blackpool, Liverpool, Stoke) (22): 2007 v A, Fi; 2010 v J, CzR; 2011 v Se, Sp, Fi, Ni, Br, W, Ei; 2012 v D, CzR, Sp, Slo; 2013 v Aus, Mac, W (2), Bel, Est, Ser.
ADAMS, J. (Hearts) (3): 1889 v Ni; 1892 v W; 1893 v Ni.
AGNEW, W. B. (Kilmarnock) (3): 1907 v Ni; 1908 v W, Ni.
AIRD, J. (Burnley) (4): 1954 v N (2); A, U.
AITKEN A. (Newcastle Utd, Middlesbrough, Leicester Fosse) (14): 1901 v E; 1902 v E; 1903 v E, W; 1904 v E; 1905 v E, W; 1906 v E; 1907 v E, W; 1908 v E; 1910 v E; 1911 v E, Ni.
AITKEN, G, G. (East Fife, Sunderland) (8): 1949 v E, Fr; 1950 v W, Ni, Sw; 1953 v W, Ni; 1954 v E.
AITKEN, R. (Dumbarton) (2): 1886 v E: 1888 v Ni.
AITKEN, R. (Celtic, Newcastle Utd, St Mirren) (57): 1980 v Pe, Bel, W, E, Pol; 1983 v Bel, Ca (2); 1984 v Bel, Ni, W; 1985 v E, Ice; 1986 v W, EG, Aus (2), Is, R, E, D, WG, U; 1987 v Bul, Ei (2), L, Bel, E, Br; 1988 v H, Bel, Bul, L, S.Ar., Ma, Sp, Co, E; 1989 v N, Y, I, Cy, (2), Fr, E, Ch; 1990 v Y, Fr, N, Arg, Pol, Ma, Cr, Se, Br; 1992 v R.
AITKENHEAD, W. A. C. (Blackburn R.) (1): 1912 v Ni.
ALBISTON, A. (Manchester Utd) (14): 1982 v Ni; 1984 v U, Bel, EG, W, E; 1985 v Y, Ice, Sp (2), W; 1986 v EG, Holl, U.
ALEXANDER, D. (East Stirlingshire) (2): 1894 v W, Ni.
ALEXANDER, G. (Preston, Burnley) (40): 2002 v Nig, Skor, SA, HK; 2003 v D, Fi, Can, Por, Ei, Ice, Lth, Nz; 2004 v Lth; 2004 v R; 2005 v Mo, Blr; 2006 v A, I, N, Blr, Slo, US, Sw; 2007 v Lth, Fr, Uk, Geo, I, A, Fi; 2008 v Fr, Geo, Cro; 2009 v Ni, Mac, Ice, Arg, Holl; 2010 v N, Mac.
ALEXANDER, N. (Cardiff) (3): 2006 v Sw, Bul, J.
ALLAN, D. S. (Queen's Park) (3): 1885 v E, W; 1886 v W.
ALLAN, G. (Liverpool) (1): 1897 v E.
ALLAN, H. (Hearts) (1): 1902 v W.
ALLAN, J. (Queen's Park) (2): 1887 v E, W.
ALLAN, T. (Dundee) (2): 1974 v WG, N.
ANCELL, R. F. D. (Newcastle Utd) (2): 1937 v W, Ni.
ANDERSON, A. (Hearts) (23): 1933 v E; 1934 v A, E, W, Ni; 1935 v E, W, Ni; 1936 v E, W, Ni; 1937 v G, E, W, Ni, A; 1938 v E, W, Ni, Cz, Holl; 1939 v W, H.
ANDERSON, F. (Clydesdale) (1): 1874 v E.
ANDERSON, G. (Kilmarnock) (1): 1901 v Ni.
ANDERSON, H. A. (Raith Rovers) (1): 1914 v W.
ANDERSON, J. (Leicester City) (1): 1954 v Fin.
ANDERSON, K. (Queen's Park) (3): 1896 v Ni; 1898 v E, Ni.
ANDERSON, R. (Aberdeen, Sunderland) (11): 2003 v Ice, Can, Por, Ei; 2005 v N, Se; 2006 v A, Bul, J; 2008 v Cro, SA.
ANDERSON, W. (Queen's Park) (6): 1882 v E: 1883 v E, W; 1884 v E; 1885 v E, W.
ANDREWS, P. (Eastern) (1): 1875 v E.
ARCHIBALD, A. (Rangers) (8): 1921 v W; 1922 v W, E; 1923 v Ni; 1924 v E, W; 1931 v E; 1932 v E.
ARCHIBALD, S. (Aberdeen, Tottenham H., Barcelona) (27): 1980 v Por, Ni, Pol, H; 1981 v Se, Is (2), Ni (2), E; 1982 v Ni, Por, Sp, Holl, Nz, Br, USSR; 1983 v EG, Sw, Bel; 1984 v EG, E, Fr; 1985 v Sp, E, Ice; 1986 v WG.

ARMSTRONG, M. W. (Aberdeen) (3): 1936 v W, Ni; 1937 v G.
ARNOTT, W. (Queen's Park) (14): 1883 v W; 1884 v E, Ni; 1885 v E, W; 1886 v E; 1887 v E, W; 1888 v E; 1889 v E; 1890 v E; 1891 v E; 1892 v E; 1893 v E.
AULD, J. R. (Third Lanark) (3): 1887 v E, W; 1889 v W.
AULD, R. (Celtic) (3): 1959 v H, Por; 1960 W.

BAIRD, A. (Queen's Park) (2): 1892 v Ni; 1894 v W.
BAIRD, D. (Hearts) (3): 1890 v Ni; 1891 v E; 1892 v W.
BAIRD, H. (Airdrie) (1): 1956 v A.
BAIRD, J. C. (Vale of Leven) (3): 1876 v E; 1878 v W; 1880 v E.
BAIRD, S. (Rangers) (7): 1957 v Y, Sp (2), Sw, WG: 1958 v Fr, Ni.
BAIRD, W. U. (St Bernard's) (1): 1897 v Ni.
BANNAN, B. (Aston Villa) (11): 2011 v Fi, Ni, Br, W, Ei; 2012 v D, Lth, Sp, Slo, US; 2013 v Cro.
BANNON, E. (Dundee Utd) (11): 1980 v Bel; 1983 v Ni, W, E, Ca; 1984 v EG; 1986 v Is, R, E, D, WG.
BARBOUR, A. (Renton) (1): 1885 v Ni.
BARDSLEY, P. (Sunderland) (11): 2011 v Sp, Fi, Ni, W, Ei; 2012 v D, CzR, Lth, Sp, Cy, US.
BARKER, J. B. (Rangers) (2): 1893 v W: 1894 v W.
BARR, D. (Falkirk) (1): 2009 v Ni
BARRETT, F. (Dundee) (2): 1894 v Ni; 1895 v W.
BATTLES, B. (Celtic) (3): 1901 v E, W, Ni.
BATTLES, B. (Hearts) (1): 1931 v W.
BAULD, W. (Hearts) (3): 1950 v E, Sw, Por.
BAXTER, J. C. (Rangers, Sunderland) (34): 1961 v Ni, Ei (2), Cz; 1962 v Ni, W, E, Cz (2), U; 1963 v W, Ni, E, A, N, Ei, Sp; 1964 v W, E, N, WG; 1965 v W, Ni, Fin; 1966 v Por, Br, Ni, W, E, I; 1967 v W, E, USSR; 1968 v W.
BAXTER, R. D. (Middlesbrough) (3): 1939 v E, W, H.
BEATTIE, A. (Preston NE) (7): 1937 v E, A, Cz; 1938 v E; 1939 v W, Ni, H.
BEATTIE, C. (Celtic, West Bromwich Albion) (7): 2006 v I, N; 2007 v Geo, I; 2008 v SA, Lth, Geo.
BEATTIE, R. (Preston NE) (1): 1939 v W.
BEGBIE, I. (Hearts) (4): 1890 v Ni; 1891 v E; 1892 v W; 1894 v E.
BELL, A. (Manchester Utd) (1): 1912 v Ni.
BELL, C. (Kilmarnock) (1): 2011 v Fi.
BELL, J. (Dumbarton, Everton, Celtic) (10): 1890 v Ni; 1892 v E; 1896 v E; 1897 v E; 1898 v E; 1899 v E, W, Ni; 1900 v E, W.
BELL, M. (Hearts) (1): 1901 v W.
BELL, W. J. (Leeds Utd) (2): 1966 v Por, Br.
BENNETT, A. (Celtic, Rangers) (11): 1904 v W; 1907 v Ni; 1908 v W: 1909 v W, Ni, E; 1910 v E, W; 1911 E, W; 1913 v Ni.
BENNIE, R. (Airdrie) (3): 1925 v W, Ni; 1926 v Ni.
BERNARD, P. (Oldham Ath.) (2): 1995 v J, Ec.
BERRA, C. (Hearts, Wolves) (26): 2008 v CzR; 2009 v Ni, Arg, Holl; 2010 v N, J, CzR; 2011 v Se, Lth, Ni, Br, W, Ei; 2012 v CzR, Lth, Sp, Cy, Slo, US; 2013 v Aus, Mac, W, Bel, Lux, Est, Ser.
BERRY, D. (Queen's Park) (3): 1894 v W; 1899 v W, Ni.
BERRY, W. H. (Queen's Park) (4): 1888 v E; 1889 v E; 1890 v E; 1891 v E.
BETT, J. (Rangers, Lokeren, Aberdeen) (25): 1982 v Holl; 1983 v Bel; 1984 v Bel, W, E, Fr; 1985 v Y, Ice, (2), Sp (2), W, E; 1986 v W, Is, Holl; 1987 v Bel; 1988 v H; 1989 v Y; 1990 v Fr, N, Arg, Eg, Ma, Cr.
BEVERIDGE, W. W. (Glasgow University) (3): 1879 v E, W; 1880 v W.

BLACK, A (Hearts) (3): 1938 v Cz, Holl; 1939 v H.
BLACK, D. (Hurlford) (1): 1889 v Ni.
BLACK, E. (Metz) (2): 1988 v H, L.
BLACK, I. (Rangers) (1): 2013 v Aus.
BLACK, I. H. (Southampton) (1): 1948 v E.
BLACKBURN, J. E. (Royal Engineers) (1): 1873 v E.
BLACKLAW, A. S. (Burnley) (3): 1963 v N, Sp; 1966 v I.
BLACKLEY, J. (Hibernian) (7): 1974 v Cz, E, Bel, Z; 1976 v Sw; 1977 v W, Se.
BLAIR, D. (Clyde, Aston Villa) (8): 1929 v W, Ni; 1931 v E, A, I; 1932 v W, Ni; 1933 v W.
BLAIR, J. (Sheffield W., Cardiff City) (8): 1920 v E, Ni; 1921 v E; 1922 v E; 1923 v E, W, Ni; 1924 v W.
BLAIR, J. (Motherwell) (1): 1934 v W.
BLAIR, J. A. (Blackpool) (1): 1947 v W.
BLAIR, W. (Third Lanark) (1): 1896 v W.
BLESSINGTON, J. (Celtic) (4): 1894 v E, Ni; 1896 v E, Ni.
BLYTH, J. A. (Coventry City) (2): 1978 v Bul, W.
BONE, J. (Norwich City) (2): 1972 v Y; 1973 v D.
BOOTH, S. (Aberdeen, Twente Enschede) (22): 1993 v G, Est (2); 1994 v Sw, Ma; 1995 v Fi, Ru; 1996 v Fin, Sm, Aus, US, Holl, Sw; 1998 v D, Fin, Co, M, US; 2001 v Pol; 2002 v Cro, Bel, La.
BOWIE, J. (Rangers) (2): 1920 v E, Ni.
BOWIE, W. (Linthouse) (1): 1891 v Ni.
BOWMAN, D. (Dundee United) (6): 1992 v Fin, US; 1993 v G, Est; 1994 v Sw, I.
BOWMAN, G. A. (Montrose) (1): 1892 v Ni.
BOYD, J. M. (Newcastle Utd) (1): 1934 v Ni.
BOYD, K. (Rangers, Middlesbrough) (18): 2006 v Bul, J; 2007 v Fi (2), Lth, Uk, Geo, I, A; 2008 v SA, Lth, Geo, I, Cro; 2009 v Mac; 2010 v CzR; 2011 v Se, Li.
BOYD, R. (Mossend Swifts) (2): 1889 v Ni; 1891 v W.
BOYD, T. (Motherwell, Chelsea, Celtic) (72): 1991 v R (2), Sw, Bul, USSR; 1992 Sw, Fin, Ca, N, CIS; 1993 v Sw, Por, I, Ma, G, Est (2); 1994 v I, Ma, Holl, A; 1995 v Fin, Fi, Ru (2), Gr, Sm. 1996 v Gr, Fin, Se, Sm, Aus, D, US, U, Holl, E, Sw; 1997 v A (2), La, Se (2), Est (2), W, Ma, Blr; 1998 v Blr, La, Fr, D, Fin, Co, US, Br, N, M. 1999 v Lth, Est, Fi, CzR (2), G, Fi; 2001 v La, Cro, Aus, Bel, Sm, Pol; 2002 v Bel.
BOYD, W. G. (Clyde) (2): 1931 v I, Sw, Fin.
BRACKENBRIDGE, T. (Hearts) (1): 1888 v Ni.
BRADSHAW, T. (Bury) (1): 1928 v E.
BRAND, R. (Rangers) (8): 1961 v Ni, Cz, Ei. (2); 1962 v Ni, W, Cz, U.
BRANDEN, T. (Blackburn R.) (1): 1896 v E.
BRAZIL, A. (Ipswich Town, Tottenham) (13): 1980 v Pol, H; 1982 v Sp, Holl, Ni, W, E, Nz, USSR; 1983 v EG, Sw, W, E.
BREMNER, D. (Hibernian) (1): 1976 v Sw.
BREMNER, W. J. (Leeds Utd) (54): 1965 v Sp; 1966 v E, Pol, P, Br, I (2); 1967 v W, Ni, E; 1968 v W, E; 1969 v W, E, Ni, D, A, WG, Cy (2); 1970 v Ei, WG, A; 1971 v W, E; 1972 v Por, Bel, Holl, Ni, W, E, Y, Cz (cont...)

GORDON STRACHAN (right) selected Mark McGhee as No.2 when taking up the reins as Scotland boss

BREMNER, W. J. Br; 1973 v D (2), E (2), Ni, Sw, Br; 1974 v Cz, WG, Ni, W, E, Bel, N, Z, Br, Y; 1975 v Sp (2); 1976 v D.
BRENNAN, F. (Newcastle Utd) (7): 1947 v W, Ni; 1953 v W, Ni, E; 1954 v Ni, E.
BRESLIN, B. (Hibernian) (1): 1897 v W.
BREWSTER, G. (Everton) (1): 1921 v E.
BROADFOOT, K. (Rangers) (4): 2009 v Ice, N, Arg; 2011 v Se.
BROGAN, J. (Celtic) (4): 1971 v W, Ni, Por, E.
BROWN, A. (Middlesbrough) (1): 1904 v E.
BROWN, A. (St Mirren) (2): 1890 v W; 1891 v W.
BROWN, A. D. (East Fife, Blackpool) (14): 1950 v Sw, Por, Fr; 1952 v USA, D, Se; 1953 v W; 1954 v W, E, N (2), Fin, A, U.
BROWN, G. C. P. (Rangers) (19): 1931 v W; 1932 v E, W, Ni; 1933 v E; 1935 v A, E, W; 1936 v E, W; 1937 v G, E, W, Ni, Cz; 1938 v E, W, Cz, Holl.
BROWN, H. (Partick Th.) (3): 1947 v W, Bel, L.
BROWN, J. (Cambuslang) (1): 1890 v W.
BROWN, J. B. (Clyde) (1): 1939 v W.
BROWN, J. G. (Sheffield U.) (1): 1975 v R.
BROWN, R. (Dumbarton) (2): 1884 v W, Ni.
BROWN, R. (Rangers) (3): 1947 v Ni; 1949 v Ni; 1952 v E.
BROWN, R. (Dumbarton) (1): 1885 v W.
BROWN, S. (Hibernian, Celtic) (30): 2006 v US; 2007 v Geo, I; 2008 v SA, Lth, Fr, Uk, I, Cro; 2009 v Ni, Mac, Ice (2), N, Arg, Holl; 2010 v N, Mac, Holl, CzR; 2011 v Lth, Li, Br, W, Ei; 2012 v D, CzR, US. 2013 v W, Est.
BROWN, W. D. F. (Dundee, Tottenham H.) (28): 1958 v Fr; 1959 v E, W, Ni; 1960 v W, Ni, Pol, A, H, T; 1962 v Ni, W, E, Cz; 1963 v W, Ni, E, A; 1964 v Ni, W, N; 1965 v E, Fin, Pol, Sp; 1966 v Ni, Pol, I.
BROWNING, J. (Celtic) (1): 1914 v W.
BROWNLIE, J. (Hibernian) (7): 1971 v USSR; 1972 v Pe, Ni, E; 1973 v D (2); 1976 v R.
BROWNLIE, J. (Third Lanark) (16): 1909 v E, Ni; 1910 v E, W, Ni; 1911 v W, Ni; 1912 v W, Ni, E; 1913 v W, Ni, E; 1914 v W, Ni, E.
BRUCE, D. (Vale of Leven) (1): 1890 v W.
BRUCE, R. F. (Middlesbrough) (1): 1934 v A.
BRYSON, C. (Kilmarnock) (1): 2011 v Fi.
BUCHAN, M. M. (Aberdeen, Manchester Utd.) (34): 1972 v Por, Bel, W, Y, Cz, Br; 1973 v D (2), E; 1974 v WG, Ni, W, N, Br, Y; 1975 v EG, Sp, Por; 1976 v D, R; 1977 v Fin, Cz, Ch, Arg, Br; 1978 v EG, W, Ni, Pe, Ir, Holl; 1979 v A, N, Por.
BUCHANAN, J. (Cambuslang) (1): 1889 v Ni.
BUCHANAN, J. (Rangers) (2): 1929 v E; 1930 v E.
BUCHANAN, P. S. (Chelsea) (1): 1938 v Cz.
BUCHANAN, R. (Abercorn) (1): 1891 v W.
BUCKLEY, P. (Aberdeen) (3): 1954 v N; 1955 v W, Ni.
BUICK, A. (Hearts) (2): 1902 v W, Ni.
BURCHILL, M. (Celtic) (6): 2000 v Bos, Lth, E (2), Fr, Holl.
BURKE, C. (Rangers, Birmingham) (4): 2006 v Bul, J; 2013 v Est, W.
BURLEY C. (Chelsea, Celtic, Derby) (46): 1995 v J, Ec, Fi. 1996 v Gr, Se, Aus, D, US, Co, Ho, E, Sw; 1997 v A (2), La, Se (2), Est, Ma, Blr.

1998 v Blr, La, Fr, Co, US, Br, N, M. 1999 v Fi, CzR. 2000 v Bos (2), Est, Lth, E (2), Holl, Ei; 2001 v Cro, Aus, Bel, Sm; 2002 v Cro, Bel, La; 2003 v A.

BURLEY, G. (Ipswich Town) (11): 1979 v W, Ni, E, Arg, N; 1980 v Por, Ni, E, Pol; 1982 v W, E.

BURNS, F. (Manchester Utd) (1): 1970 v A.

BURNS, K. (Birmingham City, Nottingham F.) (20): 1974 v WG; 1975 v EG, Sp (2); 1977 v Cz, W, (2), Se; 1978 v Ni, W, E, Pe, Ir; 1979 v N; 1980 v Pe, A, Bel; 1981 v Is, Ni, W.

BURNS, T. (Celtic) (8): 1981 v Ni; 1982 v Holl, W; 1983 v Bel, Ni, Ca (2); 1988 v E.

BUSBY, M. W. (Manchester City) (1): 1934 v W.

CAIRNS, T. (Rangers) (8): 1920 v W; 1922 v E; 1923 v E, W; 1924 v Ni; 1925 v W, E, Ni.

CALDERHEAD, D. (Q.O.S. Wanderers) (1): 1889 v Ni.

CALDERWOOD, C. (Tottenham Hotspur, Aston Villa) (36): 1995 v Ru, Sm, J, Ec, Fi. 1996 v Gr, Fin, Se, Sm, US, U, Holl, E, Sw; 1997 A (2), La, Se (2), Est (2); 1998 v Blr, La, Fr, D, Fin, Co, US, Br, N. 1999 v Lth, Est, Fi, CzR. 2000 v Bos (2).

CALDERWOOD, R. (Cartvale) (3): 1885 v Ni, E, W.

CALDOW, E. (Rangers) (40): 1957 Sp (2), Sw, WG, E; 1958 v Ni, W, Sw, Par, H, Pol, Y, Fr; 1959 v E, W, Ni, WG, Holl, Por; 1960 v E, W, Ni, A, H, T; 1961 v E, W, Ni, Ei (2), Cz; 1962 v Ni, W, E, Cz (2), U; 1963 v W, Ni, E.

CALDWELL, G. (Newcastle, Hibernian, Celtic, Wigan) (54): 2002 v Fr, Nig, Skor, SA, HK; 2004 v R, D, Est, Trin; 2005 v H, Sp, Slo, N, Mo, I, Blr; 2006 v Slo, US, Sw, Bul, J; 2007 v Lth, Fr, Uk, A; 2008 v SA, Cro, CzR; 2009 v Mac, Ice (2), N, Arg, Holl; 2010 v N, J, W, CzR; 2011 v CzR, Br, W; 2012 v D, CzR, Lth, Sp, Cy, Slo, US; 2013 v Aus, Mac, W (2), Bel, Ser.

CALDWELL, S. (Newcastle, Sunderland, Burnley, Wigan) (12): 2001 v Pol; 2003 v Ei; 2004 v W, Trin; 2005 v Mo; 2006 v A, Slo, US, Sw; 2010 v N; 2011 v Fi, Ni.

CALLAGHAN, P. (Hibernian) (1): 1900 v Ni.

CALLAGHAN, W. C. Dunfermline Ath.) (2): 1970 v Ei, W.

CAMERON, C. (Hearts, Wolves) (28): 1999 v G, Fi; 2000 v Lth, Fr, Ei; 2001 v La, Sm, Cro, Aus, Sm, Pol; 2002 v Cro, Bel, La, Fr; 2003 v Ei, A, Lth, G; 2004 v N, Fi, G, Lth, W, R, D, 2005 v Sp, Mo.

CAMERON, J. (Rangers) (1): 1886 v NI.

CAMERON, J. (Queen's Park) (1): 1896 v Ni.

CAMERON, J. (St Mirren, Chelsea) (2): 1904 v Ni; 1909 v E.

CAMPBELL, C. (Queen's Park) (13): 1874 v E; 1876 v W; 1877 v E, W; 1878 v E; 1879 v E; 1880 v E; 1881 v E; 1882 v E, W; 1884 v E; 1885 v E; 1886 v E.

CAMPBELL, H. (Renton) (1): 1889 v W.

CAMPBELL, J. (Sheffield W.) (1): 1913 v W.

CAMPBELL, J. (South Western) (1): 1880 v W.

CAMPBELL, J. (Kilmarnock) (2): 1891 v Ni; 1892 v W.

CAMPBELL, J. (Celtic) (12): 1893 v E, Ni; 1898 v E, Ni; 1900 v E, Ni; 1901 v E, W, Ni; 1902 v W, Ni; 1903 v W.

CAMPBELL, J. (Rangers) (4): 1899 v E, W, Ni; 1901 v Ni.
CAMPBELL, K. (Liverpool, Partick Th.) (8): 1920 v E, W, Ni; 1921 v W, Ni; 1922 v W. Ni, E.
CAMPBELL, P. (Rangers) (2): 1878 v W; 1879 v W.
CAMPBELL, P. (Morton) (1): 1898 v W.
CAMPBELL, R. (Falkirk, Chelsea) (5): 1947 v Bel, L; 1950 v Sw, Por, Fr.
CAMPBELL, W. (Morton) (5): 1946 v Sw; 1947 v Ni; 1948 v E, Bel, Sw.
CANERO, P. (Leicester) (1): 2004 v D.
CARABINE, J. (Third Lanark) (3): 1938 v Holl; 1939 v E, Ni.
CARR, W. M. (Coventry City) (6): 1970 v Ni, W, E; 1971 v D; 1972 v Pe; 1973 v D.
CASSIDY, J. (Celtic) (4): 1921 v W, Ni; 1923 v Ni; 1924 v W.
CHALMERS, S. (Celtic) (5): 1965 v W, Fin; 1966 v Por, Br; 1967 v Ni.
CHALMERS, W. (Rangers) (1): 1885 v Ni.
CHALMERS, W. S. (Queen's Park) (1): 1929 v Ni.
CHAMBERS, T. (Hearts) (1): 1894 v W.
CHAPLIN, G. D. (Dundee) (1): 1908 v W.
CHEYNE, A. G. (Aberdeen) (5): 1929 v E, N, G, Holl; 1930 v Fr.
CHRISTIE, A. J. (Queen's Park) (3): 1898 v W; 1899 v E, Ni.
CHRISTIE, R. M. (Queen's Park) (1): 1884 v E.
CLARK, J. (Celtic) (4): 1966 v Br; 1967 v W, Ni, USSR.
CLARK, R. B. (Aberdeen) (17): 1968 v W, Holl; 1970 v Ni; 1971 v W, Ni, E, D, Por, USSR; 1972 v Bel, Ni, W, E, Cz, Br; 1973 v D, E.
CLARKE, S. (Chelsea) (6): 1988 v H, Bel, Bul, S.Ar, Ma; 1984 v Holl.
CLARKSON, D. (Motherwell) (2): 2008 v CzR; 2009 v Arg.
CLELAND, J. (Royal Albert) (1): 1891 v Ni.
CLEMENTS, R. (Leith Ath.) (1): 1891 v Ni.
CLUNAS, W. L. (Sunderland) (2): 1924 v E; 1926 v W.
COLLIER, W. (Raith R.) (1): 1922 v W.
COLLINS, J. (Hibs, Celtic, Monaco, Everton) (58): 1988 v S.Ar; 1990 v EG, Pol, Ma; 1991 v Sw, Bul, Ni, Fin; 1993 v Por (2), Ma, G, Est (2); 1994 v Sw, Holl (2), A; 1995 v Fin, Fi (2), Ru (2), Gr, Sm. 1996 v Gr, Fin, Se, Sm, Aus, D, US, U, Holl, E, Sw; 1997 v A (2), La, Se (2), Est, Ma; 1998 v Blr, La, Fr, Fin, Co, US, Br, M, N. 1999 v Lth. 2000 v Bos (2), Est, E (2).
COLLINS, R. Y. (Celtic, Everton, Leeds Utd) (31): 1951 v W, Ni, A; 1955 v Y, A, H; 1956 v Ni, W; 1957 v E, W, Sp (2), Sw, WG; 1958 v Ni, W, Sw, H, Pol, Y, Fr, Par; 1959 v E, W, Ni, WG, Holl, Por; 1965 v E, Pol, Sp.
COLLINS, T. (Hearts) (1): 1909 v W.
COLMAN, D. (Aberdeen) (4): 1911 v E, W, Ni; 1913 v Ni.
COLQUHOUN, E. P. (Sheffield Utd) (9): 1972 v Por, Holl, Pe, Y, Cz, Br; 1973 v D (2), E.
COLQUHOUN, J. (Hearts) (2): 1988 v S.Ar, Malta.
COMBE, J. R. (Hibernian) (3): 1948 v E, Bel, Sw.
COMMONS. K (Derby, Celtic) (12): 2009 v Ni, Mac, Ice, Arg; 2010 v N, Holl; 2011 v Fi, Ni, Br; 2013 v W, Bel, Est.
CONN, A. (Hearts) (1): 1956 v A.
CONN, A. (Tottenham H.) (2): 1975 v Ni, E.

CONNACHAN, E. D. (Dunfermline Ath.) (2): 1962 v Cz, U.
CONNELLY, G. (Celtic) (2): 1974 v Cz, WG.
CONNOLLY, J. (Everton) (1): 1973 v Sw.
CONNOR, J. (Airdrie) (1): 1886 v Ni.
CONNOR, J. (Sunderland) (4): 1930 v Fr; 1932 v Ni; 1934 v E; 1935 v Ni.
CONNOR, R. (Dundee, Aberdeen) (4): 1986 v Holl; 1988 v S.Ar; 1989 v E; 1991 v R.
CONWAY, C. (Dundee United, Cardiff) (4): 2010 v J; 2011 v Ni; 2012 v Cy; 2013 v Cro.
COOK, W. L. (Bolton W.) (3): 1934 v E; 1935 v W, Ni.
COOKE, C. (Dundee, Chelsea) (16): 1966 v W, I, Por, Br; 1968 v E, Holl; 1969 v W, Ni, A, WG, Cy (2); 1970 v A; 1971 v Bel; 1975 v Sp, Por.
COOPER, D. (Rangers, Motherwell) (22): 1980 v Pe, A; 1984 v W, E; 1985 v Y, Ice, Sp (2), W; 1986 v W, EG, Aus (2), Holl, WG, U; 1987 v Bul, L, Ei, Br; 1990 v N, Eg.
CORMACK, P. B. (Hibernian, Nottingham F.) (9): 1966 v Br; 1969 v D; 1970 v Ei, WG; 1971 v D, W, Por, E; 1972 v Holl.
COWAN, J. (Aston Villa) (3): 1896 v E; 1897 v E; 1898 v E.
COWAN, J. (Morton) (25): 1948 v Bel, Sw, Fr; 1949 v E, W, Fr; 1950 v E, W, Ni, Sw, Por, Fr; 1951 v E, W, Ni, A (2), D, Fr, Bel; 1952 v Ni, W, USA, D, Se.
COWAN, W. D. (Newcastle Utd) (1): 1924 v E.
COWIE, D. (Dundee) (20): 1953 v E, Se; 1954 v Ni, W, Fin, N, A, U; 1955 v W, Ni, A, H; 1956 v W, A; 1957 v Ni, W; 1958 v H, Pol, Y, Par.
COWIE, D. (Watford, Cardiff) (9): 2010 v J, W; 2011 V Br; 2012 v D, CzR, Lth, Sp, Cy, US.
COX, S. (Rangers) (25): 1948 v Fr; 1949 v E, Fr; 1950 v E, Fr, W, Ni, Sw, Por; 1951 v E, D, Fr, Bel, A; 1952 v Ni, W, USA, D, Se; 1953 v W, Ni, E; 1954 v W, Ni, E.
CRAIG, A. (Motherwell) (3): 1929 v Ni, Holl; 1932 v E.
CRAIG, J. (Celtic) (1): 1977 v Se.
CRAIG, J. P. (Celtic) (1): 1968 v W.
CRAIG, T. (Rangers) (8): 1927 v Ni; 1928 v Ni; 1929 v N, G, Holl; 1930 v Ni, E, W.
CRAIG, T. B. (Newcastle Utd) (1): 1976 v Sw.
CRAINEY, S (Celtic, Southampton, Blackpool) (12): 2002 v Fr, Nig; 2003 v D, Fi; 2004 v R, D; 2011 v Fi, Br, W; 2012 v D, Lth, Cy.
CRAPNELL, J. (Airdrie) (9): 1929 v E, N, G; 1930 v Fr; 1931 v Ni, Sw; 1932 v E, Fr; 1933 v Ni.
CRAWFORD, D. (St Mirren, Rangers) (3): 1894 v W, Ni; 1900 v W.
CRAWFORD, J. (Queen's Park) (5): 1932 v Fr, Ni; 1933 v E, W, Ni.
CRAWFORD, S. (Raith Rovers, Dunfermline, Plymouth) (25): 1995 v Ec; 2001 v Pol; 2002 v Fr; 2003 v Fi, Ice (2), Can, Por, Ei, A, Lth, Nz, G; 2004 v N, Fi, Lth, Holl, R, Est, Trin; 2005 v H, Sp, Slo, Mo, Se.
CRERAND, P. T. (Celtic, Manchester Utd) (16): 1961 v Ei (2), Cz; 1962 v Ni, W, E, Cz (2), U; 1963 v W, Ni; 1964 v Ni; 1965 v E, Pol, Fin; 1966 v Pol.
CRINGAN, W. (Celtic) (5): 1920 v W; 1922 v E, Ni; 1923 v W, E.
CROSBIE, J. A. (Ayr Utd, Birmingham C) (2): 1920 v W; 1922 v E.
CROAL, J. A. (Falkirk) (3): 1913 v Ni; 1914 v E, W.

JORDAN RHODES earned his ninth cap for Scotland when he came on as a substitute against Croatia

CROPLEY, A. J. (Hibernian) (2): 1972 v Por, Bel.
CROSS, J. H. (Third Lanark) (1): 1903 v Ni.
CRUICKSHANK, J. (Hearts) (6): 1964 v WG; 1970 v W, E; 1971 v D, Bel; 1976 v R.
CRUM, J. (Celtic) (2): 1936 v E; 1939 v Ni.
CULLEN, M. J. (Luton Town) (1): 1956 v A.
CUMMING, D. S. (Middlesbrough) (1): 1938 v E.
CUMMING, J. (Hearts) (9): 1955 v E, H, Por, Y; 1960 v E, Pol, A, H, T.
CUMMINGS, G. (Partick Th., Aston Villa) (9): 1935 v E; 1936 v W, Ni, E; 1937 v G; 1938 v W, Ni, Cz; 1939 v E.
CUMMINGS, W. (Chelsea) (1): 2002 v HK.
CUNNINGHAM, A. N. (Rangers) (12): 1920 v Ni; 1921 v W, E; 1922 v Ni; 1923 v E, W; 1924 v E, Ni; 1926 v E, Ni; 1927 v E, W.
CUNNINGHAM, W. C. (Preston NE) (8): 1954 v N (2), U, Fin, A; 1955 v W, E, H.
CURRAN, H. P. (Wolves) (5): 1970 v A; 1971 v Ni, E, D, USSR.

DAILLY, C. (Derby, Blackburn, West Ham, Rangers) (67): 1997 v W, Ma, Blr; 1998 v Blr, La, Fr, D, Fin, Co, US, Br, N, M; 1999 v Lth; 2000 v Bos (2), Est, Lth, E (2), Fr, Holl, Ei; 2001 v La, Sm, Aus, Pol; 2002 v Cro, Bel, La, Fi, Nig, Skor, SA, HK; 2003 v D, Fi, Ice (2), Can, Por, Ei, A, Lth, Nz, G; 2004 v N, G, Lth, Holl, W, R, D; 2005 v Mo, Blr; 2006 v A, I, Blr, Slo, US, Sw; 2007 v Fi, Lth, Fr, A; 2008 v Uk, CzR.
DALGLISH, K. (Celtic, Liverpool) (102): 1972 v Bel, Holl; 1973 v D (2), E (2), W, Ni, Sw, Br; 1974 v Cz (2), WG (2), Ni, W, E, Bel, N, Z, Br, Y; 1975 v EG, Sp (2), Se, Por, W, Ni, E, R; 1976 v D (2), R, Sw, Ni, E; 1977 v Fin, Cz, W (2), Se, Ni, E, Ch, Arg, Br; 1978 v EG, Cz, W, Bul, Ni, W, E, Pe, Ir, Holl; 1979 v A, N, Por, W, Ni, E, Arg, N; 1980 v Pe, A, Bel (2), Por, Ni, W, E, Pol, H; 1981 v Se, Por, Is; 1982 v Se, Ni, Por, Sp, Holl, Ni, W, E, Nz, Br; 1983 v Bel, Sw; 1984 v U, Bel, EG; 1985 v Y, Ice, Sp, W; 1986 v EG, Aus, R; 1987 v Bul, L.
DAVIDSON, C. (Blackburn Rovers, Leicester, Preston NE) (19): 1999 v Lth, Est, Fi, CzR (2), G, Fi; 2000 v Est, Bos, Lth, E, Fr; 2001 v La, Pol; 2002, La; 2003 v Ice, Can; 2010 v N, Mac.
DAVIDSON, D. (Queen's Park) (5): 1878 v W; 1879 v W; 1880 v W; 1881 v E, W.
DAVIDSON, J. A. (Partick Th.) (8): 1954 v N (2), A, U; 1955 v W, Ni, E, H.
DAVIDSON, M. (St Johnstone) (1): 2013 v Lux.
DAVIDSON, S. (Middlesbrough) (1): 1921 v E.
DAWSON, A. (Rangers) (5): 1980 v Pol, H; 1983 v Ni, Ca (2).
DAWSON, J. (Rangers) (14): 1935 v Ni; 1936 v E; 1937 v G, E, W, Ni, A, Cz; 1938 v W, Holl, Ni; 1939 v E, Ni, H.
DEANS, J. (Celtic) (2): 1975 v EG, Sp.
DELANEY, J. (Celtic, Manchester Utd) (13): 1936 v W, Ni; 1937 v G, E, A, Cz; 1938 v Ni; 1939 v W, Ni; 1947 v E; 1948 v E, W, Ni.
DEVINE, A. (Falkirk) (1): 1910 v W.
DEVLIN, P. (Birmingham City) (10): 2003 v Can, Por, Ei, A, Ice, Lth, Nz, G; 2004 v N, Fi.
DEWAR, G. (Dumbarton) (2): 1888 v Ni; 1889 v E.

DEWAR, N. (Third Lanark) (3): 1932 v E, Fr; 1933 v W.
DICK, J. (West Ham Utd) (1): 1959 v E.
DICKIE, M. (Rangers) (3): 1897 v Ni; 1899 v Ni; 1900 v W.
DICKOV, P. (Manchester City, Leicester, Blackburn) (10): 2001 v Sm, Cro, Aus; 2003 v Fi; 2004 v Fi, Holl (2), W; 2005 v N, Slo.
DICKSON, W. A (Dundee Strathmore) (1): 1888 v Ni.
DICKSON, W. (Kilmarnock) (5): 1970 v Ni, W, E; 1971 v D, USSR.
DIVERS, J. (Celtic) (1): 1895 v W.
DIXON, P. (Dundee Utd) (3): 2013 v Mac, Lux, Ser.
DAVIDSON, S. (Middlesbrough) (1): 1921 v E.
DOBIE, S. (WBA) (6): 2002 v Skor, SA, HK; 2003 v D, Fi, Por.
DOCHERTY, T. H. (Preston NE, Arsenal) (25): 1952 v W; 1953 v E, Se; 1954 v N (2), A, U; 1955 v W, E, H (2), A; 1957 v E, Y, Sp (2), Sw, WG; 1958 v Ni, W, E, Sw; 1959 v W, E, Ni.
DODDS, D. (Dundee Utd) (2): 1984 v U, Ni.
DODDS, J. (Celtic) (3): 1914 v E, W, Ni.
DODDS, W. (Aberdeen, Dundee Utd, Rangers) (26): 1997 v La, W, Blr; 1998 v Blr. 1999 v Est, Fi, G, Fi, CzR. 2000 v Bos (2), Est, Lth, E (2), Fr, Holl, Ei; 2001 v La, Sm (2), Aus, Bel, Pol; 2002 v Cro, Bel.
DOIG, J. E. (Arbroath, Sunderland) (5): 1887 v Ni; 1889 v Ni; 1896 v E; 1899 v E; 1903 v E.
DONACHIE, W. (Manchester City) (35): 1972 v Pe, Ni, E, Y, Cz, Br; 1973 v D, E, W, Ni; 1974 v Ni; 1976 v R, Ni, W, E,; 1977 v Fin, Cz, W (2), Se, Ni, E, Ch, Arg, Br; 1978 v EG, W (2), Bul, E, Ir, Holl; 1979 v A, N, Por.
DONALDSON, A. (Bolton) (6): 1914 v E, Ni, W; 1920 v E, Ni; 1922 v Ni.
DONNACHIE, J. (Oldham Ath.) (3): 1913 v E; 1914 v E, Ni.
DONNELLY, S. (Celtic) (10): 1997 v W, Ma; 1998 La, Fr, D, Fin, Co, US. 1999 v Est. Fi.
DORRANS, G. (West Bromwich Albion) (9): 2010 v J, W, CzR; 2011 v CzR, Sp; 2012 v D, Lth, Slo; 2013 v W.
DOUGALL, C. (Birmingham City) (1): 1947 v W.
DOUGALL, J. (Preston NE) (1): 1939 v E.
DOUGAN, R. (Hearts) (1): 1950 v Sw.
DOUGLAS, A. (Chelsea) (1): 1911 v Ni.
DOUGLAS, J. (Renfrew) (1): 1880 v W.
DOUGLAS, R. (Celtic, Leicester) (18): 2002 v Nig, SA, HK; 2003 v D, Fi, Ice (2), Por, Nz, G; 2004 v N, Fi, G, Lth, Holl (2), W; 2005 v I; 2006 v A.
DOWDS, P. (Celtic) (1): 1892 v Ni.
DOWNIE, R. (Third Lanark) (1): 1892 v W.
DOYLE, D. (Celtic) (8): 1892 v E; 1893 v W; 1894 v E; 1895 v E, Ni; 1897 v E; 1898 v E, Ni.
DOYLE, J. (Ayr Utd) (1): 1976 v R.
DRUMMOND, J. (Falkirk, Rangers) (14): 1892 v Ni; 1894 v Ni; 1895 v Ni, E; 1896 v E, Ni; 1897 v Ni; 1898 v E; 1900 v E; 1901 v E; 1902 v E, W, Ni; 1903 v Ni.
DUNBAR, M. (Cartvale) (1): 1886 v Ni.
DUNCAN, A. (Hibernian) (6): 1975 v Por, W, Ni, E, R; 1976 v D.

DUNCAN, D. (Derby Co.) (14): 1933 v E, W; 1934 v A, W; 1935 v E, W; 1936 v E, W, Ni; 1937 v G, E, W, Ni; 1938 v W.
DUNCAN, D. M. (East Fife) (3): 1948 v Bel, Sw, Fr.
DUNCAN, J. (Alexandra Ath.) (2): 1878 v W; 1882 v W.
DUNCAN, J. (Leicester City) (1): 1926 v W.
DUNCANSON, J. (Rangers) (1): 1947 v Ni.
DUNLOP, J. (St Mirren) (1): 1890 v W.
DUNLOP, W. (Liverpool) (1): 1906 v E.
DUNN, J. (Hibernian, Everton) (6): 1925 v W, Ni; 1927 v Ni; 1928 v Ni, E; 1929 v W.
DURIE, G. S. (Chelsea, Tottenham, Rangers) (43): 1988 v Bul; 1989 v I, Cy; 1990 v Y, EG, Eg, Se; 1991 v Sw, Bul (2), USSR, Sm (2), 1992 v Sw, R, Ni, Fin, Ca, N, Holl, G; 1993 v Sw, I; 1994 v Sw, I, Holl (2). 1996 US, Holl, E, Sw; 1997 v A, Se, Ma, Blr; 1998 Blr, La, Fr, Fin, Co, Br, N, M.
DURRANT, I. (Rangers, Kilmarnock) (20): 1988 v H, Bel, Ma, Sp; 1989 v N; 1993 v Sw, Por (2), I; 1994 v I, Ma. 1999 v Est, Fi, G, Fi, CzR. 2000 v Bos; Est, Holl, Ei.
DYKES, J. (Hearts) (2): 1938 v Holl; 1939 v Ni.

EASSON, J. F. (Portsmouth) (3): 1931 v A, Sw; 1934 v W.
ELLIOTT, M. (Leicester City) (18): 1998 v Fr, D, Fin. 1999, v Lth, Fi, CzR, Fi, Holl, Ei; 2001 v La, Sm (2), Cro, Aus, Bel; 2002 v Cro, Bel, La.
ELLIS, J. (Mossend Swifts) (1): 1892 v Ni.
EVANS, A. (Aston Villa) (4): 1982 v Holl, Ni, E, Nz.
EVANS, R. (Celtic, Chelsea) (48): 1949 v E, W, Ni, Fr; 1950 v W, Ni, Sw, Por; 1951 v E, A; 1952 v Ni; 1953 v Se; 1954 v Ni, W, E, N, Fin; 1955 v Ni, Por, Y, A, H; 1956 v E, Ni, W, A; 1957 v WG, Sp; 1958 v Ni, W, E, Sw, H, Pol, Y, Par, Fr; 1959 v E, WG, Holl, Por; 1960 v E, Ni, W, Pol; 1960 v A, H, T.
EWART, J. (Bradford City) (1): 1921 v E.
EWING, T. (Partick Th.) (2): 1958 v W, E.

FARM, G. N. (Blackpool) (10): 1953 v W, Ni, E, Se; 1954 v Ni, W, E; 1959 v WG, Holl, Por.
FERGUSON, B. (Rangers, Blackburn, Rangers) (45): 1999 v Lth. 2000 v Bos, Est, E (2), Fr, Ei; 2001 v La, Aus, Bel; 2003 v D, Fi, Ice (2), Ei; 2004 v N, Fi, G, Lth, Holl (2); 2005 v H, Sp, Slo, N, Mo (2), I, Blr; 2006: v I, N, Blr, Sw; 2007 v Fr, Uk, Geo, I, A, Fi; 2008 v Fr, Uk, Geo, I; 2009 v Arg, Holl.
FERGUSON, D. (Rangers) (2): 1988 v Ma, Co.
FERGUSON, D. (Dundee United, Everton) (7): 1992 v US, Ca, Holl; 1993 v G; 1995 v Gr; 1997 v A, Est.
FERGUSON, I. (Rangers) (9): 1989 v I, Cy, Fr; 1993 v Ma, Est; 1994 v Ma, A, Holl; 1997 v Est.
FERGUSON, J. (Vale of Leven) (6): 1874 v E; 1876 v E, W; 1877 v E, W; 1878 v W.
FERGUSON, R. (Kilmarnock) (7): 1966 v W, E, Holl, Por, Br; 1967 v W, Ni.

FERNIE, W. (Celtic) (12): 1954 v Fin, A, U; 1955 v W, Ni; 1957 v E, Ni, W, Y; 1958 v W, Sw, Par.
FINDLAY, R. (Kilmarnock) (1): 1898 v W.
FITCHIE, T. T. (Woolwich Arsenal, Queen's Park) (4): 1905 v W: 1906 v W, Ni; 1907 v W.
FLAVEL, R. (Airdrie) (2): 1947 v Bel, L.
FLECK, R. (Norwich City) (4): 1990 v Arg, Se, Br; 1991 v USSR.
FLEMING, C. (East Fife) (1): 1954 v Ni.
FLEMING, J. W. (Rangers) (3): 1929 v G, Holl; 1930 v E.
FLEMING, R. (Morton): 1886 v Ni.
FLETCHER, D. (Manchester Utd) (61): 2004 v N, Lth, Holl (2), W, D, Est, Trin; 2005 v H, Sp, Slo, N, Mo (2), Blr; 2006 v I, N, Blr, Slo, US, Sw, Bul, J; 2007 v Fi (2), Lth, Fr, Uk, A; 2008 v SA, Lth, Fr, Geo, I, Cro, CzR. 2009 v Ni, Mac, Ice (2), N, Holl; 2010 v N, Mac, Holl, W, CzR; 2011 v Se, Lth, Li, CzR, Sp, Fi. 2012 v CzR, Lth, Sp, Cy; 2013 v W, Bel, Lux.
FLETCHER, S. (Hibs, Wolves, Sunderland) (12): 2008 v Cro; 2009 v N, Holl, Ice; 2010 v Mac, W, J; 2011 v Se; 2013 v W (2), Bel, Est.
FORBES, A. R. (Sheffield Utd, Arsenal) (14): 1947 v Bel, L, E; 1948 v W, Ni; 1950 v E, Por, Fr; 1951 v W, Ni, A; 1952 v W, D, Se.
FORBES, J. (Vale of Leven) (5): 1884 v E, W, Ni; 1887 v W, E.
FORD, D. (Hearts) (3): 1974 v Cz, WG, W.
FORREST, J. (Rangers, Aberdeen) (5): 1966 v W, I; 1971 v Bel, D, USSR.
FORREST, J. (Motherwell) (1): 1958 v E.
FORREST, J. (Celtic) (6): 2011 v Ei; 2012 v D, Sp, Slo; 2013 v Mac, Ser.
FORSYTH, A. (Partick Th., Manchester Utd) (10): 1972 v Y, Cz, Br; 1973 v D, E; 1975 v Sp, Ni, R, EG; 1976 v D.
FORSYTH, C. (Kilmarnock) (4): 1964 v E; 1965 v W, Ni, Fin.
FORSYTH, T. (Motherwell, Rangers) (22): 1971 v D; 1974 v Cz; 1976 v Sw, Ni, W, E; 1977 v Fin, Se, W, Ni, E, Ch, Arg, Br; 1978 v Cz, W, Ni, W, E, Pe, Ir, Holl.
FOX, D. (Celtic, Southampton) (4): 2010 v W; 2013 v Aus, W, Bel.
FOYERS, R. (St Bernard's) (2): 1893 v W; 1894 v W.
FRASER, D. M. (WBA) (2): 1968 v Holl; 1969 v Cy.
FRASER, J. (Moffat) (1): 1891 v Ni.
FRASER, M. J. E. (Queen's Park) (5): 1880 v W; 1882 v W, E; 1883 v W, E.
FRASER, J. (Dundee) (1): 1907 v Ni.
FRASER, W. (Sunderland) (2): 1955 v W, Ni.
FREEDMAN, D. (Crystal Palace) (2): 2002 v L1, Fr.
FULTON, W. (Abercorn) (1): 1884 v Ni.
FYFE, J. H. (Third Lanark) (1): 1895 v W.
GABRIEL, J. (Everton) (2): 1961 v W; 1964 v N.
GALLACHER, K. W. (Dundee Utd, Coventry, Blackburn Rov, Newcastle) (53): 1988 v Co, E; 1989 v N; I; 1991 v Sm (2); 1992 v R, Ni, N, Holl, G, CIS; 1993 v Sw, Por (2), Est (2); 1994 v I, Ma; 1996 v Aus, D, U, Holl; 1997 v Se (2), Est (2), A, W, Ma, Blr; 1998 v Blr, La, Fr, Fin, US, Br, N, M. 1999 v Lth, Est, Fi, CzR. 2000 v Bos (2), Lth, E, Fr, Ei; 2001 v Sm (2), Cro, Bel.
GALLACHER, P. (Sunderland) (1): 1935 v Ni.

GALLACHER, P. (Dundee United) (8): 2002 v HK; 2003 v Can, Ei, A, Lth, R, D, Est.
GALLAGHER, H. K. (Airdrie, Newcastle Utd, Chelsea, Derby C.) (20): 1924 v Ni; 1925 v E, W, Ni; 1926 v W, E, Ni; 1927 v E, W, Ni; 1928 v E, W; 1929 v E, W, Ni; 1930 v W, Ni, Fr; 1934 v E; 1935 v E.
GALLOWAY, M. (Celtic) (1): 1992 v R.
GALLAGHER, P. (Blackburn Rov) (1): 2004 v W.
GALT, J. H. (Rangers) (2): 1908 v W, Ni.
GARDINER, I. (Motherwell) (1): 1958 v W.
GARDNER, D. R. (Third Lanark) (1): 1897 v W.
GARDNER, R. (Queen's Park, Clydesdale) (5): 1872 v E; 1873 v E; 1874 v E; 1875 v E; 1878 v E.
GEMMELL, T. (St Mirren) (2): 1955 v Por, Y.
GEMMELL, T. (Celtic) (18): 1966 v E; 1967 v W, Ni, E, USSR; 1968 v Ni, E; 1969 v W, Ni, E, D, A, WG, Cy; 1970 v E, Ei, WG; 1971 v Bel.
GEMMILL, A. (Derby Co., Nottingham F., Birmingham City) (43): 1971 v Bel; 1972 v Por, Holl, Pe, Ni, W, E; 1976 v D, R, Ni, W, E; 1977 v Fin, Cz, W (2), Ni, E, Ch, Arg, Br; 1978 v EG, Bul, Ni, W, E, Pe, Ir, Holl; 1979 v A, N. Por, N; 1980 v A, Por, Ni, W, E, H; 1981 v Se, Por, Is, Ni.
GEMMILL, S. (Nottingham F, Everton) (25): 1995 v J, Ec, Fi; 1996 v Sm, D, US; 1997 v Est, Se, W, Ma, Blr; 1998 v D, Fin; 1999 v G, Fi; 2001 v Sm; 2002 v Cro, Fr, Nig, Skor, SA, HK; 2003 v Can, Ei, A.
GIBB, W. (Clydesdale) (1): 1873 v E.
GIBSON, D. W. (Leicester City) (7): 1963 v A, N, Ei, Sp; 1964 v Ni; 1965 v W, Fin.
GIBSON, J. D. (Partick Th., Aston Villa) (8): 1926 v E; 1927 v E, W, Ni; 1928 v E, W; 1930 v W. Ni.
GIBSON, N. (Rangers, Partick Th.) (14): 1895 v E, Ni; 1896 v E, Ni; 1897 v E, Ni; 1898 v E; 1899 v E, W, Ni; 1900 v E, Ni; 1901 v W; 1905 v Ni.
GILCHRIST, J. E. (Celtic) (1): 1922 v E.
GILHOOLEY, M. (Hull City) (1): 1922 v W.
GILKS, M. (Blackpool) (2): 2013 v Aus, Lux.
GILLESPIE, G. (Rangers, Queen's Park) (7): 1880 v E, W; 1882 v E; 1886 v W; 1890 v W; 1891 v Ni.
GILLESPIE, G. T. (Liverpool) (13): 1988 v Bel, Bul, Sp; 1989 v N, Fr, Ch; 1990 v Y, EG, Eg, Pol, Ma, Br; 1991 v Bul.
GILLESPIE, Jas. (Third Lanark) (1): 1898 v W.
GILLESPIE, John (Queen's Park) (1): 1896 v W.
GILLESPIE, R. (Queen's Park) (4): 1927 v W; 1931 v W; 1932 v Fr; 1933 v E.
GILLICK, T. (Everton) (5): 1937 v A, Cz; 1939 v W, Ni, H.
GILMOUR, J. (Dundee) (1): 1931 v W.
GILZEAN, A. J. (Dundee, Tottenham H.) (22): 1964 v W, E, N, WG; 1965 v Ni, Sp; 1966 v Ni, W, Pol, I; 1968 v W; 1969 v W, E, WG, Cy (2), A; 1970 v Ni, E, WG, A; 1971 v Por.

GLAVIN, R. (Celtic) (1): 1977 v Se.
GLASS S. (Newcastle Utd) (1): 1999 v Fi.
GLEN, A. (Aberdeen) (2): 1956 v E, Ni.
GLEN, R. (Renton, Hibernian) (3): 1895 v W; 1896 v W; 1900 v Ni.
GOODWILLIE, D. (Dundee Utd, Blackburn) (3): 2011 v Fi; 2012 v Lth, Sp.
GORAM, A. L. (Oldham, Hibs, Rangers) (42): 1986 v EG, R, Holl; 1987 v Br; 1989 v Y, I; 1990 v EG, Pol, Ma; 1991 v R (2), Sw, Bul (2), USSR, Sm (2); 1992 v Sw, Fin, N, Holl, G, CIS; 1993 v Sw, Por (2), I, Ma; 1994 v Holl; 1995 v Fin, Fi, Ru, Gr; 1996 v Se, D, Holl, Sw, E, Col; 1997 A, La, Est; 1998 v D.
GORDON, C. (Hearts, Sunderland) (40): 2004 v Trin; 2005 v Sp, Slo, N, Mo (2), I, Blr; 2006 v A, I, N, Blr, Slo, US, Sw; 2007 v Fi (2), Lth, Fr, Uk, Geo, I, A; 2008 v SA, Lth, Fr, Uk, Geo, I, Cro, CzR; 2009 v Ni, Mac, Ice (2), N; 2010 v Mac, J, CzR; 2011 v Fi.
GORDON, J. E. (Rangers) (10): 1912 v E, Ni; 1913 v E, Ni, W; 1914 v E, Ni; 1920 v W, E, Ni, U.
GOSSLAND, J. (Rangers) (1): 1884 v Ni.
GOUDLE, J. (Abercorn) (1): 1884 v Ni.
GOUGH, C. R. (Dundee Utd, Tottenham H., Rangers) (61): 1983 v Sw, Ni, W, E, Ca (3); 1984 v U, Bel, EG, Ni, W, E, Fr; 1985 v Sp, E, Ice; 1986 v W, EG, Aus, Is, R, E, D, WG, U; 1987 v Bul, L, Ei (2), Bel, E, Br; 1988 v H, S.Ar, Sp, Co, E; 1989 v Y, I, Cy (2), Fr; 1990 v Fr, Arg, EG, Pol, Ma, Cr; 1991 v USSR, Bul; 1992 v Sm, Ni, Ca, N, Holl, G, CIS; 1993 v Sw, Por.
GOULD, J. (Celtic) (2): 2000 v Lth; 2001 v Aus.
GOURLAY, J. (Cambuslang) (2): 1886 v Ni; 1888 v W.
GOVAN, J. (Hibernian) (6): 1948 v E, W, Bel, Sw, Fr; 1949 v Ni.
GOW, D. R. (Rangers) (1): 1888 v E.
GOW, J. J. (Queen's Park) (1): 1885 v E.
GOW, J. R. (Rangers) (1): 1888 v Ni.
GRAHAM, A. (Leeds Utd) (11): 1978 v EG; 1979 v A, N, W, Ni, E, Arg, N; 1980 v A, Pe; 1981 v W.
GRAHAM, G. (Arsenal, Manchester Utd) (12): 1972 v Por, Holl, Ni, Y, Cz, Br; 1973 v D (2), E, W, Ni, Br.
GRAHAM, J. (Annbank) (1): 1884 v Ni.
GRAHAM, J. A. (Arsenal) (1): 1921 v Ni.
GRANT, J. (Hibernian) (2): 1959 v W, Ni.
GRANT, P. (Celtic) (2): 1989 v E, Ch.
GRAY, A, (Hibernian) (1): 1903 v Ni.
GRAY, A. (Bradford) (2): 2003 v Lth, Nz.
GRAY, A. M. (Aston Villa, Wolverhampton W., Everton) (20): 1976 v R, Sw; 1977 v Fin, Cz; 1979 v A, N; 1980 v Por, E; 1981 v Se, Por, Is, Ni; 1982 v Se, Ni; 1983 v Ni, W, E, Ca (2); 1985 v Ice.
GRAY, D. (Rangers) (10): 1929 v W, Ni, G, Holl; 1930 v W, E, Ni; 1931 v W; 1933 v W, Ni.
GRAY, E. (Leeds Utd) (12): 1969 v E, Cy; 1970 v WG, A; 1971 v W, Ni; 1972 v Bel, Holl; 1976 v W, E; 1977 v Fin, W.
GRAY, F. T. (Leeds Utd, Nottingham F.) (32): 1976 v Sw; 1979 v N, Por, W, Ni, E, Arg; 1980 v Bel; 1981 v Se, Por, Is (2), Ni, (2), W, E; 1982 v Se, Ni, Por, Sp, Holl, W, Nz, Br, USSR; 1983 v EG, Sw, (2), Bel, W, E, Ca.

GRAY, W. (Pollokshields Ath.) (1): 1886 v E.
GREEN, A. (Blackpool, Newcastle) (6): 1971 v Bel, Por, Ni, E; 1972 v W, E.
GREIG, J. (Rangers) (44): 1964 v E, WG; 1965 v W, Ni, E, Fin (2), Sp, Pol; 1966 v Ni, W, E, Pol, I (2), Por, Holl, Br; 1967 v W, Ni, E; 1968 v Ni, W, E, Holl; 1969 v W, Ni, E, D, A, WG, Cy (2); 1970 v W, E, Ei, WG, A; 1971 v D, Bel, W, Ni, E; 1976 v D.
GRAY, W. (Pollokshields Ath.) (1): 1886 v E.
GRIFFITHS, L. (Wolves) (2): 2013 v Lux, Cro.
GUILLILAND, W. (Queen's Park) (4): 1891 v W; 1892 v Ni; 1894 v E; 1895 v E.
GUNN, B. (Norwich City) (6): 1990 v Eg; 1993 v Est (2); 1994 v Sw, I, Holl.
HADDOCK, H. (Clyde) (6): 1955 v E, H (2), Por, Y; 1958 v E.
HADDOW, D. (Rangers) (1): 1894 v E.
HAFFEY, F. (Celtic) (2): 1960 v E; 1961 v E.
HAMILTON, A. (Queen's Park) (4): 1885 v E, W; 1886 v E; 1888 v E.
HAMILTON, A. W. (Dundee) (24): 1962 v Cz, U, W, E; 1963 v W, Ni, E, A, N, Ei; 1964 v Ni, W, E, N, WG; 1965 v Ni, W, E, Fin (2), Pol, Sp; 1966 v Pol, Ni.
HAMILTON, G. (Aberdeen) (5): 1947 v Ni; 1951 v Bel, A; 1954 v N (2).
HAMILTON, G. (Port Glasgow Ath.) (1): 1906 v Ni.
HAMILTON, J. (Queen's Park) (3): 1892 v W; 1893 v E, Ni.
HAMILTON, J. (St Mirren) (1): 1924 v Ni.
HAMILTON, R. C. (Rangers, Dundee) (11): 1899 v E, W, Ni; 1900 v W; 1901 v E, Ni; 1902 v W, Ni; 1903 v E; 1904 v Ni; 1911 v W.
HAMILTON, T. (Hurlford) (1): 1891 v Ni.
HAMILTON, T. (Rangers) (1): 1932 v E.
HAMILTON, W. M. (Hibernian) (1): 1965 v Fin.
HAMMELL, S. (Motherwell) (1): 2005 v Se.
HANLEY, G (Blackburn Rovs) (6): 2011 v W, Ei; 2012 v D; 2013 v Lux, W, Cro.
HANNAH, A. B., (Renton) (1): 1888 v W.
HANNAH, J. (Third Lanark) (1): 1889 v W.
HANSEN, A. D. (Liverpool) (26): 1979 v W, Arg; 1980 v Bel, Por; 1981 v Se, Por, Is; 1982 v Se, Ni (2), Por, Sp, W, E, Nz, Br, USSR; 1983 v EG, Sw (2), Bel; 1985 v W; 1986 v R; 1987 v Ei (2), L.
HANSEN, J. (Partick Th.) (2): 1972 v Bel, Y.
HARKNESS, J. D. (Queen's Park, Hearts) (12): 1927 v E, Ni; 1928 v E; 1929 v W, E, Ni; 1930 v E, W; 1932 v W, Fr; 1934 v Ni, W.
HARPER, J. M. (Aberdeen, Hibernian) (4): 1973 v D (2); 1976 v D; 1978 v Ir.
HARPER, W. (Hibernian, Arsenal) (11): 1923 v E, Ni, W; 1924 v E, Ni, W; 1925 v E, Ni, W; 1926 v E, Ni.
HARRIS, J. (Partick Th.) (2): 1921 v W, Ni.
HARRIS, N. (Newcastle Utd) (1): 1924 v E.
HARROWER, W. (Queen's Park) (3): 1882 v E; 1884 v Ni; 1886 v W.
HARTFORD, R. A. (WBA, Manchester City, Everton) (50): 1972 v Pe, W, E, Y, Cz, Br; 1976 v D, R, Ni; 1977 v Cz, W, (2), Se, Ni, E, Ch, Arg, (cont..)

HARTFORD, R. A. Br; 1978 v EG, Cz, W (2), Bul, E, Pe, Ir, Holl; 1979 v A, N, Por, W, Ni, E, Arg, N; 1980 v Pe, Bel; 1981 v Ni (2), Is, W, E; 1982 v Se, Ni (2), Por, Sp, W, E, Br.
HARTLEY, P. (Hearts, Celtic, Bristol City) (25): 2005 v I, Mo; 2006 v I, N, Blr, Slo, US; 2007 v Fi (2), Lth, Fr, Uk, Geo, I, A; 2008 v Fr, I, Cro, CzR; 2009 v Mac, Ice, Arg; 2010 v Mac, Holl, CzR.
HARVEY, D. (Leeds Utd.) (16): 1973 v D; 1974 v Cz, WG, Ni, W, E, Bel, Z, Br, Y; 1975 v EG, Sp (2); 1976 v D (2); 1977 v Fin.
HASTINGS, A. C. (Sunderland) (2): 1936 v Ni; 1938 v Ni.
HAUGHNEY, M. (Celtic) (1): 1954 v E.
HAY, D. (Celtic) (27): 1970 v Ni, W, E; 1971 v D, Bel, W, Por, Ni; 1972 v Por, Bel, Holl; 1973 v W, Ni, E, Sw, Br; 1974 v Cz (2), WG, Ni, W, E, Bel, N, Z, Br.
HAY, J. (Celtic, Newcastle Utd) (11): 1905 v Ni; 1909 v Ni; 1910 v W, Ni, E; 1911 v Ni, E; 1912 v E, W; 1914 v E, Ni.
HEGARTY, P. (Dundee Utd.) (8): 1979 v W, Ni, E, Arg, N; 1980 v W, E; 1983 v Ni.
HEGGIE, C. (Rangers) (1): 1886 v Ni.
HENDERSON, G. H. (Rangers) (1): 1904 v Ni.
HENDERSON, J. G. (Portsmouth, Arsenal) (7): 1953 v Se; 1954 v Ni, E, N; 1956 v W; 1959 v W, Ni.
HENDERSON, W. (Rangers) (30): 1963 v W, Ni, E, A, N, Ei, Sp; 1964 v W, Ni, E, N, WG; 1965 v Fin, Pol, E, Sp; 1966 v Ni, W, Pol, I, Holl; 1967 v W, Ni; 1968 v Holl; 1969 v Ni, E, Cy; 1970 v Ei; 1971 v Por.
HENDRY C. (Blackburn R., Rangers, Bolton) (51): 1993 v Est (2); 1994 v Ma, Holl (2), A; 1995 v Fin, Fi, Gr, Ru, Sm; 1996 v Fin, Se, Sm, Aus, D, US, U, Holl, E, Sw; 1997 A (2), Se (2), Est (2); 1998 La, D, Fin, Co, US, Br, N, M. 1999 v Lth, Est, Fi, G. 2000 v Bos (2), Est, E (2), Fr; 2001 v La, Sm (2), Cro, Aus, Bel.
HEPBURN, J. (Alloa Ath.) (1) 1891 v W.
HEPBURN, R. (Ayr Utd) (1): 1932 v Ni.
HERD, A. C. (Hearts): (1): 1935 v Ni.
HERD, D. G. (Arsenal): (5): 1959 v E, W, Ni; 1961 v E, Cz.
HERD, G. (Clyde) (5): 1958 v E; 1960 v H, T; 1961 v W, Ni.
HERRIOT, J. (Birmingham City) (8): 1969 v Ni, E, D, Cy (2), W; 1970 v Ei, WG.
HEWIE, J. D. (Charlton Ath.) (19): 1956 v E, A; 1957 v E, Ni, W, Y, Sp (2), Sw, WG; 1958 v H, Pol, Y, Fr; 1959 v Holl, Por; 1960 v Ni, W, Pol.
HIGGINS, A. (Kilmarnock) (1): 1885 v Ni.
HIGGINS, A. (Newcastle Utd) (4): 1910 v E, Ni; 1911 v E, Ni.
HIGHET, T. C. (Queen's Park) (4): 1875 v E; 1876 v E, W; 1878 v E.
HILL, D. (Rangers) (3): 1881 v E, W; 1882 v W.
HILL, D. A. (Third Lanark) (1): 1906 v Ni.
HILL, F. R. (Aberdeen) (3): 1930 v Fr; 1931 v W, Ni.
HILL, J. (Hearts) (2): 1891 v E; 1892 v W.
HOGG, G. (Hearts) (2): 1896 v E, Ni.
HOGG, J. (Ayr Utd.) (1): 1922 v Ni.
HOGG, R. M. (Celtic) (1): 1937 v Cz.

HOLM, A. H. (Queen's Park) (3): 1882 v W; 1883 v E, W.
HOLT, D. D. (Hearts) (5): 1963 v A, N, Ei, Sp; 1964 v WG.
HOLT, G. (Kilmarnock, Norwich) (10): 2001 v La, Cro; 2002 v Fr; 2004 v W, Est, Trin; 2005 v H, Slo, N, Mo.
HOLTON, J. A. (Manchester Utd.) (15): 1973 v W, Ni, E, Sw, Br; 1974 v Cz, WG, Ni, W, E, N, Z, Br, Y; 1975 v EG.
HOPE, R. (WBA) (2): 1968 v Holl; 1969 v D.
HOPKIN, D. (Crystal Palace, Leeds) (7): 1997 v Ma, Blr; 1998 v Blr, La; 1999 v CzR. 2000 v Bos (2).
HOULISTON, W. (Queen of the South) (3): 1949 v E, Ni, Fr.
HOUSTON, S. M. (Manchester Utd.) (1): 1976 v D.
HOWDEN, W. (Partick Th.) (1): 1905 v Ni.
HOWE, R. (Hamilton Accies) (2): 1929 v N, Holl.
HOWIE, J. (Newcastle Utd.) (3): 1905 v E; 1906 v E; 1908 v E.
HOWIE, H. (Hibernian) (1): 1949 v W.
HOWIESON, J. (St Mirren) (1): 1927 v Ni.
HUGHES, J. (Celtic) (8): 1965 v Pol, Sp; 1966 v Ni, I (2); 1968 v E; 1969 v A; 1970 v Ei.
HUGHES, R. (Portsmouth, Grimsby) (5): 2004 v Est, Trin; 2005 v N, Se; 2006 v A.
HUGHES, S. (Norwich City) (1): 2010 v J.
HUGHES, W. (Sunderland) (1): 1975 v Se.
HUMPHRIES, W. (Motherwell) (1): 1952 v Se.
HUNTER, A. (Kilmarnock, Celtic) (4): 1972 v Pe, Y; 1973 v E; 1974 v Cz.
HUNTER, J. (Dundee) (1): 1909 v W.
HUNTER, J. (Third Lanark, Eastern) (4): 1874 v E, 1875 v E, 1876 v E, 1877 v W.
HUNTER, R. (St Mirren) (1): 1890 v Ni.
HUNTER, W. (Motherwell) (3): 1960 v H, T; 1961 v W.
HUSBAND, J. (Partick Th.) (1): 1947 v W.
HUTCHISON, D. (Everton, Sunderland, West Ham) (26): 1999 v CzR, G; 2000 v. Bos, Est, Lth, E (2), Fr, Holl, Ei; 2001 v La, Sm (2), Cro, Aus, Bel; 2002 v Cro, Bel, La; 2003 v Ei, A, Ice, Lth; 2004 v N, Lth, Holl.
HUTCHISON, T. (Coventry City) (17): 1974 v Cz (2), WG (2), Ni, W, Bel, N, Z, Y; 1975 v EG, Sp (2), Por, E, R; 1976 v D.
HUTTON, A. (Rangers, Tottenham, Aston Villa) (30): 2007 v A; 2008 v SA, Lth, Fr, Uk, I, Cro; 2009 v Arg, Holl, Ice; 2010 v N, Mac, Holl, W, CzR; 2011 v Lth, Li, CzR, Ni, Br; 2012 v CzR, Sp; 2013 v Aus, Mac, W (2), Bel, Est, Ser, Cro.
HUTTON, J. (Aberdeen, Blackburn R.) (10): 1923 v E, W, Ni; 1924 v Ni; 1926 v W, E, Ni; 1927 v Ni; 1928 v W, Ni.
HUTTON, J. (St Bernard's) (1): 1887 v Ni.
HYSLOP, T. (Stoke City, Rangers) (2): 1896 v E; 1897 v E.
IMLACH, J. J. S. (Nottingham F.) (4): 1958 v H, Pol, Y. Fr.
IMRIE, W. N. (St Johnstone) (2): 1929 v N, G.
INGLIS, J. (Kilmarnock Ath.) (1): 1884 v Ni.
INGLIS, J. (Rangers) (2): 1883 v E, W.
IRONS, J. H. (Queen's Park) (1): 1900 v W.
IRVINE, B. (Aberdeen) (9): 1991 v R; 1993 v G, Est (2); 1994 v Sw, I, Ma, A, Holl.
IWELUMO, C. (Wolves) (4): 2009 v N, Arg; 2011 v Se, CzR.

JACKSON, A. (Cambuslang) (2): 1886 v W, 1888 v Ni.
JACKSON, A. (Aberdeen, Huddersfield Town) (17): 1925 v E, W, Ni; 1926 v E, W, Ni; 1927 v W, Ni; 1928 v E, W; 1929 v E, W, Ni; 1930 v E, W, Ni, Fr.
JACKSON, C. (Rangers) (8): 1975 v Se, Por, W; 1976 v D, R, Ni, W, E.
JACKSON D. (Hibs, Celtic) (28): 1995 v Ru, Sm, J, Ec, Fi. 1996 v Gr, Fin, Se, Sm, Aus, D, US; 1997 v La, Se (2), Est, A, W, Ma, Blr; 1998 v D, Fin, Co, US, Br, N. 1999 v Lth, Est.
JACKSON, J. (Partick Th., Chelsea) (8): 1931 v A, I, Sw; 1933 v E; 1934 v E; 1935 v E; 1936 v W, Ni.
JACKSON, T. A. (St Mirren) (6): 1904 v W, E, Ni; 1905 v W; 1907 v W, Ni.
JAMES, A. (Preston NE, Arsenal) (8): 1926 v W; 1928 v E; 1929 v E, Ni; 1930 v E, W, Ni; 1933 v W.
JARDINE, A. (Rangers) (38): 1971 v D; 1972 v Por, Bel, Holl; 1973 v E, Sw, Br; 1974 v Cz (2), WG (2), Ni, W, E, Bel, N, Z, Br, Y; 1975 v EG, Sp (2), Se, Por, W, Ni, E; 1977 v Se, Ch, Br; 1978 v Cz, W, Ni, Ir; 1980 v Pe, A. Bel (2).
JARVIE, A. (Airdrie) (3): 1971 v Por, Ni, E.
JESS, E. (Aberdeen) (18): 1993 v I, Ma; 1994 v Sw, I, Holl (2), A; 1995 v Fin; 1996 v Se, Sm, US, U, E; 1998 v D; 1999 v CzR (2), G, Fi.
JENKINSON, T. (Hearts) (1): 1887 v Ni.
JOHNSTON, A. (Sunderland, Rangers, Middlesbrough) (18): 1999 v Est, Fi, CzR (2), G, Fi; 2000 v Est, Fr, Ei; 2001 v Sm (2), Cro; 2002 v Nig, Skor, SA, HK; 2003 v D, Fi.
JOHNSTON, L. H. (Clyde) (2): 1948 v Bel, Sw.
JOHNSTON, M. (Watford, Celtic, Nantes, Rangers) (38): 1984 v W, E, Fr; 1985 v Y, Ice, Sp (2), W; 1986 v EG; 1987 v Bul, Ei (2), L; 1988 v H, Bel, L. S.Ar, Sp, Co, E; 1989 v N, Y, I, Cy (2), Fr, E, Ch; 1990 v Fr, N, EG, Pol, Ma, Cr, Se, Br; 1992 v Sw, Sm.
JOHNSTON, R. (Sunderland) (1): 1938 v Cz.
JOHNSTON, W. (Rangers, WBA) (22): 1966 v W, E, Pol, Holl; 1968 v W, E; 1969 v Ni; 1970 v Ni; 1971 v D; 1977 v Se, W, Ni, E, Ch, Arg, Br; 1978 v EG, Cz, W (2), E, Pe.
JOHNSTONE, D. (Rangers) (14): 1973 v W, Ni, E, Sw, Br; 1975 v EG, Se; 1976 v Sw, Ni, E; 1978 v Bul, Ni, W; 1980 v Bel.
JOHNSTONE, J. (Abercorn) (1): 1888 v W.
JOHNSTONE, J. (Celtic) (23): 1965 v W, Fin; 1966 v E; 1967 v W, USSR; 1968 v W; 1969 v A, WG; 1970 v E, WG; 1971 v D, E; 1972 v Por, Bel, Holl, Ni, E; 1974 v W, E, Bel, N; 1975 v EG, Sp.
JOHNSTONE, JAS. (Kilmarnock) (1): 1894 v W.
JOHNSTONE, J. A. (Hearts) (3): 1930 v W; 1933 v W, Ni.
JOHNSTONE, R. (Hibernian, Manchester City) (17): 1951 v E, D, Fr; 1952 v Ni, E; 1953 v E, Se; 1954 v W, E, N, Fin; 1955 v Ni, H, E; 1956 v E, Ni, W.
JOHNSTONE, W. (Third Lanark) (3): 1887 v Ni; 1889 v W; 1890 v E.

JORDAN, J. (Leeds Utd, Manchester Utd, AC Milan) (52): 1973 v E, Sw, Br; 1974 v Cz (2), WG, Ni, W, E, Bel, N, Z, Br, Y; 1975 v EG, Sp (2); 1976 v Ni, W, E; 1977 v Cz, W, Ni, E; 1978 v EG, Cz, W, Bul, Ni, E, Pe, Ir, Holl; 1979 v A, Por, W, Ni, E, N; 1980 v Bel, Ni, W, E, Pol; 1981 v Is, W, E; 1982 v Se, Holl, W, E, USSR.

KAY, J. L. (Queen's Park) (6): 1880 v E; 1882 v E, W; 1883 v E, W; 1884 v W.
KEILLOR, A. (Montrose, Dundee) (6): 1891 v W; 1892 v Ni; 1894 v Ni; 1895 v W; 1896 v W; 1897 v W.
KEIR, L. (Dumbarton) (5): 1885 v W: 1886 v Ni; 1887 v E, W; 1888 v E.
KELLY, H. T. (Blackpool) (1): 1952 v USA.
KELLY, J. (Renton, Celtic) (8): 1888 v E; 1889 v E; 1890 v E; 1892 v E; 1893 v E, Ni; 1894 v W; 1896 v Ni.
KELLY, J. C. (Barnsley) (2): 1949 v W, Ni.
KELLY, L (Kilmarnock) (1): 2013 v Lux.
KELSO, R. (Renton, Dundee) (8): 1885 v W, Ni; 1886 v W; 1887 v E, W; 1888 v E, Ni; 1898 v Ni.
KELSO, T. (Dundee) (1): 1914 v W.
KENNAWAY, J. (Celtic) (1): 1934 v A.
KENNEDY, A. (Eastern, Third Lanark) (6): 1875 v E; 1876 v E, W; 1878 v E; 1882 v W; 1884 v W.
KENNEDY, J. (Celtic) (6): 1964 v W, Fr, WG; 1965 v W, Ni, Fin.
KENNEDY, J. (Celtic) (1): 2004 v R.
KENNEDY, J. (Hibernian) (1): 1897 v W.
KENNEDY, S. (Aberdeen) (8): 1978 v Bul, W, E, Pe, Holl; 1979 v A, Por; 1982 v Por.
KENNEDY, S, (Partick Th.) (1): 1905 v W.
KENNEDY, S. (Rangers) (5): 1975 v Se, Por, W, Ni, E.
KENNETH, G. (Dundee United) (2): 2011 v Se, Fi.
KER, G. (Queen's Park) (5): 1880 v E; 1881 v E, W; 1882 v W, E.
KER, W. (Granville, Queen's Park) (2): 1872 v E; 1873 v E.
KERR, A. (Partick Th.) (2): 1955 v A, H.
KERR, B. (Newcastle Utd, Coventry) (3): 2003 v Nz; 2004 v Est; 2004: v Trin.
KERR, P. (Hibernian) (1): 1924 v Ni.
KEY, G. (Hearts) (1): 1902 v Ni.
KEY, W. (Queen's Park) (1): 1907 v Ni.
KING, A. (Hearts, Celtic) (6): 1896 v E, W; 1897 v Ni; 1898 v Ni; 1899 v Ni, W.
KING, J. (Hamilton Accies) (2): 1933 v Ni; 1934 v Ni.
KING, W. S. (Queen's Park) (1): 1929 v W.
KINLOCH, J. D. (Partick Th.) (1): 1922 v Ni.
KINNAIRD, A. F. (Wanderers) (1): 1873 v E.
KINNEAR, D. (Rangers) (1): 1938 v Cz.
KYLE, K. (Sunderland, Kilmarnock) (10): 2002 v Skor, SA, HK; 2003 v D, Fi, Can, Por, Nz; 2004 v D; 2010 v W.

LAMBERT, P. (Motherwell, Borussia Dortmund, Celtic) (40): 1995 v J, Ec; 1997 v La, Se (2), A, Blr; 1998 v Blr, La, Fin, Co, US, Br, N, M. (cont)...

LAMBERT, P. 1999 v Lth, CzR (2), G, Fi; 2000 v Bos, Lth, Holl, Ei; 2001 v Bel, Sm; 2002 v Cro, Bel, Fr, Nig; 2003 v D, Fi, Ice (2), Por, Ei, Lth, G; 2004 v N, G.
LAMBIE, J. A. (Queen's Park) (3): 1886 v Ni; 1887 v Ni; 1888 v E.
LAMBIE, W. A. (Queen's Park) (9): 1892 v Ni; 1893 v W; 1894 v E; 1895 v E, Ni; 1896 v E, Ni; 1897 v E, Ni.
LAMONT, D. (Pilgrims): 1885 v Ni.
LANG, A. (Dumbarton) (1): 1880 v W.
LANG, J. J. (Clydesdale, Third Lanark) (2): 1876 v W; 1878 v W.
LATTA, A. (Dumbarton) (2): 1888 v W; 1889 v E.
LAW, D. (Huddersfield Town, Manchester Utd, Torino, Manchester City) (55): 1959 v W, Ni, Holl, Por; 1960 v Ni, W; 1960 v E, Pol, A; 1961 v E, Ni; 1962 v Cz (2), E; 1963 v W, Ni, E, A, N, Ei, Sp; 1964 v W, E, N, WG;1965 v W, Ni, E, Fin (2), Pol, Sp; 1966 v Ni, E, Pol; 1967 v W, E, USSR; 1968 v Ni; 1969 v Ni, A, WG; 1972 v Pe, Ni, W, E, Y, Cz, Br; 1974 v Cz (2), WG (2), Ni, Z.
LAW, G. (Rangers) (3): 1910 v E, Ni, W.
LAW, T. (Chelsea) (2): 1928 v E, 1930 v E.
LAWRENCE, J. (Newcastle Utd.) (1): 1911 v E.
LAWRENCE, T. (Liverpool) (3): 1963 v Ei; 1969 v W, WG.
LAWSON, D. (St Mirren) (1): 1923 v E.
LECKIE, R. (Queen's Park) (1): 1872 v E.
LEGGAT, G. (Aberdeen, Fulham) (18): 1956 v E; 1957 v W; 1958 v Ni, H, Pol, Y, Par; 1959 v E, W, Ni, WG, Holl; 1960 v E, Ni, W, Pol, A, H.
LEIGHTON, J. (Aberdeen, Manchester Utd, Hibernian, Aberdeen) (91): 1983 v EG, Sw (2), Bel, W, E, Ca (2); 1984 v U, Bel, Ni, W, E, Fr; 1985 v Y, Ice, Sp (2), W, E, Ice; 1986 v W, EG, Aus (2), Is, D, WG, U; 1987 v Bul, Ei (2), L, Bel, E; 1988 v H, Bel, Bul, L, S.Ar, Ma, Sp, Co, E; 1989 v N, Cy (2), Fr, E, Ch; 1990 v Y, Fr, N, Arg, Ma, Cr, Se, Br; 1994 v Ma, A, Holl; 1995 v Gr, Ru, Sm, J, Ec, Fi. 1996 v Gr, Fin, Se, Sm, Aus, D, US;1997 v Se (2), Est, A, W, Ma, Blr.1998 v Blr, La, D, Fin, US, Br, N, M. 1999 v Lth, Est.
LENNIE, W. (Aberdeen) (2): 1908 v W, Ni.
LENNOX, R. (Celtic) (10): 1967 v Ni, E, USSR; 1968 v W, L; 1969 v D, A. WG, Cy; 1970 v W.
LESLIE, L. G. (Airdrie) (5): 1961 v W, Ni, Ei (2), Cz.
LEVEIN, C. (Hearts) (16): 1990 v Arg, EG, Eg, Pol, Ma, Se; 1991 R, Sm; 1993 v Por (2), G; 1994 v Sw, Holl; 1995 v Fin, Fi, Ru.
LIDDELL, W. (Liverpool) (28): 1947 v W, Ni; 1948 v E, W, Ni; 1950 v E, W, Por, Fr; 1951 v W, Ni, E, A; 1952 v W, Ni, E, USA, D, Se; 1953 v W, Ni, E; 1954 v W; 1955 v Por, Y, A, H; 1956 v Ni.
LIDDLE, D. (East Fife) (3): 1931 v A, I, Sw.
LINDSAY, D. (St Mirren) (1): 1903 v Ni.
LINDSAY, J. (Dumbarton) (8): 1880 v W; 1881 v W, E; 1884 v W, E; 1885 v W, E; 1886 v E.
LINDSAY, J. (Renton) (3): 1888 v E; 1893 v E, Ni.

LINWOOD, A. B. (Clyde) (1): 1950 v W.
LITTLE, R. J. (Rangers) (1): 1953 v Se.
LIVINGSTONE, G. T. (Man City, Rangers) (2): 1906 v E; 1907 v W.
LOCHHEAD, A. (Third Lanark) (1): 1889 v W.
LOGAN, J. (Ayr Utd) (1): 1891 v W.
LOGAN, T. (Falkirk) (1): 1913 v Ni.
LOGIE, J. T. (Arsenal) (1): 1953 v Ni.
LONEY, W. (Celtic) (2): 1910 v W, Ni.
LONG, H. (Clyde) (1): 1947 v Ni.
LONGAIR, W. (Dundee) (1): 1894 v Ni.
LORIMER, P. (Leeds Utd) (21): 1970 v A; 1971 v W, Ni; 1972 v Ni, W, E; 1973 v D (2), E (2); 1974 v WG, E, Bel, N, Z, Br, Y; 1975 v Sp; 1976 v D (2), R.
LOVE, A. (Aberdeen) (3): 1931 v A, I, Sw.
LOW, A. (Falkirk) (1): 1934 v Ni.
LOW, T. P. (Rangers) (1): 1897 v Ni.
LOW, W. L. (Newcastle U) (5): 1911 v E, W; 1912 v Ni; 1920 v E, Ni.
LOWE, J. (Cambuslang) (1): 1891 v Ni.
LOWE, J. (St Bernard's) (1): 1887 v Ni.
LUNDIE, J. (Hibernian) (1): 1886 v W.
LYALL, J. (Sheffield W.) (1): 1905 v E.

McADAM, J. (Third Lanark) (1): 1880 v W.
McALLISTER, B. (Wimbledon) (3): 1997 v W, Ma, Blr.
McALLISTER, G. (Leicester City, Leeds Utd, Coventry) (57): 1990 v EG, Pol, Ma; 1991 v R, Sw (2), Bul, USSR, Sm, (2); 1992 v Ni, Fin, US, Ca, N, Holl, G, CIS; 1993 v Sw, Por, I, Ma; 1994 v Sw, I, Ma, Holl (2), A; 1995 v Fin, Ru (2), Gr, Sm. 1996 v Gr, Fin, Se, Sm, Aus, D, US, U, Holl, E, Sw; 1997 v A (2), La, Est (2), Se, W, Ma, Blr; 1998 v Blr, La, Fr; 1999 v CzR.
McALLISTER, J. (Livingston) (1): 2004 v Trin.
McARTHUR, D. (Celtic) (3): 1895 v E, Ni; 1899 v W.
McARTHUR, J. (Wigan) (11): 2011 v Fi, Ni, Br, W; 2012 v Cy, Slo, US; 2013 v Bel, Est, W, Cro.
McATEE, A. (Celtic) (1): 1913 v W.
McAULAY, J. (Dumbarton, Arthurlie) (2): 1882 v W; 1884 v Ni.
McAULAY, J. (Dumbarton) (8): 1883 v E, W; 1884 v E; 1885 v E, W; 1886 v E; 1887 v E, W.
McAULEY, R. (Rangers) (2): 1932 v Ni, W.
McAVENNIE, F. (West Ham Utd., Celtic) (5): 1986 v Aus (2), D, WG; 1988 v S.Ar.
McBAIN, E. (St Mirren) (1): 1894 v W.
McBAIN, N. (Manchester Utd., Everton) (3): 1922 v E; 1923 v Ni; 1924 v W.
McBRIDE, J. (Celtic) (2): 1967 v W, Ni.
McBRIDE, P. (Preston NE) (6): 1904 v E; 1906 v E; 1907 v E, W; 1908 v E; 1909 v W.
McCALL, J. (Renton) (5): 1886 v W; 1887 v E, W; 1888 v E; 1890 v E.

McCALL, S. M. (Everton, Rangers) (40) 1990 v Arg, EG, Eg, Pol, Ma, Cr, Se, Br; 1991 v Sw, USSR, Sm (2); 1992 v Sw, R, US, Ca, N, Holl, G, CIS; 1993 v Sw, Por (2); 1994 v I, Holl (2), A; 1995 v Fin, Ru, Gr; 1996 v Gr, D, US, U, Holl, E, Sw; 1997 v A, La; 1998 v D.
McCALLIOG, J. (Sheffield W., Wolverhampton W.) (5): 1967 v E, USSR; 1968 v Ni; 1969 v D; 1971 v Por.
McCALLUM, N. (Renton) (1): 1888 v Ni.
McCANN, N. (Hearts, Rangers, Southampton) (26): 1999 v Lth, CzR. 2000 v Bos; Est, E, Fr, Holl, Ei; 2001 v La, Sm, Aus; 2002 v Cro, La, Fr, Nig; 2003 v Ei; 2004 v Fi, G, Holl (2), R, D; 2005 v I; 2006 v I, N, US.
McCANN, R. J. (Motherwell) (5): 1959 v WG; 1960 v E, Ni, W; 1961 v E.
McCARTNEY, W. (Hibernian) (1): 1902 v Ni.
McCLAIR, B. (Celtic, Manchester Utd) (30): 1987 v L, Ei, E, Br; 1988 v Bul, Ma, Sp; 1989 v N, Y, I, Cy, Fr; 1990 v N, Arg; 1991 v Bul (2), Sm; 1992 v Sw, R, Ni, US, Ca, N, Holl, G, CIS; 1993 v Sw, Por, Est (2).
McCLORY, A. (Motherwell) (3): 1927 v W; 1928 v Ni; 1935 v W.
McCLOY, P. (Ayr Utd) (2): 1924 v E; 1925 v E.
McCLOY, P. (Rangers) (4): 1973 v W, Ni, Sw, Br.
McCOIST, A. (Rangers, Kilmarnock) (61): 1986 v Holl; 1987 v L, Ei, Bel, E, Br; 1988 v H, Bel, Ma, Sp, Co, E; 1989 v Y, Fr, Cy, E; 1990 v Y, Fr, N, EG, Eg, Pol, Ma, Cr, Se, Br; 1991 v R, Sw, Bul (2), USSR; 1992 v Sw, Sm, Ni, Fin, US, Ca, N, Holl, G, CIS; 1993 v Sw, Por (2), I, Ma. 1996 v Gr, Fin, Sm, Aus, D, U, E, Sw; 1997 v A (2), Se, Est; 1998 v Blr. 1999 v Lth, Est.
McCOLL, A. (Renton) (1): 1888 v Ni.
McCOLL, I. M. (Rangers) (14): 1950 v E, Fr; 1951 v W, Ni, Bel; 1957 v E, Ni, W, Y, Sp, Sw, WG; 1958 v Ni, E.
McCOLL, R. S. (Queen's Park, Newcastle Utd.) (13): 1896 v W, Ni; 1897 v Ni; 1898 v Ni; 1899 v Ni; E, W; 1900 v E, W; 1901 v E, W; 1902 v E; 1908 v Ni.
McCOLL, W. (Renton) (1): 1895 v W.
McCOMBIE, A. (Sunderland, Newcastle (4): 1903 v E, W; 1905 v E, W.
McCORKINDALE, J. (Partick Th.) (1): 1891 v W.
McCORMACK, R. (Motherwell, Cardiff), Leeds (8): 2008 v CzR; 2009 v Holl, Ice; 2010 v N, W; 2011 v W, Ei; 2013 v Aus.
McCORMICK, R. (Abercorn) (1): 1886 v W.
McCRAE, D. (St Mirren) (2): 1929 v N, G.
McCREADIE, A. (Rangers) (2): 1893 v W; 1894 v E.
McCREADIE, E. G. (Chelsea) (23): 1965 v E, Sp, Fin, Pol; 1966 v Por, Ni, W, Pol, I; 1967 v E, USSR; 1968 v Ni, W, E, Holl; 1969 v W, Ni, E, D, A. WG, Cy (2).
McCULLOCH, D. (Hearts, Brentford, Derby Co.) (7): 1935 v W; 1936 v E; 1937 v W, Ni; 1938 v Cz; 1939 v H, W.
McCULLOCH, L. (Wigan, Rangers) (18): 2005 v Mo (2), I, Blr; 2006 v Blr, Bul, J; 2007 v Fr, Geo, I, A; 2008 v Lth, Fr, Uk, I; 2011 v Lth, Li, Sp.

MacDONALD, A. (Rangers) (1): 1976 v Sw.
McDONALD, J. (Edinburgh University) (1): 1886 v E.
McDONALD, J. (Sunderland) (2): 1956 v W, Ni.

MacDOUGALL, E. J. (Norwich City) (7): 1975 v Se, Por, W, Ni, E; 1976 v D, R.
McDOUGALL, J. (Liverpool) (2): 1931 v I, A.
McDOUGALL, J. (Airdrie) (1): 1926 v Ni.
McDOUGALL, J. (Vale of Leven) (5): 1877 v E, W; 1878 v E; 1879 v E, W.
McEVELEY, J. (Derby County) (3): 2008 v SA, Lth, Cro.
McFADDEN, J. (Motherwell, Everton, Birmingham) (48): 2002 v SA; 2003 v Can, A, Nz; 2004 v Fi, G, Lth, Holl (2), W, R, D, Est, Trin; 2005 v H, Sp, Slo, N, Se, Mo, Blr; 2006 v N, Slo, US, Sw, Bul, J; 2007 v Fi, Lth, Fr, Uk; 2008 v SA, Lth, Fr, Uk, Geo, I; 2009 v Ni, Mac, Ice, N, Arg; 2010 v N, Mac, W; 2011 v Se, Lth, Li.
McFADYEN, W. (Motherwell) (2): 1934 v A, W.
MACFARLANE, A. (Dundee) (5): 1904 v W; 1906 v W; 1908 v W; 1909 v Ni; 1911 v W.
MACFARLANE, W. (Hearts) (1): 1947 v L.
McFARLANE, R. (Morton) (1): 1896 v W.
McGARR, E. (Aberdeen) (2): 1970 v Ei, A.
McGARVEY, F. (Liverpool, Celtic) (7): 1979 v Ni, Arg; 1984 v U, Bel, EG, Ni, W.
McGEOCH, A. (Dumbreck) (4): 1876 v E, W; 1877 v E, W.
McGHEE, J. (Hibernian) (1): 1886 v W.
McGHEE, M. (Aberdeen) (4): 1983 v Ca (2); 1984 v Ni, E.
McGINLAY, J. (Bolton W.) (13): 1994 v A, Holl; 1995 v Fi (2), Ru (2), Gr, Sm; 1996 v Se; 1997 v Se, Est (2), A.
McGONAGLE, W. (Celtic) (6): 1933 v E; 1934 v A, E, Ni; 1935 v Ni, W.
McGOWAN, J. (Partick Thistle) (1): 1946 v Bel.
McGRAIN, D. (Celtic) (62): 1973 v W, Ni, E, Sw, Br; 1974 v Cz (2), WG, W, E, Bel, N, Z, Br, Y; 1975 v Sp, Se, Por, W, Ni, E, R; 1976 v D (2), Sw, Ni, W, E; 1977 v Fin, Cz, W (2), Se, Ni, E, Ch, Arg, Br; 1978 v EG, Cz; 1980 v Bel, Por, Ni, W, E, Pol, H; 1981 v Se, Por, Is, (2), Ni (2), W, E; 1982 v Se, Sp, Holl, Ni, E, Nz, USSR.
McGREGOR, A. (Rangers, Besiktas) (27): 2007 v A; 2009 v Ni, Arg, Holl; 2011 v Se, Lth, Li, CzR, Sp, Ni, Br, W, Ei; 2012 v D, CzR, Lth, Sp, Cy, Slo, US; 2013 v Aus, Mac, W (2), Est, Serb, Cro.
McGREGOR, J. C. (Vale of Leven) (4): 1877 v E, W; 1878 v E; 1880 v E.
McGRORY, J. E. (Kilmarnock) (3): 1965 v Ni, Fin; 1966 v Por.
McGRORY, J. (Celtic) (7): 1928 v Ni; 1931 v E; 1932 v Ni, W; 1933 v E, Ni; 1934 v Ni.
McGUIRE, W. (Beith) (2): 1881 v E, W.
McGURK, F. (Birmingham City) (1): 1934 v W.
McHARDY, H. (Rangers) (1): 1885 v Ni.
McINALLY, A. (Aston Villa, Bayern Munich) (8): 1989 v Cy, Ch; 1990 v Y, Fr, Arg, Pol, Ma, Cr.
McINALLY, J. (Dundee Utd) (10): 1987 v Bel, Br; 1988 v Ma; 1991 v Bul (2); 1992 v US, N, CIS; 1993 v G, Por.
McINALLY, T. B. (Celtic) (2): 1926 v Ni; 1927 v W.
McINNES, D. (WBA) (2): 2003 v D, Por.
McINNES, T. (Cowlairs) (1): 1889 v Ni.
McINTOSH, W. (Third Lanark) (1): 1905 v Ni.

ALLAN McGREGOR has continued to star in goal for Scotland since his move to Turkey's Besiktas

McINTYRE, A. (Vale of Leven) (2): 1878 v E; 1882 v E.
McINTYRE, H. (Rangers) (1): 1880 v W.
McINTYRE, J. (Rangers) (1): 1884 v W.
McKAY, D. (Celtic) (14): 1959 v E, WG, Holl, Por; 1960 v E, Pol, A, H, T; 1961 v W, Ni; 1962 v Ni, Cz, U.
McKAY, J. (Blackburn R.) (1): 1924 v W.
McKAY, R. (Newcastle Utd.) (1): 1928 v W.
McKEAN, R. (Rangers) (1): 1976 v Sw.
McKENZIE, D. (Brentford) (1): 1938 v Ni.
MACKENZIE, J. A. (Partick Th.) (9): 1954 v W, E, N, Fin, A, U; 1955 v E, H; 1956 v A.
McKEOWN, M. (Celtic) (2): 1889 v Ni; 1890 v E.
McKIE, J. (East Stirling) (1): 1898 v W.
McKILLOP, T. R. (Rangers) (1): 1938 v Holl.
McKIMMIE, S. (Aberdeen) (40): 1989 v E, Ch; 1990 v Arg, Eg, Cr, Br; 1991 v R (2), Sw, Bul, Sm; 1992 v Sw, Ni, Fin, US, Ca, N, Holl, G, CIS. 1993 v Por, Est; 1994 v Sw, I, Holl (2), A; 1995 v Fin, Fi (2), Ru (2), Gr. 1996 v Gr, Fin, Se, D, U, Holl, E.
McKINLAY, D. (Liverpool) (2): 1922 v W, Ni.
McKINLAY, T. (Celtic) (22): 1996 v Gr, Fin, D, U, E, Sw; 1997 v A (2), La, Se (2), Est (2), W, Ma, Blr; 1998 v Blr, La, Fr, US, Br, M.
McKINLAY, W. (Dundee Utd, Blackburn R.) (29): 1994 v Ma, Holl (2), A; 1995 v Fi (2), Ru (2), Gr, Sm, J, Ec; 1996 v Fin, Se, Sm, Aus, D, Holl; 1997 v Se, Est; 1998 v La, Fr, D, Fin, Co, US, Br. 1999 v Est, Fi.
McKINNON, A. (Queen's Park) (1): 1874 v E.
McKINNON, R. (Rangers) (28): 1966 v W, E, I (2), Holl, Br; 1967 v W, Ni, E; 1968 v Ni, W, E, Holl; 1969 v D, A, WG, Cy; 1970 v Ni, W, E, Ei, WG, A; 1971 v D, Bel, Por, USSR, D.
McKINNON, R. (Motherwell) (3): 1994 v Ma; 1995 v J, Fi.
MACKINNON, W. (Dumbarton) (4): 1883 v E, W; 1884 v E, W.
McKINNON, W. W. (Queen's Park) (9): 1872 v E; 1873 v E; 1874 v E; 1875 v E; 1876 v E, W; 1877 v E; 1878 v E; 1879 v E.
McLAREN, A. (St Johnstone) (5): 1929 v N, G, Holl; 1933 v W, Ni.
McLAREN, A. (Preston NE) (4): 1947 v E, Bel, L; 1948 v W.
McLAREN, A. (Hearts, Rangers) (24): 1992 v US, Ca, N; 1993 v I, Ma, G, Est (2); 1994 v I, Ma, Holl, A; 1995 v Fin, Fi (2), Ru (2), Gr, Sm, J, Ec; 1996 v Fin, Se, Sm.
McLAREN, A. (Kilmarnock) (1): 2001 v Pol.
McLAREN, J. (Hibernian, Celtic) (3): 1888 v W; 1889 v E; 1890 v E.
McLEAN, A. (Celtic) (4): 1926 v W, Ni; 1927 v W, E.
McLEAN, D. (St Bernard's) (2): 1896 v W; 1897 v Ni.
McLEAN, D. (Sheffield W.) (1): 1912 v E.
McLEAN, G. (Dundee) (1): 1968 v Holl.
McLEAN, T. (Kilmarnock) (6): 1969 v D. Cy, W; 1970 v Ni, W; 1971 v D.
McLEISH, A. (Aberdeen) (77): 1980 v Por, Ni, W, E, Pol, H; 1981 v Se, (cont...)

DAVE McPHERSON and Alan McLaren move in on Italy's Gigi Lentini in a Scotland clash in 1992

McLEISH, A. Is (2), Ni (2), E; 1982 v Se, Sp, Ni, Br; 1983 v Bel, Sw, W, E, Ca (3); 1984 v U, Bel, EG, Ni, W, E, Fr; 1985 v Y, Ice, (2), Sp (2), W, E; 1986 v W, EG, Aus (2), E, Holl, D; 1987 v Bel, E, Br; 1988 v Bel, Bul, L, S.Ar, Ma, Sp, Co, E; 1989 v N, Y, I, Cy (2), Fr, E, Ch; 1990 v Y, Fr, N, Arg, EG, Eg, Cr, Se, Br; 1991 v R, Sw, USSR, Bul; 1993 v Ma.
McLEOD, D. (Celtic) (4): 1905 v Ni; 1906 v E, W, Ni.
McLEOD, J. (Dumbarton) (5): 1888 v Ni; 1889 v W; 1890 v Ni; 1892 v E; 1893 v W.
MacLEOD, J. M. (Hibernian) (4): 1961 v E, Ei (2), Cz.
MacLEOD, M. (Celtic, Borussia Dort., Hibernian) (20): 1985 v E; 1987 v Ei, L, E, Br; 1988 v Co, E; 1989 v I, Ch; 1990 v Y, Fr, N, Arg, EG, Pol, Se, Br; 1991 v R, Sw, USSR.
McLEOD, W. (Cowlairs) (1): 1886 v Ni.
McLINTOCK, A. (Vale of Leven) (3): 1875 v E; 1876 v E; 1880 v E.
McLINTOCK, F. (Leicester City, Arsenal) (9): 1963 v N, Ei, Sp; 1965 v Ni; 1967 v USSR; 1970 v Ni; 1971 v W, Ni, E.
McLUCKIE, J. S. (Manchester City) (1): 1934 v W.
McMAHON, A. (Celtic) (6): 1892 v E; 1893 v E, Ni; 1894 v E; 1901 v Ni. 1902 v W.
McMANUS S. (Celtic) (26): 2007 v Uk, Geo, I, Fi, A; 2008 v SA, Lth, Fr, Uk, Geo, I, Cro, CzR; 2009 v Ni, Mac, Ice (2), Arg; 2010 v Mac, Holl, J, W; 2011 v Lth, Li, CzR, Sp.
McMENEMY, J. (Celtic) (12): 1905 v Ni; 1909 v Ni; 1910 v E, W; 1911 v Ni, W, E; 1912 v W; 1914 v W, Ni, E; 1920 v Ni.
McMENEMY, J. (Motherwell) (1): 1934 v W.
McMILLAN, J. (St Bernard's) (1): 1897 v W.
McMILLAN, I. L. (Airdrie, Rangers) (6): 1952 v E, USA, D; 1955 v E; 1956 v E; 1961 v Cz.
McMILLAN, T. (Dumbarton) (1): 1887 v Ni.
McMULLAN, J. (Partick Th., Manchester City) (16): 1920 v W; 1921 v W, Ni, E; 1924 v E, Ni; 1925 v E; 1926 v W, E; 1927 v E, W; 1928 v E, W; 1929 v W, E, Ni.
McNAB, A. (Morton) (2): 1921 v E, Ni.
McNAB, A. (Sunderland, WBA) (2): 1937 v A; 1939 v E.
McNAB, C. D. (Dundee) (6): 1931 v E, W, A, I, Sw; 1932 v E.
McNAB, J. S. (Liverpool) (1): 1923 v W.
McNAIR, A. (Celtic) (15): 1906 v W; 1907 v Ni; 1908 v E, W; 1909 v E; 1910 v W; 1912 v E, W, Ni; 1913 v E; 1914 v E, Ni; 1920 v E, W, Ni.
McNAMARA J. (Celtic, Wolves) (33): 1997 v La, Se, Est, W; 1998 v D, Co, US, N, M; 2000 v Holl; 2001 v Sm; 2002 v Bel, Fr; 2003 v Ice (2), Lth, Nz, G; 2004 v Fi, G, Lth, Holl (2), W, Trin; 2005 v Sp, Slo, Se, I, Mo; 2006 v A, I, N.
McNAMEE, D. (Livingston) (4): 2004 v Est, Trin; 2006 v Bul, J.
J. McNAUGHT, W. (Raith R.) (5): 1951 v A, W, Ni; 1952 v E; 1955 v Ni.
McNAUGHTON, K. (Aberdeen, Cardiff City) (4): 2002 v Nig; 2003 v D; 2005 v Se; 2008 v CzR.
McNEIL, H. (Queen's Park) (10): 1874 v E; 1875 v E; 1876 v E, W; 1877 v W; 1878 v E; 1879 v E, W; 1881 v E, W.

McNEIL, M. (Rangers) (2): 1876 v W; 1880 v E.
McNEILL, W. (Celtic) (29): 1961 v E, Ei (2), Cz; 1962 v Ni, E, Cz, U; 1963 v Ei, Sp; 1964 v W, E, WG; 1965 v E, Fin, Pol, Sp; 1966 v Ni, Pol; 1967 v USSR; 1968 v E; 1969 v Cy (2), W, E; 1970 v WG; 1972 v Ni, W, E.
McPHAIL, J. (Celtic) (5): 1950 v W; 1951 v W, Ni, A; 1954 v Ni.
McPHAIL, R. (Airdrie, Rangers) (17): 1927 v E; 1929 v W; 1931 v E, Ni; 1932 v W, Ni, Fr; 1933 v E, Ni; 1934 v A, Ni; 1935 v E; 1937 v G, E, Cz; 1938 v W, Ni.
McPHERSON, D. (Kilmarnock) (1): 1892 v Ni.
McPHERSON, D. (Hearts, Rangers) (27): 1989 v Cy, E; 1990 v N, Ma, Cr, Se, Br; 1991 v Sw, Bul (2), USSR, Sm (2); 1992 v Sw, R, Ni, Fin, US, Ca, N, Holl, G, CIS; 1993 v Sw, I, Ma, Por.
McPHERSON, J. (Clydesdale) (1): 1875 v E.
McPHERSON, J. (Vale of Leven) (8): 1879 v E, W; 1880 v E; 1881 v W; 1883 v E, W; 1884 v E; 1885 v Ni.
McPHERSON, J. (Kilmarnock, Cowlairs, Rangers) (9): 1888 v W; 1889 v E; 1890 v Ni, E; 1892 v W; 1894 v E; 1895 v E, Ni; 1897 Ni.
McPHERSON, J. (Hearts) (1): 1891 v E.
McPHERSON, R. (Arthurlie) (1): 1882 v E.
McQUEEN, G. (Leeds Utd, Manchester Utd) (30): 1974 v Bel; 1975 v Sp (2), Por, W, Ni, E, R; 1976 v D; 1977 v Cz, W (2), Ni, E; 1978 v EG, Cz, W, Bul, Ni, W; 1979 v A, N, Por, Ni, E, N; 1980 v Pe, A, Bel; 1981 v W.
McQUEEN, M. (Leith Ath.) (2): 1890 v W; 1891 v W.
McRORIE, D. M. (Morton) (1): 1931 v W.
McSPADYEN, A. (Partick Th.) (2): 1939 v E, H.
McSTAY, P. (Celtic) (76): 1984 v U, Bel, EG, Ni, W, E; 1985 v Ice, Sp (2), W; 1986 v EG, Aus, Is, U, Y; 1987 v Bul, Ei (2), L, Bel, E, Br; 1988 v H, Bel, Bul, L, S.Ar, Sp, Co, E; 1989 v N, Y, I, Cy (2), Fr, E, Ch; 1990 v Y, Fr, N, Arg, EG, Eg, Pol, Ma, Cr, Se, Br; 1991 v R, USSR, Bul; 1992 v Sm, Fin, US, Ca, N, Holl, G, CIS; 1993 v Sw, Por (2), I, Ma, Est (2); 1994 v I, Holl; 1995 v Fin, Fi, Ru; 1996 v Aus, 1997 v Est (2), A.
McSTAY, W. (Celtic) (13): 1921 v W, Ni; 1925 v E, Ni, W; 1926 v E, Ni, W; 1927 v E, Ni, W; 1928 v W, Ni.
McSWEGAN, G. (Hearts) (2): 2000 v Bos, Lth.
McTAVISH, J. (Falkirk) (1): 1910 v Ni.
McWHATTIE, G. C. (Queen's Park) (2): 1901 v W, Ni.
McWILLIAM, P. (Newcastle Utd) (8): 1905 v E; 1906 v E; 1907 v E, W; 1909 v E, W; 1910 v E; 1911 v W.
MACARI, L. (Celtic, Manchester Utd) (24): 1972 v W, E, Y, Cz, Br; 1973 v D, E (2), W, Ni; 1975 v Se, Por, W, E, R; 1977 v Ni, E, Ch, Arg; 1978 v EG, W, Bul, Pe, Ir.
MACAULEY, A. R. (Brentford, Arsenal) (7): 1947 v E; 1948 v E, W, Ni, Bel, Sw, Fr.
MACKAIL-SMITH, C. (Peterborough, Brighton) (6): 2011 v Br; 2012 v D, Sp, Cy, Slo, US.
MACKAY, D. C. (Hearts, Tottenham H) (22): 1957 v Sp; 1958 v Fr; 1959 v W, Ni, WG, E; 1960 v W, Ni, A, Pol, H, T; 1961 v W, Ni, E; 1963 v E, A, N; 1964 v Ni, W, N; 1966 v Ni.

MACKAY, G. (Hearts) (4): 1988 v Bul, L, S.Ar, Ma.
MACKAY, M. (Norwich) (5): 2004 v D, Est, Trin; 2005 v Sp, Slo.
MACKIE, J. (QPR) (9): 2011 v CzR, Sp, Fi; 2012 v Cy, Slo; 2013 v Mac, W, Bel, Ser.
MADDEN, J. (Celtic) (2): 1893 v W; 1895 v W.
MAGUIRE, C. (Aberdeen) (2): 2011 v Ni, Ei.
MAIN, F. R. (Rangers) (1): 1938 v W.
MAIN, J. (Hibernian) (1): 1909 v Ni.
MALEY, W. (Celtic) (2): 1893 v E, Ni.
MALONEY, S. (Celtic, Aston Villa, Celtic, Wigan) (28): 2006 v Blr, US; 2007 v Geo, I, Fi, A; 2008 v Lth, Uk, Geo, Cro, CzR; 2009 v Mac, Ice, N, Arg; 2010 v Mac, Holl; 2011 v Sp, Fi; 2012 v US; 2013 v Aus, Mac, W (2), Bel, Est, Ser, Cro.
MALPAS, M. (Dundee Utd) (55): 1984 v Fr; 1985 v E, Ice; 1986 v W, Aus (2), Is, R, E, Holl, D, WG; 1987 v Bul, Ei, Bel; 1988 v Bel, Bul, L, S.Ar, Ma; 1989 v N, Y, I, Cy (2), Fr, E, Ch; 1990 v Y, Fr, N, Eg, Pol, Ma, Cr, Se, Br; 1991 v R (2), Bul (2), USSR, Sm (2); 1992 v Sw, Ni, Fin, US, Ca, N, Holl, G; 1993 v Sw, Por, I.
MARSHALL, D. (Celtic, Cardiff) (5): 2005 v H, Se; 2010 v N, Holl, W.
MARSHALL, H. (Celtic) (2): 1899 v W; 1900 v Ni.
MARSHALL, G. (Celtic) (1): 1992 v US.
MARSHALL, J. (Middlesbrough, Llanelli) (7): 1921 v E, W, Ni; 1922 v E, W, Ni; 1924 v W.
MARSHALL, J. (Third Lanark) (4): 1885 v Ni; 1886 v W; 1887 v E, W.
MARSHALL, J. (Rangers) (3): 1932 v E; 1933 v E; 1934 v E.
MARSHALL, R. W. (Rangers) (2): 1892 v Ni; 1894 v Ni.
MARTIN, B. (Motherwell) (2): 1995 v. J, Ec.
MARTIN, F. (Aberdeen) (6): 1954 v N (2), A, U; 1955 v E, H.
MARTIN, N. (Hibernian, Sunderland) (3): 1965 v Fin, Pol; 1966 v I.
MARTIN, R. (Norwich) (5): 2011 v W; 2012 v Slo, US; 2013 v Aus, Cro.
MARTIS, J. (Motherwell) (1): 1961 v W.
MASON, J. (Third Lanark) (7): 1949 v E, W, Ni; 1950 v Ni; 1951 v Ni, Bel, A.
MASSIE, A. (Hearts, Aston Villa) (18): 1932 v Ni, W, Fr; 1933 v Ni; 1934 v E, Ni; 1935 v E, Ni, W; 1936 v W, Ni, E; 1937 v G, E, W, Ni, A; 1938 v W.
MASSON, D. S. (QPR, Derby Co) (17): 1976 v Ni, W, E; 1977 v Fin, Cz, W, Ni, E, Ch, Arg, Br; 1978 v EG, Cz, W, Ni, E, Pe.
MATHERS, D. (Partick Th.) (1): 1954 v Fin.
MATTEO, D. (Leeds Utd) (6): 2001 v Aus, Sm, Bel; 2002 v Cro, Bel, Fr.
MAXWELL, W. S. (Stoke City) (1): 1898 v E.
MAY, J. (Rangers) (5): 1906 v W, Ni; 1908 v E, Ni; 1909 v W.
MEECHAN, P. (Celtic) (1): 1896 v Ni.
MEIKLEJOHN, D. D. (Rangers) (15): 1922 v W; 1924 v W; 1925 v W, Ni, E; 1928 v W, Ni; 1929 v E, Ni; 1930 v E, Ni; 1931 v E; 1932 v W, Ni; 1934 v A.
MENZIES, A. (Hearts) (1): 1906 v E.
MERCER, R. (Hearts) (2): 1912 v W; 1913 v Ni.
MIDDLETON, R. (Cowdenbeath) (1): 1930 v Ni.
MILLAR, A. (Hearts) (1): 1939 v W.
MILLAR, J. (Rangers) (3): 1897 v E; 1898 v E, W.
MILLAR, J. (Rangers) (2): 1963 v A, Ei.
MILLER, C. (Dundee Utd) (1): 2001 v Pol.

MILLER, K. (Rangers, Wolves, Celtic, Derby Co, Rangers, Bursaspor, Cardiff) (68): 2001 v Pol; 2003 v A, Ice, Lth, G; 2004 v Lth, Holl (2), W, R, Est, Trin; 2005 v H, Sp, N, Mo (2), Se, I, Blr; 2006 v A, I, N, Blr, Slo, Sw; 2007 v Fi, Lth, Uk, Geo, I; 2008 v SA, Uk, Geo, I, Cro, CzR; 2009 v Ni, Mac, Ice (2), Holl; 2010 v N, Mac, Holl, W, CzR; 2011 v Lth, Li, CzR, Sp, Ni, Br, W, Ei; 2012 v D, CzR, Cy, Slo, US; 2013 v Mac, W (2), Bel, Lux, Est, Ser.
MILLER, J. (St Mirren) (5): 1931 v E, I, Sw; 1932 v Fr; 1934 v E.
MILLER, L. (Dundee Utd, Aberdeen) (3): 2006 v J; 2009 v Arg; 2010 v J.
MILLER, P. (Dumbarton) (3): 1882 v E; 1883 v E, W.
MILLER, T. (Liverpool, Manchester Utd) (3): 1920 v E; 1921 v E, Ni.
MILLER, W. (Third Lanark) (1): 1876 v E.
MILLER, W. (Celtic) (6): 1947 v E, W, Bel, L; 1948 v W, Ni.
MILLER, W. (Aberdeen) (65): 1975 v R; 1978 v Bul; 1980 v Bel, W, E, Pol, H; 1981 v Se, Por, Is, Ni (2), W, E; 1982 v Ni, Por, Holl, Br, USSR; 1983 v EG, Sw (2), W, E, Ca (3); 1984 v U, Bel, EG, W, E, Fr; 1985 v Y, Ice, Sp (2), W, E, Ice; 1986 v W, EG, Aus (2), Is, R, E, Holl, D, WG, U; 1987 v Bul, E, Br; 1988 v H, L, S.Ar, Ma, Sp, Co, E; 1989 v N, Y; 1990 Y, N.
MILLS, W. (Aberdeen) (3): 1936 v W, Ni; 1937 v W.
MILNE, J. V. (Middlesbrough) (2): 1938 v E; 1939 v E.
MITCHELL, D. (Rangers) (5): 1890 v Ni; 1892 v E; 1893 v E, Ni; 1894 v E.
MITCHELL, J. (Kilmarnock) (3): 1908 v Ni; 1910 v Ni, W.
MITCHELL, R. C. (Newcastle Utd.) (2): 1951 v D, Fr.
MOCHAN, N. (Celtic) (3): 1954 v N, A, U.
MOIR, W. (Bolton) (1): 1950 v E.
MONCUR, R. (Newcastle Utd.) (16): 1968 v Holl; 1970 v Ni, W, E, Ei; 1971 v D, Bel, W, Por, Ni, E, D; 1972 v Pe, Ni, W, E.
MORGAN, H. (St Mirren, Liverpool) (2): 1898 v W; 1899 v E.
MORGAN, W. (Burnley, Manchester Utd.) (21): 1968 v Ni; 1972 v Pe, Y, Cz, Br; 1973 v D (2), E (2), W, Ni, Sw, Br; 1974 v Cz (2), WG (2), Ni, Bel, Br, Y.
MORRIS, D. (Raith R.) (6): 1923 v Ni; 1924 v E, Ni; 1925 v E, W, Ni.
MORRIS, H. (East Fife) (1): 1950 v Ni.
MORRISON, J. (West Brom) (26): 2008 v CzR; 2009 v Ni, N, Holl, Ice; 2011 v Se, Lth, Li, CzR, Sp, Ni, Br, W; 2012 v D, CzR, Lth, Sp, Cy, Slo; 2013 v Aus, Mac, W, Bel, Est, Serb, Cro.
MORRISON, T. (St Mirren) (1): 1927 v E.
MORTON, A. L. (Queen's Park, Rangers) (31): 1920 v W, Ni; 1921 v E; 1922 v E, W; 1923 v E, W, Ni; 1924 v E, W, Ni; 1925 v E, W, Ni; 1927 v E, Ni; 1928 v E, W, Ni; 1929 v E, W, Ni; 1930 v E, W, Ni; 1931 v E, W, Ni; 1932 v E, W, Fr.
MORTON, H. A. (Kilmarnock) (2): 1929 v G, Holl.
MUDIE, J. K. (Blackpool) (17): 1957 v W, Ni, E, Y, Sw, Sp (2), WG; 1958 v Ni, E, W, Sw, H, Pol, Y, Par, Fr.
MUIR, W. (Dundee) (1): 1907 v Ni.
MUIRHEAD, T. A. (Rangers) (8): 1922 v Ni; 1923 v E; 1924 v W; 1927 v Ni; 1928 v Ni; 1929 v W, Ni; 1930 v W.
MULGREW. C (Celtic) (6): 2012 v Slo, US; 2013 v Aus, Lux, Est, W.
MULHALL, G. (Aberdeen, Sunderland) (3): 1960 v Ni; 1963 v Ni; 1964 v Ni.
MUNRO, A. D. (Hearts, Blackpool) (3): 1937 v W, Ni; 1938 v Holl.
MUNRO, F. M. (Wolverhampton W.) (9): 1971 v Ni, E, D, USSR; 1975 v Se, W, Ni, E, R.
MUNRO, I. (St Mirren) (7): 1979 v Arg, N; 1980 v Pe, A, Bel, W, E.

MUNRO, N. (Abercorn) (2): 1888 v W; 1889 v E.
MURDOCH, J. (Motherwell) (1): 1931 v Ni.
MURDOCH, R. (Celtic) (12): 1966 v W, E, I (2); 1967 v Ni; 1968 v Ni; 1969 v W, Ni, E, WG, Cy; 1970 v A.
MURPHY, F. (Celtic) (1): 1938 v Holl.
MURRAY, I. (Hibernian, Rangers) (6): 2003 v Can; 2005 v Se, Mo, Blr, Bul; 2006 v J.
MURRAY, J. (Renton) (1): 1895 v W.
MURRAY, J. (Hearts) (5): 1958 v E, H, Pol, Y, Fr.
MURRAY, J. W. (Vale of Leven) (1): 1890 v W.
MURRAY, P. (Hibernian) (2): 1896 v Ni; 1897 v W.
MURRAY, S. (Aberdeen) (1): 1972 v Bel.
MURTY, G. (Reading) (4): 2004 v W; 2006 v Bul, J; 2008 v Geo.
MUTCH, G. (Preston NE) (1): 1938 v E.

NAISMITH, S. (Kilmarnock, Rangers, Everton) (20): 2007 v Fi; 2010 v Holl, W; 2011 v Lth, Li, CzR, Sp, Ni, W, Ei; 2012 v D, CzR, Lth, Sp; 2013 v Aus, Mac, Lux, Est, Ser, Cro.
NAPIER, C. E. (Celtic, Derby County) (5): 1932 v E; 1935 v E, W; 1937 v Ni, A.
NAREY, D. (Dundee Utd.) (35): 1977 v Se; 1979 v Psor, Ni, Arg; 1980 v Por, Ni, Pol, H; 1981 v W, E; 1982 v Holl, W, E, Nz, Br, USSR; 1983 v EG, Sw, Bel, Ni, W, E, Ca (3); 1986 v Is, R, Holl, WG, U; 1987 v Bul, E, Bel; 1989 v I, Cy.
NAYSMITH, G. (Hearts, Everton, Sheffield United) (46): 2000 v Ei; 2001 v La, Sm, Cro, 2002 v Cro, Bel; 2003 v D, Ice (2), Por, Ei, A, Lth, Nz, G; 2004 v N, Fi, G, Lth, Holl (2), W; 2005 v H, Sp, Slo, N, Mo, I; 2006 v Bul, J; 2007 v Fi (2), Lth, Geo, I, A; 2008 v Uk, I, Cro, CzR; 2009 v Ni, Mac, Ice (2), N, Holl.
NEIL, R. G. (Hibernian, Rangers) (2): 1896 v W; 1900 v W.
NEILL, R. W. (Queen's Park) (5): 1876 v W; 1877 v E, W; 1878 v W; 1880 v E.
NEILSON, R. (Hearts) (1); 2007 v Uk.
NELLIES, P. (Hearts) (2): 1914 v W, Ni.
NELSON, J. (Cardiff C.) (4): 1925 v W, Ni; 1928 v E; 1930 v Fr.
NEVIN, P. (Chelsea, Everton, Tranmere) (28): 1986 v R, E; 1987 v L, Ei, Bel; 1988 v L; 1989 v Cy, E; 1991 v R, Bul, Sm; 1992 v US, G, CIS; 1993 v Ma, Por, Est; 1994 v Sw, Ma, Holl (2), A. 1995 v Fi, Ru, Sm; 1996 v Se, Sm, Aus.
NIBLO, T. (Aston Villa) (1): 1904 v E.
NIBLOE, J. (Kilmarnock) (11): 1929 v E, N, Holl; 1930 v W; 1931 v E, Ni, A, I, Sw; 1932 v E, Fr.
NICHOLAS, C. (Celtic, Arsenal, Aberdeen) (20): 1983 v Sw, Ni, E, Ca (3); 1984 v Bel, Fr; 1985 v Y, Ice, Sp, W; 1986 v Is, R, E, D, U; 1987 v Bul, E; 1989 v Cy.
NICOL, S. (Liverpool) (27): 1985 v Y, Ice, Sp, W; 1986 v W, EG, Aus, E, D, WG, U; 1988 v H, Bul, S.Ar, Sp, Co, E; 1989 v N, Y, Cy, Fr; 1990 v Y, Fr; 1991 v Sw, USSR, Sm; 1992 Sw.
NICHOLSON, B. (Dunfermline) (3): 2001 v Pol; 2002 v La; 2005 v Se.
NISBET, J. (Ayr Utd.) (3): 1929 v N, G, Holl.

NIVEN, J. B. (Moffat) (1): 1885 v Ni.

O'CONNOR, G. (Hibernian, Lokomotiv Moscow, Birmingham City) (16): 2002 v Nig, Skor, HK; 2005 v I; 2006 v A, Slo, US; 2007 v Fi (2), Fr, A; 2008 v SA, Lth, Fr, Uk; 2010 v Holl.
O'DONNELL, F. (Preston NE, Blackpool) (6): 1937 v E, A, Cz; 1938 v E, W, Holl.
O'DONNELL, P. (Motherwell) (1): 1994 v Sw.
OGILVIE, D. H. (Motherwell) (1): 1934 v A.
O'HARE, J. (Derby County) (13): 1970 v W, Ni, E; 1971 v D, Bel, W, Ni; 1972 v Por, Bel, Holl, Pe, Ni, W.
O'NEIL, J. (Hibs) (1): 2001 v Pol.
O'NEIL, B. (Celtic, Wolfsburg, Derby, Preston) (7): 1996 v Aus; 1999 v G; 2000 v Lth, Holl, Ei; 2001 v Aus; 2006 v A.
ORMOND, W. E. (Hibernian) (6): 1954 v E, N, Fin, A, U; 1959 v E.
O'ROURKE, F. (Airdrie) (1): 1907 v Ni.
ORR, J. (Kilmarnock) (1): 1892 v W.
ORR, R. (Newcastle Utd.) (2): 1902 v E; 1904 v E.
ORR, T. (Morton) (2): 1952 v Ni, W.
ORR, W. (Celtic) (3): 1900 v Ni; 1903 v Ni; 1904 v W.
ORROCK, R. (Falkirk) (1): 1913 v W.
OSWALD, J. (Third Lanark, St Bernard's, Rangers) (3): 1889 v E; 1895 v E; 1897 v W.

PARKER, A. H. (Falkirk, Everton) (15): 1955 v Por, Y, A; 1956 v E, Ni, W, A; 1957 v Ni, W, Y; 1958 v Ni, W, E, Sw, Par.
PARLANE, D. (Rangers) (12): 1973 v W, Sw, Br; 1975 v Sp, Se, Por, W, Ni, E, R; 1976 v D; 1977 v W.
PARLANE, R. (Vale of Leven) (3): 1878 v W; 1879 v E, W.
PATERSON, G. D. (Celtic) (1): 1939 v Ni.
PATERSON, J. (Leicester City) (1): 1920 v E.
PATERSON, J. (Cowdenbeath) (3): 1931 v A, I, Sw.
PATON, A. (Motherwell) (2): 1952 v D, Se.
PATON, D. (St Bernard's) (1): 1896 v W.
PATON, M. (Dumbarton) (5): 1883 E; 1884 v W; 1885 v W, E; 1886 v E.
PATON, R. (Vale of Leven) (2): 1879 v E, W.
PATRICK, J. (St Mirren) (2): 1897 E, W.
PAUL, J. McD. (Queen's Park) (3): 1909 v E, W, Ni.
PAUL, W. (Partick Th.) (3): 1888 v W; 1889 v W; 1890 v W.
PAUL, W. (Dykebar) (1): 1891 v Ni.
PEARSON, S. (Motherwell, Celtic, Derby County) (10): 2004: v Holl, W; 2005 v H, Sp, N, Se; 2008 v SA, Fr, Uk, Geo.
PEARSON, T. (Newcastle Utd.) (2): 1947 v E, Bel.
PENMAN, A. (Dundee) (1): 1966 v Holl.
PETTIGREW, W. (Motherwell) (5): 1976 v Sw, Ni, W; 1977 v W, Se.
PHILLIPS, J. (Queen's Park) (3): 1877 v E, W; 1878 v W.
PHILLIPS, M (Blackpool) (2): 2012 v US; 2013 v Bel.
PLENDERLEITH, J. B. (Manchester City) (1): 1961 v Ni.
PORTEOUS, W. (Hearts) (1): 1903 v Ni.

PRESSLEY, S. (Hearts) (32): 2000 v Fr, Ei; 2003 v Ice (2), Can, Por, A, Lth, Nz, G; 2004 v N, G, Lth, Holl (2), R, D, Est, Trin; 2005 v H, I, Mo, Blr; 2006 v A, N, Blr, Slo, US; 2007 v Fi, Lth, Fr, Uk.
PRINGLE, C. (St Mirren) (1): 1921 v W.
PROVAN, D. (Rangers) (5): 1964 v Ni, N; 1966 v I (2), Holl.
PROVAN, D. (Celtic) (10): 1980 v Bel (2), Por, Ni; 1981 v Is, W, E; 1982 v Se, Por, Ni.
PURSELL, P. (Queen's Park) (1): 1914 v W.

QUASHIE, N. (Portsmouth, Southampton, WBA) (14): 2004 v Est, Trin; 2005 v H, Sp, Slo, Se, I; 2006 v A, I, Slo, US, Sw; 2007 v Fi, Lth.
QUINN, J. (Celtic) (11): 1905 v Ni; 1906 v Ni, W; 1908 v Ni, E; 1909 v E; 1910 v E, Ni, W; 1912 v E, W.
QUINN, P. (Motherwell) (4): 1961 v E, Ei (2); 1962 v U.

RAE, G. (Dundee, Rangers, Cardiff) (14): 2001 v Pol; 2002 v La, G; 2004 v N, Fi, G, Lth, Holl, R; 2006 v Bul, J; 2008 v Cro, CzR; 2009 v Ice.
RAE, J. (Third Lanark) (2): 1889 v W; 1890 v Ni.
RAESIDE, J. S. (Third Lanark) (1): 1906 v W.
RAISBECK, A. G. (Liverpool) (8): 1900 v E; 1901 v E; 1902 v E; 1903 v E, W; 1904 v E; 1906 v E; 1907 v E.
RANKIN, G. (Vale of Leven) (2): 1890 v Ni; 1891 v E.
RANKIN, R. (St Mirren) (3): 1929 v N, G, Holl.
REDPATH, W. (Motherwell) (9): 1949 v W, Ni; 1951 v E, D, Fr, Bel, A; 1952 v Ni, E.
REID, J, G. (Airdrie) (3): 1914 v W; 1920 v W; 1924 v Ni.
REID, R. (Brentford) (2): 1938 v E, Ni.
REID, W. (Rangers) (9): 1911 v E, W, Ni; 1912 v Ni; 1913 v E, W, Ni; 1914 v E, Ni.
REILLY, L. (Hibernian) (38): 1949 v E, W, Fr; 1950 v W, Ni, Sw, Fr; 1951 v W, E, D, Fr, Bel, A; 1952 v Ni, W, E, USA, D, Se; 1953 v Ni, W, E, Se; 1954 v W; 1955 v H (2), Por, Y, A, E; 1956 v E, W, Ni, A; 1957 v E, Ni, W, Y.
RENNIE, H. G. (Hearts, Hibs) (13): 1900 v E, Ni; 1901 v E; 1902 v E, Ni, W; 1903 v Ni, W; 1904 v Ni; 1905 v W; 1906 v Ni; 1908 v Ni, W.
RENNY-TAILYOUR, H. W. (Royal Engineers) (1): 1873 v E.
RHODES, A. (Huddersfield, Blackburn) (8): 2012 v Cy; 2013 v Aus, Mac, Lux, Est, Wal, Ser, Cro.
RHIND, A. (Queen's Park) (1): 1872 v E.
RICHMOND, A. (Queen's Park) (1): 1906 v W.
RICHMOND, J. T. (Clydesdale, Queen's Park) (3): 1877 v E; 1878 v E; 1882 v W.
RING, T. (Clyde) (12): 1953 v Se; 1955 v W, Ni, E, H; 1957 v E, Sp (2), Sw, WG; 1958 v Ni, Sw.
RIOCH, B. D. (Derby County, Everton) (24): 1975 v Por, W, Ni, E, R; 1976 v D (2), R, Ni, W, E; 1977 v Fin, Cz, W (2), Ni, E, Ch, Br; 1978 v Cz, Ni, E, Pe, Holl.
RIORDAN, D. (Hibernian) (3): 2006 v A; 2010 v J, W.
RITCHIE, A. (East Stirling) (1): 1891 v W.
RITCHIE, H. (Hibernian) (2): 1923 v W; 1928 v Ni.
RITCHIE, J. (Queen's Park) (1): 1897 v W.
RITCHIE, P. (Hearts, Bolton, Walsall) (7): 1999 v G, Czr, E; 2000 v Lth, Fr, Holl; 2004 v W.

RITCHIE, W. (Rangers) (1): 1962 v U.
ROBB, D. T. (Aberdeen) (5): 1971 v W, E, Por, D, USSR.
ROBB, W. (Rangers, Hibernian) (2): 1926 v W; 1928 v W.
ROBERTSON, A. (Clyde) (5): 1955 v Por, A, H; 1958 v Sw, Par.
ROBERTSON, D. (Rangers) (3): 1991 v Ni; 1994 v Sw, Holl.
ROBERTSON, G. (Motherwell, Sheffield W.) (4): 1910 v W; 1912 v W; 1913 v E, Ni.
ROBERTSON, G. (Kilmarnock) (1): 1938 v Cz.
ROBERTSON, H. (Dundee) (1): 1962 v Cz.
ROBERTSON, J. (Dundee) (2): 1931 v A, I.
ROBERTSON, J. (Hearts) (16): 1991 v R, Sw, Bul, Sm (2); 1992 v Ni, Fin; 1993 v I, Ma, G, Est; 1995 v J, Ec, Fi. 1996 v Gr, Se.
ROBERTSON, J. N. (Nottingham F., Derby County) (28): 1978 v Ni, W, Ir; 1979 v Por, N; 1980 v Pe, A, Bel (2), Por; 1981 v Se, Por, Is, Ni (2), E; 1982 v Se, Ni (2), E, Nz, Br, USSR; 1983 v EG, Sw; 1984 v U, Bel.
ROBERTSON, J. G. (Tottenham H.) (1): 1965 v W.
ROBERTSON, J. T. (Everton, Southampton, Rangers) (16): 1898 v E; 1899 v E; 1900 v E, W; 1901 v W, Ni, E; 1902 v W, Ni, E; 1903 v E, W; 1904 v E, W, Ni; 1905 v W.
ROBERTSON, P. (Dundee) (1): 1903 v Ni.
ROBERTSON, S. (Dundee United) (2): 2009 v Arg; 2011 v Se.
ROBERTSON, T. (Queen's Park) (4): 1889 v Ni; 1890 v E; 1891 v W; 1892 v Ni.
ROBERTSON, T. (Hearts) (1): 1898 v Ni.
ROBERTSON, W. (Dumbarton) (2): 1887 v E, W.
ROBINSON, R. (Dundee) (4): 1974 v WG; 1975 v Se, Ni, R.
ROBSON, B. (Dundee United, Celtic, Middlesbrough) (16): 2008 v SA, CzR; 2009 v Ni, Mac, Ice, N; 2010 v W, CzR; 2011 v Se, Li, CzR, W, Ei; 2012 v CzR, Cy, Slo.
ROSS, M. (Rangers) (13): 2002 v Skor, SA, HK; 2003 v D, Fi, Ice, Can, Por, Nz, G; 2004 v N, G, Holl.
ROUGH, A. (Partick Th, Hibernian) (53): 1976 v Sw, Ni, W, E; 1977 v Fin, Cz, W (2), Se, Ni, E, Ch, Arg, Br; 1978 v Cz, W, Ni, E, Pe, Ir, Holl; 1979 v A, Por, W, Arg, N; 1980 v Pe, A, Bel (2), Por, W, E, Pol, H; 1981 v Se, Por, Is (2), Ni, W, E; 1982 v Se, Ni, Sp, Holl, W, E, Nz, Br, USSR; 1986 v W, E.
ROUGVIE, D. (Aberdeen) (1): 1984 v Ni.
ROWAN, A. (Caledonian, Queen's Park) (2): 1880 v E; 1882 v W.
RUSSELL, D. (Hearts, Celtic) (6): 1895 v E, Ni; 1897 v W; 1898 v Ni; 1901 v W, Ni.
RUSSELL, J. (Cambuslang) (1): 1890 v Ni.
RUSSELL W. F. (Airdrie) (2): 1924 v W; 1925 v E.
RUTHERFORD, E. (Rangers) (1): 1948 v F.

ST JOHN, I. (Motherwell, Liverpool) (21): 1959 v WG; 1960 v E, Ni, W, Pol, A; 1961 v E; 1962 v Ni, W, E, Cz (2), U; 1963 v W, Ni, (cont).. E, N, Ei, Sp; 1964 v Ni; 1965 v E.
SAUNDERS, S. (Motherwell) (1): 2011 v Fi.
SAWERS, W. (Dundee) (1): 1895 v W.

SCARFF, P. (Celtic) (1): 1931 v Ni.
SCHAEDLER, E. (Hibernian) (1): 1974 v WG.
SCOTT, A. S. (Rangers, Everton) (16): 1957 v Ni, Y, WG; 1958 v W, Sw; 1959 v Por; 1962 v Ni, W, E, Cz, U; 1964 v W, N; 1965 v Fin; 1966 v Por, Br.
SCOTT, J. (Hibernian) (1): 1966 v Holl.
SCOTT, J. (Dundee) (2): 1971 v D, USSR.
SCOTT, M. (Airdrie) (1): 1898 v W.
SCOTT, R. (Airdrie) (1): 1894 v Ni.
SCOULAR, J. (Portsmouth) (9): 1951 v D, Fr, A; 1952 v E, USA, D, Se; 1953 v W, Ni.
SELLAR, W. (Battlefield, Queen's Park) (9): 1885 v E; 1886 v E; 1887 v E, W; 1888 v E; 1891 v E; 1892 v E; 1893 v E, Ni.
SEMPLE, W. (Cambuslang) (1): 1886 v W.
SEVERIN, S. (Hearts, Aberdeen) (15): 2002 v La, Skor, SA, HK; 2003 v D, Ice, Can, Por; 2005 v H, Se; 2006 v A, Bul, J; 2007 v Fi, Lth.
SHANKLY, W. (Preston NE) (5): 1938 v E; 1939 v E, W, Ni, H.
SHARP, G. M. (Everton) (12): 1985 v Ice; 1986 v W, Aus (2), Is, R, U; 1987 v Ei; 1988 v Bel, Bul, L, Ma.
SHARP, J. (Dundee, Woolwich Arsenal, Fulham) (5): 1904 v W; 1907 v W, E; 1908 v E; 1909 v W.
SHAW, D. (Hibernian) (8): 1947 v W, Ni; 1948 v E, Bel, Sw, Fr; 1949 v W, Ni.
SHAW, F. W. (Pollokshields Ath.) (2): 1884 v E, W.
SHAW, J. (Rangers) (4): 1947 v E, Bel, L; 1948 v Ni.
SHEARER, D. (Aberdeen) (7) 1994 v A, Holl; 1995 v Fin, Ru, Sm, Fi. 1996 v Gr.
SHEARER, R. (Rangers) (4): 1961 v E, Ei (2), Cz.
SHINNIE, A. (Inverness CT) (1): 2013 v Lux.
SILLARS, D. C. (Queen's Park) (5): 1891 v Ni; 1892 v E; 1893 v W; 1894 v E; 1895 v W.
SIMPSON, J. (Third Lanark) (3): 1895 v E, W, Ni.
SIMPSON, J. (Rangers) (14): 1935 v E, W, Ni; 1936 v E, W, Ni; 1937 v G, E, W, Ni, A, Cz; 1938 v W, Ni.
SIMPSON, N. (Aberdeen) (4): 1983 v Ni; 1984 v Fr; 1987 v E; 1988 v E.
SIMPSON, R. C. (Celtic) (5): 1967 v E, USSR; 1968 v Ni, E; 1969 v A.
SINCLAIR, G. L. (Hearts) (3): 1910 v Ni; 1912 v W, Ni.
SINCLAIR, J. W. E. (Leicester City) (1): 1966 v Por.
SKENE, L. H. (Queen's Park) (1): 1904 v W.
SLOAN, T. (Third Lanark) (1): 1904 v W.
SMELLIE, R. (Queen's Park) (6): 1887 v Ni; 1888 v W; 1889 v E; 1891 v E; 1893 v E, Ni.
SMITH, A. (Rangers) (20): 1898 v E; 1900 v E, Ni, W; 1901 v E, Ni, W; 1902 v E, Ni, W; 1903 v E, Ni, W; 1904 v Ni; 1905 v W; 1906 v E, Ni; 1907 v W; 1911 v E, Ni.
SMITH, D. (Aberdeen, Rangers) (2): 1966 v Holl; 1968 v Holl.
SMITH, G. (Hibernian) (18): 1947 v E, Ni; 1948 v W, Bel, Sw, Fr; 1952

v E, USA; 1955 v Por, Y, A, H; 1956 v E, Ni, W; 1957 v Sp (2), Sw.
SMITH, H. G. (Hearts) (3): 1988 v S.Ar; 1991 Ni; 1992 v Ca.
SMITH, J. (Rangers) (2): 1935 v Ni; 1938 v Ni.
SMITH, J. (Ayr United) (1): 1924 v E.
SMITH, J. (Aberdeen, Newcastle Utd.) (4): 1968 v Holl; 1974 v WG, Ni, W.
SMITH, J. (Celtic) (2): 2003 v Ei, A.
SMITH, J. E. (Celtic) (2); 1959 v H, Por.
SMITH, Jas (Queen's Park) (1): 1872 v E.
SMITH, J. (Mauchline, Edinburgh University, Queen's Park) (10): 1877 v E, W; 1879 v E, W; 1880 v E; 1881 v W, E; 1883 v E, W; 1884 v E.
SMITH, N. (Rangers) (12): 1897 v E; 1898 v W; 1899 v E, W, Ni; 1900 v E, W, Ni; 1901 v Ni, W; 1902 v E, Ni.
SMITH, R. (Queen's Park) (2): 1872 v E; 1873 v E.
SNODGRASS, R. (Leeds Utd, Norwich) (10): 2011 v Ni, Br; 2012 v D, Lth, Slo; 2013 v Aus, Est, W, Ser, Cro.
SMITH, T. M. (Kilmarnock, Preston NE) (2): 1934 v E; 1938 v E.
SOMERS, P. (Celtic) (4): 1905 v E, Ni; 1907 v Ni; 1909 v W.
SOMERS, W. S. (Third Lanark, Queen's Park) (3): 1879 v E, W; 1880 v W.
SOMERVILLE, G. (Queen's Park) (1): 1886 v E.
SOUNESS, G. J. (Middlesbrough, Liverpool, Sampdoria, Rangers) (54): 1975 v EG, Sp, Se; 1978 v Bul, W, E, Holl; 1979 v A. N, W, Ni, E; 1980 v Pe, A, Bel, Por, Ni; 1981 v Por, Is (2); 1982 v Ni, Por, Sp, W, E, Nz, Br, USSR; 1983 v EG, Sw (2), Bel, W, E, Ca (3); 1984 v U, Ni, W; 1985 v Y, Ice (2), Sp (2), W, E; 1986 v EG, Aus (2), R, E, D, WG.
SPEEDIE, D. R. (Chelsea, Coventry City) (10): 1985 v E; 1986 v W, EG, Aus, E; 1989 v Y, I, Cy (2), Ch.
SPEEDIE, F. (Rangers) (3): 1903 v E, W, Ni.
SPENCER, J. (Chelsea, QPR) (14): 1995 v Ru, Gr, Sm, J; 1996 v Fin, Aus, D, US, U, Holl, E, Sw; 1997 v La, W.
SPEIRS, J. H. (Rangers) (1): 1908 v W.
STANTON, P. (Hibernian) (16): 1966 v Holl; 1969 v Ni; 1970 v Ei, A; 1971 v D, Bel, Por, USSR, D; 1972 v Por, Bel, Holl, W; 1973 v W, Ni; 1974 v WG.
STARK. J. (Rangers) (2): 1909 v E, Ni.
STEEL, W. (Morton, Derby County, Dundee) (30): 1947 v E, Bel, L; 1948 v Fr, E, W, Ni; 1949 v E, W, Ni, Fr; 1950 v E, W, Ni, Sw, Por, Fr; 1951 v W, Ni, E, A (2), D, Fr, Bel; 1952 v W; 1953 v W, E, Ni, Se.
STEELE, D. M. (Huddersfield) (3): 1923 v E, W, Ni.
STEIN, C. (Rangers, Coventry City) (21): 1969 v W, Ni, D, E, Cy (2); 1970 v A, Ni, W, E, Ei, WG; 1971 v D. USSR, Bel, D; 1972 v Cz; 1973 v E (2), W, Ni.
STEPHEN, J. F. (Bradford) (2): 1947 v W; 1948 v W.
STEVENSON, G. (Motherwell) (12): 1928 v W, Ni; 1930 v Ni, E, Fr; 1931 v E, W; 1932 v W, Ni; 1933 v Ni; 1934 v E; 1935 v Ni.
STEWART, A. (Queen's Park) (2): 1888 v Ni; 1889 v W.
STEWART, A. (Third Lanark) (1): 1894 v W.

STEWART, D. (Dumbarton) (1): 1888 v Ni.
STEWART, D. (Queen's Park) (3): 1893 v W; 1894 v Ni; 1897 v Ni.
STEWART, D. S. (Leeds Utd.) (1): 1978 v EG.
STEWART, G. (Hibernian, Man City) (4): 1906 v W, E; 1907 v E, W.
STEWART, J. (Kilmarnock, Middlesbrough) (2): 1977 v Ch; 1979 v N.
STEWART, M. (Manchester Utd, Hearts) (4): 2002 v Nig, Skor, SA; 2009 v Ni.
STEWART, R. (West Ham Utd.) (10): 1981 v W, Ni, E; 1982 v Ni, Por, W; 1984 v Fr; 1987 v Ei (2), L.
STEWART, W. E. (Queen's Park) (2): 1898 v Ni; 1900 v Ni.
STOCKDALE, R. (Middlesbrough) (5): 2002 v Nig, Skor, SA, HK; 2003 v D.
STORRIER, D. (Celtic) (3): 1899 v E, W, Ni.
STRACHAN, G. (Aberdeen, Manchester Utd., Leeds Utd.) (50): 1980 v Ni, W, E, Pol, H; 1981 v Se, Por; 1982 v Ni, Por, Sp, Holl, Nz, Br, USSR; 1983 v EG, Sw (2), Bel, Ni, W, E, Ca (3); 1984 v EG, Ni, E, Fr; 1985 v Sp, E, Ice; 1986 v W, Aus, R, D, WG, U; 1987 v Bul, Ei (2); 1988 v H; 1989 v Fr; 1990 v Fr; 1991 v USSR, Bul, Sm; 1992 v Sw, R, Ni, Fin.
STURROCK, P. (Dundee Utd.) (20): 1981 v W, Ni, E; 1982 v Por, Ni, W, E; 1983 v EG, Sw, Bel, Ca (3); 1984 v W; 1985 v Y; 1986 v Is, Holl, D, U; 1987 v Bel.
SULLIVAN, N. (Wimbledon, Spurs) (28): 1997 v W; 1998 Fr, Co. 1999 v Fi (2), CzR (2), G. 2000 v Bos (2), Est, E (2) Fr, Holl, Ei; 2001 v La, Sm (2), Cro, Bel, Pol; 2002 v Cro, Bel, La, Fr, Skor; 2003 v Ei.
SUMMERS, W. (St Mirren) (1): 1926 v E.
SYMON, J. S. (Rangers) (1): 1939 v H.

TAIT, T. S. (Sunderland) (1): 1911 v W.
TAYLOR, J. (Queen's Park) (6): 1872 v E; 1873 v E; 1874 v E; 1875 v E; 1876 v E, W.
TAYLOR, J. D. (Dumbarton, St Mirren) (4): 1892 v W; 1893 v W; 1894 v Ni; 1895 v Ni.
TAYLOR, W. (Hearts) (1): 1892 v E.
TEALE, G. (Wigan, Derby) (13): 2006 v Sw, Bul, J; 2007 v Fi (2), Fr, Geo, I; 2008 v SA, Lth, Cro; 2009 v Holl, Ice.
TELFER, P. (Coventry) (1): 2000 v Fr.
TELFER, W. (Motherwell) (2): 1933 v Ni; 1934 v Ni.
TELFER, W. D. (St Mirren) (1): 1954 v W.
TEMPLETON, R. (Aston Villa, Newcastle Utd., Woolwich Arsenal, Kilmarnock) (11): 1902 v E; 1903 v E, W; 1904 v E; 1905 v W; 1908 v Ni; 1910 v E, Ni; 1912 v E, Ni; 1913 v W.
THOMPSON, S. (Dundee United, Rangers) (16): 2002 v Fr, Nig, HK; 2003 v D, Fi, Ice, Can, Ei, A, G; 2004 v Fi, G, R; 2005 v H, N, Mo.
THOMSON, A. (Arthurlie) (1): 1886 v Ni.
THOMSON, A. (Third Lanark) (1): 1889 v W.
THOMSON, A. (Airdrie) (1): 1909 v Ni.

THOMSON, A. (Celtic) (3): 1926 v E; 1932 v Fr; 1933 v W.
THOMSON, C. (Hearts, Sunderland) (21): 1904 v Ni; 1905 v E, Ni, W; 1906 v W, Ni; 1907 v E, W, Ni; 1908 v E, W, Ni; 1909 v W; 1910 v E; 1911 v Ni; 1912 v E, W; 1913 v E, W; 1914 v E, Ni.
THOMSON, C. (Sunderland) (1): 1937 v Cz.
THOMSON, D. (Dundee) (1): 1920 v W.
THOMSON, J. (Celtic) (4): 1930 v Fr; 1931 v E, W, Ni.
THOMSON, J. J. (Queen's Park) (3): 1872 v E; 1873 v E; 1874 v E.
THOMSON, J. R. (Everton) (1): 1933 v W.
THOMSON, K. (Rangers) (3): 2009 v Ni; 2010 v CzR; 2011 v Se.
THOMSON, R. (Celtic) (1): 1932 v W.
THOMSON, R. W. (Falkirk) (1): 1927 v E.
THOMSON, S. (Rangers) (2): 1884 v W, Ni.
THOMSON, W. (Dumbarton) (4): 1892 v W; 1893 v W; 1898 v Ni, W.
THOMSON, W. (Dundee) (1): 1896 v W.
THOMSON, W. (St Mirren) (7): 1980 v Ni; 1981 v Ni (2); 1982 v Por; 1983 v Ni, Ca; 1984 v EG.
THORNTON, W. (Rangers) (7): 1947 v W, Ni; 1948 v E, Ni; 1949 v Fr; 1952 v D, Se.
TONER, W. (Kilmarnock) (2): 1959 v W, Ni.
TOWNSLEY, T. (Falkirk) (1926 v W.
TROUP, A. (Dundee, Everton) (5): 1920 v E; 1921 v W, Ni; 1922 v Ni; 1926 v E.
TURNBULL, E. F. (Hibernian) (9): 1948 v Bel, Sw, Fr; 1951 v A; 1958 v H, Pol, Y, Par, Fr.
TURNER, T. (Arthurlie) (1): 1884 v W.
TURNER, W. (Pollokshields Ath.) (2): 1885 v Ni; 1886 v Ni.

URE, J. F. (Dundee, Arsenal) (11): 1962 v W, Cz; 1963 v W, Ni, E, A, N, Sp; 1964 v Ni, N; 1968 v Ni.
URQUHART, D. (Hibernian) (1): 1934 v W.

VALLANCE, T. (Rangers) (7): 1877 v E, W; 1878 v E; 1879 v E, W; 1881 v E, W.
VENTERS, A. (Cowdenbeath, Rangers) (3): 1934 v Ni; 1936 v E; 1939 v E.

WADDELL, T. S. (Queen's Park) (6): 1891 v Ni; 1892 v E; 1893 v E, Ni; 1895 v E, Ni.
WADDELL, W. (Rangers) (17): 1947 v W; 1949 v E, W, Ni, Fr; 1950 v E, Ni; 1951 v E, D, Fr, Bel, A; 1952 v Ni, W; 1954 v Ni; 1955 v W, Ni.
WALES, H. M. (Motherwell) (1): 1933 v W.
WALKER, A. (Celtic) (3): 1988 v Co; 1995 v Fin, Fi.
WALKER, F. (Third Lanark) (1): 1922 v W.
WALKER, G. (St Mirren) (4): 1930 v Fr; 1931 v Ni, A, Sw.
WALKER, J. (Hearts, Rangers) (5): 1895 v Ni; 1897 v W; 1898 v Ni; 1904 v W, Ni.
WALKER, J. (Swindon T.) (9): 1911 v E, W, Ni; 1912 v E, W, Ni; 1913 v E, W, Ni.
WALKER, N. (Hearts, Partick Thistle) (2): 1993 v G, 1996 US.
WALKER, R. (Hearts) (29): 1900 v E, Ni; 1901 v E, W; 1902 v E, W, Ni;

1903 v E, W, Ni; 1904 v E, W, Ni; 1905 v E, W, Ni; 1906 v Ni; 1907 v E, Ni; 1908 v E, W, Ni; 1909 v E, W; 1912 v E, W, Ni; 1913 v E, W.
WALKER, T. (Hearts) (20): 1935 v E, W; 1936 v E, W, Ni; 1937 v G, E, W, Ni, A, Cz; 1938 v E, W, Ni, Cz, Holl; 1939 v E, W, Ni, H.
WALKER, W. (Clyde) (2): 1909 v Ni; 1910 v Ni.
WALLACE, I. A. (Coventry City) (3): 1978 v Bul; 1979 v Por, W.
WALLACE, L. (Hearts, Rangers) (6): 2010 v J, W CzR; 2011 v Se, Li; 2012 v US.
WALLACE, R. (Preston NE) (1): 2010 v J.
WALLACE, W. S. B. (Hearts, Celtic) (7): 1965 v Ni; 1966 v E, Holl; 1967 v E, USSR; 1968 v Ni; 1969 v E.
WARDHAUGH, J. (Hearts) (2): 1955 v H; 1957 v Ni.
WARK, J. (Ipswich Town, Liverpool) (29): 1979 v W, Ni, E, Arg, N; 1980 v Pe, A, Bel (2); 1981 v Is, Ni; 1982 v Se, Sp, Holl, Ni, Nz, Br, USSR; 1983 v EG, Sw (2), Ni, E; 1984 v U, Bel, EG, E, Fr; 1985 v Y.
WATSON, A. (Queen's Park) (3): 1881 v E, W; 1882 v E.
WATSON, J. (Sunderland, Middlesbrough) (6): 1903 v E, W; 1904 v E; 1905 v E; 1909 v E, Ni.
WATSON, J. (Motherwell, Huddersfield) (2): 1948 v Ni; 1954 v Ni.
WATSON, J. A. K. (Rangers) (1): 1878 v W.
WATSON, P. R. (Blackpool) (1): 1934 v A.
WATSON, R. (Motherwell) (1): 1971 v USSR.
WATSON, W. (Falkirk) (1): 1898 v W.
WATT, F. (Kilbirnie) (4): 1889 v W, Ni; 1890 v W; 1891 v E.
WATT, W. W. (Queen's Park) (1): 1887 v Ni.
WAUGH, W. (Hearts) (1): 1938 v Cz.
WEBSTER, A. (Hearts, Rangers) (28): 2003 v A, Nz, G; 2004 v N, Fi, W, Est, Trin; 2005 v H, Sp, Slo, N, Mo (2), Se, Blr; 2006 v A, I, N, Slo, US, Sw; 2010 v CzR; 2012 v US; 2013 v Aus, Mac, Est, Ser.
WEIR, A. (Motherwell) (6): 1959 v WG; 1960 v E, Por, A, H, T.
WEIR, D. (Hearts, Everton, Rangers) (69): 1997 v W, Ma; 1998 Fr, D, Fin, N, M; 1999 v Est, Fi, CzR (2), G, Fi; 2000 v Bos (2), Est, Lth, E (2), Holl; 2001 v La, Sm (2), Cro, Aus, Bel, Pol; 2002 v Cro, Bel, La, Fr, Nig, Skor, SA, HK; 2003 v D, Fi; 2005 v I, Mo, Blr; 2006 v I, N, Blr, Slo, US, Sw, Bul, J; 2007 v Fi (2), Lth, Fr, Uk, Geo, I, A; 2008 v Lth, Fr, Uk, Geo, I; 2009 v Ni, N; 2010 v Mac, Holl; 2011 v Lth, Li, CzR, Sp.
WEIR, J. (Third Lanark) (1): 1887 v Ni.
WEIR, J. B. (Queen's Park) (4): 1872 v E; 1874 v E; 1875 v E; 1878 v W.
WEIR, P. (St Mirren, Aberdeen) (6): 1980 v N, W, Pol, H; 1983 v Sw; 1984 v Ni.
WHITE, J. (Albion Rovers, Hearts) (2): 1922 v W; 1923 v Ni.
WHITE, J. A. (Falkirk, Tottenham H.) (22): 1959 v WG, Holl, Por; 1960 v Ni, W, Pol, A, T; 1961 v W; 1962 v Ni, W, E, Cz (2); 1963 v W, Ni, E; 1964 v Ni, W, E, N, WG.
WHITE, W. (Bolton W.) (2): 1907 v E; 1908 v E.
WHITELAW, A. (Vale of Leven) (2): 1887 v Ni; 1890 v W.
WHITTAKER, S. (Rangers, Norwich) (18): 2010 v N, Mac, Holl, J, CzR; 2011 v Se, Lth, CzR, Sp, Br, W, Ei; 2012 v Lth, Cy, Lux, US; 2013 v Lux, Cro.
WHYTE, D. (Celtic, Middlesbrough, Aberdeen) (12): 1988 v Bel, L; 1989 v Ch; 1992 v US; 1993 v Por, I; 1995 v J, Ec, US; 1997 v La; 1998 v Fin: 1999 v G.
WILKIE, L. (Dundee) (11): 2002 v SA, HK; 2003 v Ice (2), Can, Por, A, Lth; 2004 v Fi, Holl (2).

WILLIAMS, G. (Nottingham Forest) (5): 2002 v Nig, Skor, SA, HK, Por.
WILSON, A. (Sheffield W.) (6): 1907 v E; 1908 v E; 1912 v I; 1913 v E, W; 1914 v Ni.
WILSON, A. (Portsmouth) (1): 1954 v Fin.
WILSON, A. N. (Dunfermline, Middlesbrough) (12): 1920 v E, W, Ni; 1921 v E, W, Ni; 1922 v E, W, Ni; 1923 v E, W, Ni.
WILSON, D. (Queen's Park) (1): 1900 v W.
WILSON, D. (Oldham) (1): 1913 v E.
WILSON, D. (Rangers) (22): 1961 v E, W, Ni, Ei (2), Cz; 1962 v Ni, W, E, Cz, U; 1963 v W, E, A, N, Ei, Sp; 1964 v E, WG; 1965 v Ni, E, Fin.
WILSON, D. (Liverpool) (5): 2011 v Fi, Ni, Br; 2012 v D, CzR.
WILSON, G. W. (Hearts, Everton, Newcastle Utd.) (6): 1904 v W; 1905 v E, Ni; 1906 v W; 1907 v E; 1909 v E.
WILSON, H. (Newmilns, Sunderland, Third Lanark) (4): 1890 v W; 1897 v E; 1902 v W; 1904 v Ni.
WILSON, I. A. (Leicester, Everton) (5): 1987 v E, Br; 1988 v Bel, Bul, L.
WILSON, J. (Vale of Leven) (4): 1888 v W; 1889 v E; 1890 v E; 1891 v E.
WILSON, M. (Celtic) (1): 2011 v Ni.
WILSON, P. (Celtic) (4): 1926 v Ni; 1930 v Fr; 1931 v Ni; 1933 v E.
WILSON, P. (Celtic) (1): 1975 v Sp.
WILSON, R. P. (Arsenal) (2): 1972 v Por, Holl.
WINTERS, R. (Aberdeen) (1): 1999 v G.
WISEMAN, W. (Queen's Park) (2): 1927 v W; 1930 v Ni.
WOOD, G. (Everton, Arsenal) (4): 1979 v Ni, E, Arg; 1982 v Ni.
WOODBURN, W. A. (Rangers) (24): 1947 v E, Bel, L; 1948 v W, Ni; 1949 v E, Fr; 1950 v E, W, Ni, Por, Fr; 1951 v E, W, Ni, A (2), D, Fr, Bel; 1952 v E, W, Ni, USA.
WOTHERSPOON, D. N. (Queen's Park) (2): 1872 v E; 1873 v E.
WRIGHT, K. (Hibs) (1): 1992 v Ni.
WRIGHT, S. (Aberdeen) (2): 1993 v G, Est.
WRIGHT, T. (Sunderland) (3): 1953 v W, Ni, E.
WYLIE, T. G. (Rangers) (1): 1890 v Ni.

YEATS, R. (Liverpool) (2): 1965 v W; 1966 v I.
YORSTON, B. C. (Aberdeen) (1): 1931 v Ni.
YORSTON, H. (Aberdeen) (1): 1955 v W.
YOUNG, A. (Hearts, Everton) (8): 1960 v E, A, H, T; 1961 v W, Ni, Ei; 1966 v Por.
YOUNG, A. (Everton) (2): 1905 v E; 1907 v W.
YOUNG, G. A. (Rangers) (53): 1947 v E, Ni, Bel, L; 1948 v E, Ni, Bel, Sw, Fr; 1949 v E, W, Ni, Fr; 1950 v E, W, Ni, Sw, Por, Fr; 1951 v E, W, Ni, A (2), D, Fr, Bel; 1952 v E, W, Ni, USA, D, Se; 1953 v W, E, Ni, Se; 1954 v Ni, W; 1955 v W, Ni, Por, Y; 1956 v Ni, W, E, A; 1957 v E, Ni, W, Y, Sp, Sw.
YOUNG, J. (Celtic) (1): 1906 v Ni.
YOUNGER, T. (Hibernian, Liverpool) (24): 1955 v Por, Y, A, H; 1956 v E, Ni, W, A: 1957 v E, Ni, W, Y, Sp (2), Sw, WG; 1958 v Ni, W, E, Sw, H, Pol, Y, Par.

WORLD CUP WINNERS

Year	Winners		Runners-up		Venue
1930	URUGUAY	4	Argentina	2	Uruguay
1934	ITALY	2	Czechoslovakia	1	Italy
	(after extra time)				
1938	ITALY	4	Hungary	2	France
1950	URUGUAY	2	Brazil	1	Brazil
1954	W GERMANY	3	Hungary	2	Switzerland
1958	BRAZIL	5	Sweden	2	Sweden
1962	BRAZIL	3	Czechosl'kia	1	Chile
1966	ENGLAND	4	W Germany	2	England
	(after extra time)				
1970	BRAZIL	4	Italy	1	Mexico
1974	W GERMANY	2	Holland	1	W Germany
1978	ARGENTINA	3	Holland	1	Argentina
	(after extra time)				
1982	ITALY	3	W Germany	1	Spain
1986	ARGENTINA	3	W Germany	2	Mexico
1990	W GERMANY	1	Argentina	0	Italy
1994	BRAZIL	0	Italy	0	America
	(after extra time, Brazil won 3-2 on penalties)				
1998	FRANCE	3	Brazil	0	France
2002	BRAZIL	2	Germany	0	Japan
2006	ITALY	1	France	1	Germany
	(after extra time, Italy won 5-3 on penalties)				
2010	SPAIN	1	Holland	0	South Africa
	(after extra time)				

EUROPEAN CHAMPIONSHIP WINNERS

Year	Winners		Runners-up		Venue
1960	RUSSIA	2	Yugoslavia	1	France
1964	SPAIN	2	Russia	1	Spain
1968	ITALY	2	Yugoslavia	0	Italy
	(aet in replay after 1-1 draw)				
1972	W GERMANY	3	Russia	0	Belgium
1976	CZECHOSLOVAKIA	2	W Germany	2	Yugoslavia
	(Czechoslovakia won 5-3 on penalties)				
1980	W GERMANY	2	Belgium	1	Italy
1984	FRANCE	2	Spain	0	France
1988	HOLLAND	2	Russia	0	West Germany
1992	DENMARK	2	Germany	0	Sweden
1996	GERMANY	2	Czech Rep	1	England
	(1-1 full time. Germany scored Golden Goal in extra time)				
2000	FRANCE	2	Italy	1	Holland
	(1-1 full time. France scored Golden Goal in extra time)				
2004	GREECE	1	Portugal	0	Portugal
2008	SPAIN	1	Germany	0	Austria
2012	SPAIN	4	Italy	0	Ukraine

EUROPEAN SUPER CUP

Year	Home		Away	
1972	AJAX	3	Rangers	2
	Rangers	1	AJAX	3
1973	AC Milan	0	AJAX	1
	AJAX	6	AC Milan	0
	1974 – Not contested			
1975	Bayern Munich	0	DYNAMO KIEV	1
	DYNAMO KIEV	2	Bayern Munich	0

Year	Team	Score	Team	Score
1976	Bayern Munich	2	ANDERLECHT	1
	ANDERLECHT	4	Bayern Munich	1
1977	Hamburg	1	LIVERPOOL	1
	LIVERPOOL	6	Hamburg	0
1978	ANDERLECHT	3	Liverpool	1
	Liverpool	2	ANDERLECHT	1
1979	NOTTS FOREST	1	Barcelona	0
	Barcelona	1	NOTTS FOREST	1
1980	Nottingham Forest	2	VALENCIA	1
	VALENCIA	1	Nottingham Forest	0
	1981 – Not contested			
1982	Barcelona	1	ASTON VILLA	0
	ASTON VILLA	3	Barcelona	0
1983	Hamburg	0	ABERDEEN	0
	ABERDEEN	2	Hamburg	0
1984	JUVENTUS	2	Liverpool	0
1985	Juventus v Everton not played due to Uefa ban on English clubs			
1986	ST BUCHREST	1	Dynamo Kiev	0
1987	Ajax	0	FC PORTO	1
	FCPORTO	1	Ajax	0
1988	MECHELEN	3	PSV Eindhoven	0
	PSV Eindhoven	1	MECHELEN	0
1989	Barcelona	1	AC MILAN	1
	AC MILAN	1	Barcelona	0
1990	Sampdoria	1	AC MILAN	1
	AC MILAN	2	Sampdoria	0
1991	MANCHESTER UTD	1	Red Star Belgrade	0
1992	Werder Bremen	1	BARCELONA	1
	BARCELONA	2	Werder Bremen	1
1993	PARMA	0	AC Milan	1
	AC Milan	0	PARMA	2
	(aet, 90mins 0-1, agg.1-2 for Parma)			
1994	Arsenal	0	AC MILAN	0
	AC MILAN	2	Arsenal	0
1995	Real Zaragoza	1	AJAX	1
	AJAX	4	Real Zaragoza	0
1996	Paris St Germain	0	JUVENTUS	1
	JUVENTUS	6	Paris St Germain	1
1997	BARCELONA	0	Borussia Dortmund	0
	Borussia Dortmund	1	BARCELONA	1
1998	Real Madrid	0	CHELSEA	1
1999	LAZIO	1	Manchester United	0
2000	GALATASARAY	2	Real Madrid	1
	(1-1 full time. Galatasaray scored golden goal in extra time)			
2001	LIVERPOOL	3	Bayern Munich	2
2002	REAL MADRID	3	Feyenoord	1
2003	AC MILAN	1	FC Porto	0
2004	Porto	1	VALENCIA	2
2005	LIVERPOOL	3	CSKA Moscow	1
	(aet, 90mins 1-1)			
2006	SEVILLA	3	Barcelona	0
2007	AC MILAN	3	Sevilla	1
2008	Manchester Utd	1	ZENIT	2
2009	BARCELONA	1	Shakhtar Donetsk	0
	(after extra time)			
2010	Inter Milan	0	ATLETICO MADRID	2
2011	BARCELONA	2	Porto	0
2012	ATLETICO MADRID	4	Chelsea	1

EUROPEAN CUP FINALS

Year	Winners		Runners-up	
1956	REAL MADRID	4	Rheims	3
	(Paris, 38,000)			
1957	REAL MADRID	2	Fiorentina	0
	(Madrid, 124,000)			
1958	REAL MADRID	3	AC Milan	2
	After extra time (Brussels, 67,000)			
1959	REAL MADRID	2	Rheims	0
	(Stuttgart, 80,000)			
1960	REAL MADRID	7	Eintracht	3
	(Glasgow, 127,261)			
1961	BENFICA	3	Barcelona	2
	(Berne, 28,000)			
1962	BENFICA	5	Real Madrid	3
	(Amsterdam, 65,000)			
1963	AC MILAN	2	Benfica	1
	(Wembley, 45,000)			
1964	INTER MILAN	3	Real Madrid	1
	(Vienna, 74,000)			
1965	INTER MILAN	1	Benfica	0
	(Milan, 80,000)			
1966	REAL MADRID	2	Partisan Belgrade	1
	(Brussels, 55,000)			
1967	CELTIC	2	Inter Milan	1
	(Lisbon, 56,000)			
1968	MAN UNITED	4	Benfica	1
	(Wembley, 100,000)			
1969	AC MILAN	4	Ajax	1
	(Madrid, 50,000)			
1970	FEYENOORD	2	Celtic	1
	(Milan, 50,000)			
1971	AJAX	2	Panathinaikos	0
	(Wembey, 90,000)			
1972	AJAX	2	Inter Milan	0
	(Rotterdam, 67,000)			
1973	AJAX	1	Juventus	0
	(Belgrade, 93,500)			
1974	BAYERN MUNICH	4	Atletico Madrid	0
	(Brussels, 65,000) (after 1-1 draw)			
1975	BAYERN MUNICH	2	Leeds	0
	(Paris, 50,000)			
1976	BAYERN MUNICH	1	St Etienne	0
	(Glasgow, 54,864)			

FORMER Scotland defender Graham Alexander keeps a close eye on French star Franck Ribery

EUROPEAN CUP FINALS (continued)

1977 LIVERPOOL.............3 Borussia MG 1
(Rome, 57,000)
1978 LIVERPOOL............1 Bruges......................... 0
(Wembley, 92,000)
1979 NOTTS FOREST......1 Malmo 0
(Munich, 57,500)
1980 NOTTS FOREST......1 Hamburg 0
(Madrid, 50,000)
1981 LIVERPOOL............1 Real Madrid................. 0
(Paris, 48,360)
1982 ASTON VILLA..........1 Bayern Munich............ 0
(Rotterdam, 46,000)
1983 HAMBURG ....1 Juventus...................... 0
(Athens, 75,000)
1984 LIVERPOOL............1 Roma........................... 1
(Rome, 69,693)
Liverpool won 4-2 on penalties
1985 JUVENTUS ....1 Liverpool 0
(Brussels, 58,000)
1986 S BUCHAREST ....0 Barcelona.................... 0
Steaua Bucharest won 2-0 on penalties (Seville, 70,000)
1987 PORTO ....2 Bayern Munich............ 1
(Vienna, 59,000)
1988 PSV.........................0 Benfica 0
(Stuttgart, 70,000)
PSV Eindhoven won 6-5 on penalties
1989 AC MILAN ....4 Steau Bucharest.......... 0
(Barcelona, 97,000)
1990 AC MILAN ....1 Benfica 0
(Vienna, 57,500)
1991 R.S. BELGRADE......0 Marseille..................... 0
(Bari, 56,000)
Red Star won 5-3 on penalties

1992 BARCELONA..........1 Sampdoria..................0
After extra time
(Wembley, 70,000)
1993 MARSEILLE............1 AC Milan.....................0
(Munich, 65,000)
1994 AC MILAN ....4 Barcelona...................0
(Athens, 75,000)
1995 AJAX.......................1 AC Milan.......................0
(Vienna, 49,000)
1996 JUVENTUS.............1 Ajax 1
(Rome, 67,000)
(1-1 full time. Juventus won 4-2 on penalties)
1997 B DORTMUND........3 Juventus.......................1
(Munich, 55,500)
1998 REAL MADRID ....1 Juventus.......................0
(Amsterdam, 45,000)
1999 MANCHESTER UTD2 Bayern Munich.............1
(Barcelona, 90,000)
2000 REAL MADRID ....3 Valencia........................0
(Paris, 73,000)
2001 BAYERN MUNICH...1 Valencia........................1
(1-1 full-time, Bayern won 5-4 on penalties)
(Milan, 80,000)
2002 REAL MADRID ....2 Bayer Leverkusen 1
(Glasgow, 52,000)
2003 AC MILAN ....0 Juventus.......................0
(0-0 after extra time. AC Milan won 3-2 on penalties)
(Manchester, 63,000)
2004 PORTO ....3 Monaco 0
(Gelsenkirchen, 52,000)
2005 LIVERPOOL............3 AC Milan.......................3
(3-3 after extra time, Liverpool won 3-2 on penalties)
(Istanbul, 65,000)
2006 BARCELONA..........2 Arsenal 1
(Paris, 79,500)
2007 AC MILAN ....2 Liverpool 1
(Athens, 74,000)
2008 MANCHESTER UTD...1 Chelsea 1
(1-1 full-time, Manchester Utd won 6-5 on penalties)
(Moscow, 69,552)
2009 BARCELONA..........2 Manchester Utd 0
(Rome, 72,700)
2010 INTER MILAN.........2 Bayern Munich.............0
(Madrid, 80,100)
2011 BARCELONA..........3 Manchester Utd 1
(Wembley, 87,695)
2012 CHELSEA................1 Bayern Munich.............1
(1-1 full-time, Chelsea won 4-3 on penalties)
(Munich, 69,901)
2013 BAYERN MUNICH...2 B Dortmund.................1
(Wembley, 86,298)

EUROPEAN CUP-WINNERS' CUP FINALS

1961 Rangers..................... 0 FIORENTINA......................2
(Ibrox, 80,000)
FIORENTINA............. 2 Rangers.............................1
(Florence, 50,000)
Aggregate 4-1

1962 ATLETICO MADRID... 1 Fiorentina...........................1
(Glasgow, 27,389)
ATLETICO MADRID... 3 Fiorentina...........................0
(Stuttgart, 45,000)

1963 SPURS...................... 5 Atletico Madrid.................1
(Rotterdam, 25,000)

1964 SPORTING LISBON.. 1 MTK Budapest...................0
(Antwerp, 18,000)
After 3-3 draw in Brussels

1965 WEST HAM............... 2 Munich 1860......................0
(Wembley, 100,000)

1966 BOR. DORTMUND.... 2 Liverpool...........................1
(Hampden, 41,657)

1967 BAYERN MUNICH .... 1 Rangers.............................0
(Nuremberg, 69,480 aet)

1968 AC MILAN................. 2 S.V. Hamburg.....................0
(Rotterdam, 60,000)

1969 S BRATISLAVIA......... 3 Barcelona..........................2
(Basle, 40,000)

1970 MANCHESTER CITY. 2 Gornik...............................1
(Vienna, 10,000)

1971 CHELSEA.................. 2 Real Madrid.......................1
(Athens, 24,000, after 1-1 draw)

1972 RANGERS................. 3 Moscow Dynamo...............2
(Barcelona, 35,000)

1973 AC MILAN................. 1 Leeds United.....................0
(Salonika, 45,000)

1974 AC MAGDEBURG..... 2 AC Milan............................0
(Rotterdam, 5,000)

1975 DYNAMO KIEV.......... 3 Ferencvaros.......................0
(Basle, 13,000)

1976 ANDERLECHT........... 4 West Ham.........................2
(Brussels, 58,000)

1977 SV HAMBURG........... 2 Anderlecht.........................0
(Amsterdam, 65,000)

1978 ANDERLECHT........... 4 Austria Wein.......................0
(Paris, 48,679)

1979 BARCELONA..............4 Fortuna Dusseldorf 3
(Basel, 58,000)
1980 VALENCIA ....0 Arsenal 0
(Brussels, 40,000, Valencia won 5-4 on penalties)
1981 DYNAMO TBILISI ....2 Carl Zeiss Jena 1
(Dusseldorf, 9,000)
1982 BARCELONA..............2 Standard Liege 1
(Barcelona, 100,000)
1983 ABERDEEN ....2 Real Madrid 1
(Gothenburg, 17,804)
1984 JUVENTUS ....2 FC Porto 1
(Basle, 60,000)
1985 EVERTON ....3 Rapid Vienna......................1
(Rotterdam, 30,000)
1986 DYNAMO KIEV ....3 Atletico Madrid ....0.
(Lyon, 39,300)
1987 AJAX...........................1 Lokomotiv Leipzig..............0
(Athens, 35,000)
1988 KV MECHELEN ....1 Ajax 0
(Strasbourg, 39,446)
1989 BARCELONA..............2 Sampdoria 0
(Berne, 45,000)
1990 SAMPDORIA ....2 Anderlecht..........................0
(Gothenburg, 20,103)
1991 MANCHESTER UTD...2 Barcelona...........................1
(Rotterdam, 50,000)
1992 WERDER BREMEN ....2 Monaco 0
(Lisbon, 50,000)
1993 Antwerp ....1 PARMA...............................3
(Wembley, 50,000)
1994 Parma ....0 ARSENAL...........................1
(Copenhagen, 33,765)
1995 Arsenal ....1 REAL ZARAGOZA..............2
(aet, 90 minutes 1-1) (Paris, 42,000)
1996 PARIS ST GERMAIN ..1 Rapid Vienna......................0
(Brussels, 50,000)
1997 BARCELONA..............1 Paris St Germain................0
(Rotterdam, 40,000)
1998 CHELSEA ....1 VfB Stuttgart 0
(Stockholm, 30, 216)
1999 LAZIO ....2 Real Mallorca 1
(Villa Park, 30,000)

EUROPA LEAGUE FINALS

(FORMERLY FAIRS CITIES CUP, UEFA CUP)

Year	Team	Score	Team	Score
1958	London	2	BARCELONA	2
	BARCELONA	6	London	0
	(agg: 8-2)			
1960	Birmingham	0	BARCELONA	0
	BARCELONA	4	Birmingham	1
	(agg: 4-1)			
1961	Birmingham	2	ROMA	2
	ROMA	2	Birmingham	0
	(agg: 4-2)			
1962	VALENCIA	6	Barcelona	2
	Barcelona	1	VALENCIA	1
	(agg 7-3)			
1963	Dynamo Zagreb	1	VALENCIA	2
	VALENCIA	2	Dynamo Zagreb	0
	(agg: 4-1)			
1964	REAL ZARAGOZA	2	Valencia	1
	(Barcelona)			
1965	FERENCVAROS	1	Juventus	0
	(Turin)			
1966	BARCELONA	0	Real Zaragoza	1
	Real Zaragoza	2	BARCELONA	4
	(agg: 4-3)			
1967	DINAMO ZAGREB	2	Leeds United	0
	Leeds United	0	DINAMO ZAGREB	0
	(agg: 2-0)			
1968	LEEDS UNITED	1	Ferencvaros	0
	Ferencvaros	0	LEEDS UNITED	0
	(agg: 1-0)			
1969	NEWCASTLE UTD	3	Ujpest Dozsa	0
	Ujpest Dozsa	2	NEWCASTLE UTD	3
	(agg: 6-2)			
1970	Anderlecht	3	ARSENAL	1
	ARSENAL	3	Anderlecht	0
	(agg: 4-3)			
1971	Juventus	2	LEEDS UNITED	2
	LEEDS UNITED	1	Juventus	1
	(agg: 3-3) *Leeds won on away goals*			
1972	Wolves	1	TOTTENHAM	2
	TOTTENHAM	1	Wolves	1
	(agg: 3-2)			
1973	LIVERPOOL	3	Borussia M	0
	Borussia M	2	LIVERPOOL	0
	(agg: 3-2)			

Year	First leg		Second leg	
1974	Tottenham Hostpur	2	FEYENOORD	2
	FEYENOORD	2	Tottenham Hotspur	0
	(agg: 4-2)			
1975	BORUSSIA M	0	Twente	0
	Twente	1	BORUSSIA M	5
	(agg: 5-1)			
1976	LIVERPOOL	3	FC Bruges	2
	Bruges	1	LIVERPOOL	1
	(agg 4-3)			
1977	JUVENTUS	1	Athletic Bilbao	0
	Athletic Bilbao	2	JUVENTUS	1
	(agg: 2-2. Juventus won on away goals)			
1978	Bastia	0	PSV EINDHOVEN	0
	PSV EINDHOVEN	3	Bastia	0
	(agg: 3-0)			
1979	Red Star Belgrade	1	BORUSSIA M	1
	BORUSSIA M	1	Red Star Belgrade	0
	(agg: 2-1)			
1980	Borussia M	3	EINTRACHT	2
	EINTRACHT	1	Borussia M	0
	(agg: 3-3. Eintracht won on away goals)			
1981	IPSWICH	3	AZ 67	0
	AZ 67	4	IPSWICH	2
	(agg: 5-4)			
1982	GOTHENBURG	1	Hamburg	0
	Hamburg	0	GOTHENBURG	3
	(agg: 4-0)			
1983	ANDERLECHT	1	Benfica	0
	Benfica	1	ANDERLECHT	1
	(agg: 2-1)			
1984	Anderlecht	1	TOTTENHAM	1
	TOTTENHAM	1	Anderlecht	1
	(agg: 2-2. Tottenham won 4-3 on penalties)			
1985	Videoton	0	REAL MADRID	3
	REAL MADRID	0	Videoton	1
	(agg: 3-1)			
1986	REAL MADRID	5	Cologne	1
	Cologne	2	REAL MADRID	0
	(agg: 5-3)			
1987	GOTHENBURG	1	Dundee United	0
	Dundee United	1	GOTHENBURG	1
	(agg: 2-1)			
1988	Espanyol	3	BAYER LEVERKUSEN	0
	BAYER LEVERKUSEN	3	Espanyol	0
	(agg: 3-3. Leverkusen won 3-2 on penalties)			
1989	NAPOLI	2	Stuttgart	1
	Stuttgart	3	NAPOLI	3
	(agg: 5-4)			

Year	First leg / Final		Second leg	
1990	JUVENTUS	3	Fiorentina	1
	Fiorentina	0	JUVENTUS	0
	(agg: 3-1)			
1991	INTER MILAN	2	Roma	0
	Roma	1	INTER MILAN	0
	(agg: 2-1)			
1992	Torino	2	AJAX	2
	AJAX	0	Torino	0
	(agg: 2-2. Ajax win on away goals rule)			
1993	Borussia Dortmund	1	JUVENTUS	3
	JUVENTUS	3	Borussia Dortmund	0
	(agg: 6-1)			
1994	Salzburg	0	INTER MILAN	1
	INTER MILAN	1	Salzburg	0
	(agg: 2-0)			
1995	PARMA	1	Juventus	0
	Juventus	1	PARMA	1
	(agg: 2-1)			
1996	BAYERN MUNICH	2	Bordeaux	0
	Bordeaux	1	BAYERN MUNICH	3
	(agg: 5-1)			
1997	Schalke	1	INTER MILAN	0
	INTER MILAN	1	Schalke	0
	(agg: 1-1. Schalke win 4-1 on penalties)			
1998	INTER MILAN	3	Lazio	0
	(Paris)			
1999	PARMA	3	Marseille	0
	(Moscow)			
2000	GALATASARAY	0	Arsenal	0
	(Galatasaray won 4-1 on penalties)			
	(Copenhagen)			
2001	LIVERPOOL	5	Alaves	4
	(4-4 full-time. Liverpool win with golden goal)			
	(Dortmund)			
2002	Borussia Dortmund	2	FEYENOORD	3
	(Rotterdam)			
2003	Celtic	2	PORTO	3
	(2-2 after 90 mins.)			
	(Seville)			
2004	VALENCIA	2	Marseille	0
	(Gothenburg)			
2005	Sporting Lisbon	1	CSKA MOSCOW	3
	(Lisbon)			
2006	Middlesbrough	0	SEVILLA	4
	(Eindhoven)			
2007	SEVILLA	1	Espanyol	1
	(aet 2-2, Sevilla win 3-1 on pens)			
	(Glasgow)			
2008	ZENIT	2	Rangers	0
	(Manchester)			
2009	SHAKHTAR	2	Werder Bremen	1
	(1-1 after 90 mins.)			
	(Istanbul)			
2010	ATLETICO MADRID	2	Fulham	1
	(1-1 after 90 mins.)			
	(Hamburg)			
2011	PORTO	1	Braga	0
	(Dublin)			
2012	ATLETICO MADRID	3	Athletic Bilbao	0
	(Bucharest)			
2013	Benfica	1	CHELSEA	2
	(Amsterdam)			

GAMES TO REMEMBER

1967 England.................... 2 SCOTLAND....................... 3
(Home Internationals, Wembley, April 15. Att: 100,000)
SCOTLAND: Simpson, Gemmell, McCreadie, Greig, McKinnon, Baxter, Wallace, Bremner, McCalliog, Law, Lennox. Scorers: Law, Lennox, McCalliog.
ENGLAND: Banks, Cohen, Wilson, Stiles, J Charlton, Moore, Ball, Greaves, R Charlton, Hurst, Peters. Scorers: J. Charlton, Hurst.

1967 CELTIC..................... 2 Inter Milan......................... 1
(European Cup Final, Lisbon, May 25. Attendance 56,000)
CELTIC: Simpson, Craig, Gemmell, Murdoch, McNeill, Clark, Johnstone, Wallace, Chalmers, Auld, Lennox. Scorers: Gemmell (63), Chalmers (85).
INTER MILAN: Sarti, Burgnich, Facchetti, Bedin, Guarneri, Picchi, Domenghini, Cappellini, Mazzola, Bicicli, Corso. Scorer: Mazzola (7 pen).

1972 RANGERS................ 3 Moscow Dynamo............. 2
(Cup-Winners' Cup Final, Barcelona, May 24. Att: 35,000)
RANGERS: McCloy, Jardine, Mathieson, Greig, D Johnstone, Smith, McLean, Conn, Stein, MacDonald, W Johnston. Scorers: Stein (24), Johnston (40, 49).
MOSCOW DYNAMO: Pilgui, Basalev, Dolmatov, Zykov, Dobbonosov, (Gerschkovitch), Zhukov, Baidatchini, Jakubik (Eschtrekov), Sabo, Makovikov, Evryuzhikbin. Scorers: Eschtrekov (55) Makovikov (87).

1978 Holland..................... 2 SCOTLAND....................... 3
(World Cup finals, Mendoza, June 11. Att: 35,130)
HOLLAND: Jongbloed, Suurbier, Krol, Rijsbergen (Wildschut), Poor tvleit, W van de Kerkhof, Neeskens (Boskamp, Jansen, R van de Ker khof, Rep, Resenbrink. Scorers: Resenbrink (34pen), Rep (71).
SCOTLAND: Rough, Donachie, Buchan, Rioch, Dalglish, Jorda n, Hartford, Kennedy, Forsyth, Gemmill, Souness. Scorers: Dalglish (43), Gemmill (47pen, 68).

1983 ABERDEEN............. 2 Real Madrid...................... 1
(Cup-Winners' Cup Final, Gothenburg, May 11. Att: 17,804)
ABERDEEN: Leighton, Rougvie, McMaster, Cooper, McLeish, Miller, Strachan, Simpson, McGhee, Black (Hewitt), Weir. Subs: Kennedy, Gunn, Watson, Hewitt, Angus. Scorers: Black (7), Hewitt (112).
REAL MADRID: Agustin, Jan jose, Camacho, Metgod, Bonet, Gallego, Jaunito, Angel, Santillana, Stielike, Isidro. Scorer: Juanito (14 pen).

2007 France...................... 0 SCOTLAND....................... 1
(EURO 2008 Qualifier, Paris, September 12. Att: 42,000)
FRANCE: Landreau, Lassana Diarra, Thuram, Escude, Abidal (Benz ema), Ribery, Vieira (Nasri), Makelele, Malouda, Trezeguet, Anelka.
SCOTLAND: Gordon, Hutton, McManus, Weir, Alexander, McCulloch, Ferguson, Fletcher (Pearson), Brown, Hartley, McFadden (O'Connor). Scorer: McFadden (64).

SCOTTISH CLUBS IN EUROPE
A COMPLETE HISTORY

Abbreviations EC (European Champions Cup), ECWC (European Cup-Winners' Cup), FC (Fairs Cities Cup) UEFA (Uefa Cup) w (won) l (lost) p (preliminary) q (qualifying round)

ABERDEEN

Opponents	Venue	Res	Scorers	Rnd
		1967-68 ECWC		
KR Reykjavic (Iceland)	H	W10-1	Munro 3, Storrie 2 Smith 2, McMillan, Petersen,Taylor	1
	A	W4-1	Storrie 2 Buchan, Munro	
Standard Liege	A	L0-3		2
(Belgium)	H	W2-0	Munro, Melrose	
		1968-69 FC		
Slavia Sofia	A	D0-0		1
(Bulgaria)	H	W2-0	Robb, Taylor	
Real Zaragossa	H	W2-1	Forrest, Smith	2
(Spain)	A	L0-3		
		1970-71 ECWC		
Honved	H	W3-1	Graham, Harper, S Murray	1
(Hungary)	A	L1-3	S Murray	
		1971-72 UEFA		
Celta Vigo	A	W2-0	Harper, o.g.	1
(Spain)	H	W1-0	Harper	
Juventus	A	L0-2		2
(Italy)	H	D1-1	Harper	
		1972-73 UEFA		
Borussia Moench.	H	L2-3	Harper, Jarvie	1
(West Germany)	A	L3-6	Harper 2, Jarvie	
		1973-74 UEFA		
Finn Harps (Rep of Ireland)	H	W4-1	R Miller, Jarvie 2, Graham	1
	A	W3-1	Robb, Graham, R Miller	
Tottenham H	H	D1-1	Hermiston pen	2
(England)	A	L1-4	Jarvie	
		1977-78 UEFA		
RWD Molenbeek	A	D0-0		1
(Belgium)	H	L1-2	Jarvie	
		1978-79 ECWC		
Marek Stanke	A	L2-3	Jarvie, Harper	1
(Bulgaria)	H	W3-0	Strachan, Jarvie, Harper	
Fortuna Dusseldorf	A	L0-3		2
(West Germany)	H	W2-0	McLelland, Jarvie	
		1979-80 UEFA		
Eintracht Frankfurt	H	D1-1	Harper	1
(West Germany)	A	L0-1		
		1980-81 EC		
Austria Vienna	H	W1-0	McGhee	1
(Austria)	A	D0-0		
Liverpool	H	L0-1		2
(England)	A	L0-4		

Opponents	Venue	Res	Scorers	Rnd
		1981-82 UEFA		
Ipswich Town	A	D1-1	Hewitt	1
(England)	H	W3-1	Strachan, pen, Weir 2	
Arges Pitesti	H	W3-0	Strachan, Weir, Hewitt	2
(Romania)	A	D2-2	Strachan, pen,Hewitt	
SV Hamburg	H	W3-2	Black, Watson, Hewitt	3
(West Germany)	A	L1-3	McGhee	
		1982-83 ECWC		
Sion	H	W7-0	Black 2, Strachan,	P
(Switzerland)			Hewitt, Simpson,	
			McGhee, Kennedy	
	A	W4-1	Hewitt, Miller, McGhee 2	
Dinamo Tirana	H	W1-0	Hewitt	1
(Albania)	A	D0-0		
Lech Poznan	H	W2-0	McGhee, Weir	2
(Poland)	A	W1-0	Bell	
Bayern Munich	A	D0-0		QF
(West Germany)	H	W3-2	Simpson, McLeish, Hewitt	
Waterschei	H	W5-1	Black, Simpson	SF
(Belgium)			McGhee 2, Weir	
	A	L0-1		
Real Madrid	N	W2-1	Black, Hewitt	F
(Spain)				
		1983-84 (European Super Cup)		
Hamburg	A	D0-0		
(West Germany)	H	W2-0	Simpson, McGhee	
		1983-84 ECWC		
Akranes	A	W2-1	McGhee 2	1
(Iceland)	H	D1-1	Strachan, pen	
Beveren	A	D0-0		2
(Belgium)	H	W4-1	Strachan 2, 1 pen,	
			Simpson, Weir	
Ujpest Dozsa	A	L0-2		QF
(Hungary)	H	W3-0	McGhee 3	
Porto	A	L0-1		SF
(Portugal)	H	L0-1		
		1984-85 EC		
Dynamo Berlin	H	W2-1	Black 2	1
(East Germany)	A	L1-2	Angus	
		1985-86 EC		
Akranes	A	W3-1	Black, Hewitt, Stark	1
(Iceland)	H	W4-1	Simpson, Hewitt	
			Gray, Falconer	
Servette	A	D0-0		2
(Switzerland)	H	W1-0	McDougall	
IFK Gothenburg	H	D2-2	J Miller, Hewitt	QF
(Sweden)	A	D0-0		
		1986-87 ECWC		
Sion	H	W2-1	Bett (pen), Wright	1
(Switzerland)	A	L0-3		
		1987-88 UEFA		
Bohemians	A	D0-0		1
(Rep of Ireland)	H	W1-0	Bett pen	
Feyenoord	H	W2-1	Falconer, J Miller	2
(Holland)	A	L0-1		

Opponents	Venue	Res	Scorers	Rnd
		1988-89 UEFA		
Dynamo Dresden	H	D0-0		1
(East Germany)	A	L0-2		
		1989-90 UEFA		
Rapid Vienna	H	W2-1	C Robertson, Grant	1
(Austria)	A	L0-1		
		1990-91 ECWC		
Salamis	A	W2-0	Mason, Gillhaus	1
(Cyprus)	H	W3-0	C Robertson, Gillhaus, Jess	
Legia Warsaw	H	D0-0		2
(Poland)	A	L0-1		
		1991-92 UEFA		
BK Copenhagen	H	L0-1		1
(Denmark)	A	L0-2		
		1993-94 ECWC		
Valur	A	W3-0	Shearer, Jess 2	1
(Iceland)	H	W4-0	Jess 2, Miller, Irvine	
Torino	A	L2-3	Paatelainen, Jess	
(Italy)	H	L1-3	Richardson	
		1994-95 UEFA		
Skonto Riga	A	D0-0		P
(Latvia)	H	D1-1	Kane	
		1996-97 UEFA		
Vilnius	A	W4-1	Dodds 2, Glass, Shearer	Q
(Lithuania)	H	L1-3	Irvine	
Barry Town	H	W3-1	Windass, Glass, Young	1
(Wales)	A	D3-3	Dodds 2, Rowson	
Brondby	H	L0-2		2
(Denmark)	A	D0-0		
		2000-01 UEFA		
Bohemians	H	L1-2	Winters	Q
(Rep of Ireland)	A	W1-0	Morrison og	
		2002-2003 UEFA		
Nistru Otaci	H	W1-0	Mackie	Q
(Moldova)	A	D0-0		
Hertha Berlin	H	D0-0		1
(Germany)	A	L0-1		
		2007-08 UEFA CUP		
Dnipro	H	D0-0		1
(Ukraine)	A	D1-1	Mackie	
		GROUP STAGE		
Panai'kos (Greece)	A	L0-3		
L Moscow (Russia)	H	D1-1	Diamond	
A Madrid (Spain)	A	L0-2		
FC Cop'hagen (Den)	H	W4-0	Smith, Smith, o.g, Foster	
		LAST 32		
Bayern Munich	H	D2-2	Walker, Aluko	
(Germany)	A	L1-5	Lovell	
		2009-10 UEFA EUROPA LEAGUE		
Sigma Olomouc	H	L1-5	Mulgrew	Play-off
(Czech Rep)	A	L0-3		

AIRDRIE

1992-93 ECWC

Opponents	Venue	Res	Scorers	Rnd
Sparta Prague	H	L0-1		1
(Czechoslovakia)	A	L1-2	Black	

CELTIC

Opponents	Venue	Res	Scorers	Rnd
		1962-63 FC		
Valencia	A	L2-4	Carrol 2	1
(Spain)	H	D2-2	Crerand, o.g.	
		1963-64 ECWC		
Basle	A	W5-1	Divers, Hughes 3, Lennox	1
(Switzerland)	H	W5-0	Johnstone, Divers 2 Murdoch, Chalmers	
Dynamo Zagreb	H	W3-0	Chalmers 2, Hughes	2
(Yugoslavia)	A	L1-2	Murdoch	
Slovan Bratislava	H	W1-0	Murdoch pen	QF
(Czechoslovakia)	A	W1-0	Hughes	
MTK Budapest	H	W3-0	Johnstone, Chalmers 2	SF
(Hungary)	A	L0-4		
		1964-65 FC		
Leixoes	A	D1-1	Murdoch	1
(Portugal)	H	W3-0	Murdoch, pen, Chalmers	
Barcelona	A	L1-3	Hughes	2
(Spain)	H	D0-0		
		1965-66 ECWC		
Go Ahead	A	W6-0	Gallacher 2, Hughes Johnstone 2 Lennox	1
(Holland)				
	H	W1-0	McBride	
Aarhus	A	W1-0	McBride	2
(Denmark)	H	W2-0	McNeill, Johnstone	
Dynamo Kiev	H	W3-0	Gemmell, Murdoch 2	QF
(USSR)	A	D1-1	Gemmell	
Liverpool	H	W1-0	Lennox	SF
(England)	A	L0-2		
		1966-67 EC		
Zurich	H	W2-0	Gemmell, McBride	1
(Switzerland)	A	W3-0	Gemmell 2, 1 pen, McBride	
Nantes	A	W3-1	McBride, Lennox, Chalmers	2
(France)				
	H	W3-1	Johnstone, Lennox, Chalmers	
Vojvodina	A	L0-1		QF
(Yugoslavia)	H	W2-0	Chalmers, McNeill	
Dukla Prague	H	W3-1	Johnstone, Wallace, 2	SF
(Czechoslovakia)	A	D0-0		
Inter Milan	N	W2-1	Gemmell, Chalmers	F
(Italy)				
		1967-68 EC		
Dymano Kiev	H	L1-2	Lennox	1
(USSR)	A	D1-1	Lennox	
		1968-69 EC		
St Etienne	A	L0-2		1
(France)	H	W4-0	Gemmell pen, Craig Chalmers, McBride	
Red Star Belgrade	H	W5-1	Murdoch, Johnstone 2, Lennox, Wallace	2
(Yugoslavia)				
	A	D1-1	Wallace	
AC Milan	A	D0-0		QF
(Italy)	H	L0-1		

Opponents	Venue	Res	Scorers	Rn
		1969-70 EC		
Basle	A	D0-0		1
(Switzerland)	H	W2-0	Hood, Gemmell	
Benfica	H	W3-0	Gemmell, Wallace, Hood	2
(Portugal)	A	L0-3		
Fiorentina	H	W3-0	Auld, Wallace, o.g.	QF
(Italy)	A	L0-1		
Leeds United	A	W1-0	Connelly	SF
(England)	H	W2-1	Hughes, Murdoch	
Feyenoord	N	L1-2	Gemmell	F
(Holland)				
		1970-71 EC		
KPV Kokkola (Finland)	H	W9-0	Hood 3, Wilson 2, Hughes McNeill, Johnstone, Davidson	1
	A	W5-0	Wallace 2, Callaghan Davidson, Lennox	
Waterford (Rep of Ireland)	A	W7-0	Wallace 3, Murdoch 2 Macari 2	2
	H	W3-2	Hughes, Johnstone 2	
Ajax	A	L0-3		QF
(Holland)	H	W1-0	Johnstone	
		1971-72 EC		
BK 1903	A	L1-2	Macari	1
Copenhagen (Denmark)	H	W3-0	Wallace 2, Callaghan	
Sliema W (Malta)	H	W5-0	Gemmell, Macari 2 Hood, Brogan	2
	A	W2-1	Hood, Lennox	
Ujpest Dozsa	A	W2-1	Macari, o.g.	QF
(Hungary)	H	D1-1	Macari	
Inter Milan	A	D0-0		SF
(Italy)	H	D0-0	lost on penalties	
		1972-73 EC		
Rosenborg	H	W2-1	Macari, Deans	1
(Norway)	A	W3-1	Macari, Hood, Dalglish	
Ujpest Dozsa	H	W2-1	Dalglish 2	2
(Hungary)	A	L0-3		
		1973-74 EC		
Turku (Finland)	A	W6-1	Callaghan 2, Hood, Johnstone, Deans, Connelly, pen	1
	H	W3-0	Deans, Johnstone 2	
Vejle	H	D0-0		2
(Denmark)	A	W1-0	Lennox	
Basle	A	L2-3	Wilson, Dalglish	QF
(Switzerland)	H	W4-2	Dalglish, Deans, Callaghan, Murray	
Atletico Madrid	H	D0-0		SF
(Spain)	A	L0-2		
		1974-75 EC		
Olympiakos	H	D1-1	Wilson	1
(Greece)	A	L0-2		
		1975-76 ECWC		
Valur	A	W2-0	Wilson McDonald	1
(Iceland)	H	W7-0	Edvaldsson, Dalglish McCluskey, pen, Deans Hood 2, Callaghan	

Opponents	Venue	Res	Scorers	Rn
Boavista	A	D0-0		2
(Portugal)	H	W3-1	Dalglish, Edvaldsson, Deans	
Zwickau	H	D1-1	Dalglish	QF
(East Germany)	A	L0-1		
		1976-77 UEFA		
Wisla Krakow	H	D2-2	McDonald, Dalglish	1
(Poland)	A	L0-2		
		1977-78 EC		
Jeunesse D'Esch	H	W5-0	McDonald, Wilson, Craig 2, McLaughlin	1
(Luxembourg)	A	W6-1	Lennox 2, Glavin, Edvaldsson 2, Craig	
SW Innsbruck	H	W2-1	Craig, Burns	2
(Austria)	A	L0-3		
		1979-80 EC		
Partizan Tirana	A	L0-1		1
(Albania)	H	W4-1	McDonald, Aitken 2 Davidson	
Dundalk	H	W3-2	McDonald, Burns McCluskey	2
(Rep of Ireland)	A	D0-0		
Real Madrid	H	W2-0	McCluskey, Doyle	QF
(Spain)	A	L0-3		
		1980-81 ECWC		
Diosgyor	H	W6-0	McGarvey 2, Sullivan McCluskey 2, o.g.	P
(Hungary)	A	L1-2	Nicholas	
Timisorara	H	W2-1	Nicholas 2	1
(Romania)	A	L0-1	lost on away goals	
		1981-82 EC		
Juventus	H	W1-0	MacLeod	1
(Italy)	A	L0-2		
		1982-83 EC		
Ajax	H	D2-2	Nicholas, McGarvey	1
(Holland)	A	W2-1	Nicholas, McCluskey	
Real Sociedad	A	L0-2		2
(Spain)	H	W2-1	MacLeod 2	
		1983-84 UEFA		
Aarhus	H	1-0	Aitken	1
(Denmark)	A	W4-1	MacLeod, McGarvey, Aitken,Provan	
Sporting Lisbon	A	L0-2		2
(Portugal)	H	W5-0	Burns, McAdam, McClair MacLeod, McGarvey	
Notts Forest	A	D0-0		3
(England)	H	L1-2	MacLeod	
		1984-85 ECWC		
Gent	A	L0-1		1
(Belgium)	H	W3-0	McGarvey 2, McStay	
Rapid Vienna	A	L1-3	McClair	2
(Austria)	H	W3-0	McClair, MacLeod, Burns	
		(Uefa ordered match to be replayed)		
	N	L0-1		

Opponents	Venue	Res	Scorers	Rn
		1985-86 ECWC		
Atletico Madrid	A	D1-1	Johnston	1
(Spain)	H	L1-2	Aitken	
		1986-87 EC		
Shamrock Rov	A	W1-0	MacLeod	1
(Rep of Ireland)	H	W2-0	Johnston 2	
Dymano Kiev	H	D1-1	Johnston	2
(USSR)	A	L1-3	McGhee	
		1987-88 UEFA		
Bor Dortmund	H	W2-1	Walker, Whyte	1
(West Germany)	A	L0-2		
		1988-89 EC		
Honved	A	L0-1		1
(Hungary)	H	W4-0	Stark, Walker, McAvennie, McGhee	
Werder Bremen	H	L0-2		2
(West Germany)	A	D0-0		
		1989-90 ECWC		
Part Belgrade	A	L1-2	Galloway	1
(Yugoslavia)	H	W5-4	Dziekanowski 4 Walker	
		1991-92 UEFA		
Ekeren	H	W2-0	Nicholas 2, 1 pen	1
(Belgium)	A	D1-1	Galloway	
Neuchatel Xamax	A	L1-5	O'Neill	2
(Switzerland)	H	W1-0	Miller	
		1992-93 UEFA		
Cologne	A	L0-2		1
(Germany)	H	W3-0	McStay, Creaney, Collins	
Bor Dortmund	A	L0-1		2
(Germany)	H	L1-2	Creaney	
		1993-94 UEFA		
Young Boys	A	D0-0		1
(Switzerland)	H	W1-0	og	
Sporting Lisbon	H	W1-0	Creaney	2
(Portugal)	A	L0-2		
		1995-96 ECWC		
Dinamo Batumi	A	W3-2	Thom 2, Donnelly	1
(Georgia)	H	W4-0	Thom 2, Donnelly, Walker	
Paris St Germain	A	L0-1		2
(France)	H	L0-3		
		1996-97 UEFA		
Kosice	A	D0-0		Q
(Poland)	H	W1-0	Cadete	
Hamburg	H	L0-2		1
(Germany)	A	L0-2		
		1997-98 UEFA		
Inter Cable-Tel	A	W3-0	Thom pen, Johnson pen, Wieghorst	Q
(Wales)	H	W5-0	Thom pen, Jackson, Johnson, Hannah, Hay	
Tirol Innsbruck	A	L1-2	Stubbs	Q
(Austria)	H	W6-3	Donnelly 2, 1 pen, Thom Burley 2, Wieghorst	
Liverpool	H	D2-2	McNamara, Donnelly	1
(England)	A	D0-0		
		1998-99 EC		
St Patrick's	H	D0-0		P
(Rep of Ireland)	A	W2-0	Brattbakk, Larsson	

Opponents	Venue	Res	Scorers	Rn
Croatia Zagreb	H	W1-0	Jackson	P
(Croatia)	A	L0-3		
		UEFA		
Vitoria Guimareas	A	W2-1	Larsson, Donnelly	1
(Portugal)	H	W2-1	Stubbs, Larsson	
FC Zurich	H	D1-1	Brattbakk	2
(Switzerland)	A	L2-4	O'Donnell, Larsson	
		1999-2000 UEFA		
Cwmbran Town	A	W6-0	Berkovic, Larsson 2, Tebily, Viduka, Brattbakk	Q
(Wales)				
	H	W4-0	Brattbakk, Smith, Mjallby, Johnson	
Hapoel Tel Aviv	H	W2-0	Larsson 2	1
(Israel)	A	W1-0	Larsson	
Lyon	A	L0-1		2
(France)	H	L0-1		
		2000-2001 UEFA		
Jeunesse Esch	A	W4-0	Moravcik 2, Larsson, Petta	Q
(Luxembourg)	H	W7-0	Burchill 3, Berkovic 2, Riseth, Petrov	
HJK Helsinki	H	W2-0	Larsson 2	1
(Finland)	A	L1-2	Sutton	
Bordeaux	A	D1-1	Larsson pen	2
(France)	H	L1-2 (aet)	Moravcik	
		2001-2002 EC		
Ajax	A	W3-1	Petta, Agathe, Sutton	Q3
(Holland)	H	L0-1		
		FIRST GROUP STAGE		
Juventus	A	L2-3	Petrov, Larsson	
(Italy)				
Porto	H	W1-0	Larsson	
(Portugal)				
Rosenborg	H	W1-0	Thompson	
(Norway)				
Porto	A	L0-3		
Rosenborg	A	L0-2		
Juventus	H	W4-3	Valgaeren, Sutton 2, Larsson	
		UEFA		
Valencia	A	L0-1		3
(Spain)	H	W1-0	Larsson	
	(aet, Valencia won 5-4 on penalties)			
		2002-2003 EC		
FC Basel	H	W3-1	Larsson pen, Sutton, Sylla	Q3
(Switzerland)	A	L0-2		
		UEFA		
FK Suduva	H	W8-1	Larsson 3, Petrov, Sutton, Lambert, Hartson, Valgaeren	1
(Lithuania)				
	A	W2-0	Fernandez, Thompson	

Opponents	Venue	Res	Scorers	Rnd
Blackburn	H	W1-0	Larsson	2
(England)	A	W2-0	Larsson, Sutton	
Celta Vigo	H	W1-0	Larsson	3
(Spain)	A	L1-2	Hartson	
VfB Stuttgart	H	W3-1	Lambert, Maloney, Petrov	4
(Germany)	A	L2-3	Thompson, Sutton	
Liverpool	H	D1-1	Larsson	QF
(England)	A	W2-0	Thompson, Hartson	
Boavista	H	D1-1	Larsson	SF
(Portugal)	A	W1-0	Larsson	
Porto	N	L 2-3 (aet)	Larsson 2	F
		2003-2004 EC		
FBK Kaunas (Lithuania)	A	W4-0	Larsson, Sutton, Maloney, Miller	Q2
	H	W1-0	Gvildys (og)	
MTK Hungaria	A	W4-0	Larsson, Agathe, Petrov, Sutton	Q3
(Hungary)	H	W1-0	Sutton	
		GROUP STAGE		
Bayern Munich	A	L1-2	Thompson	
(Germany)	H	D0-0		
Lyon	H	W2-0	Miller, Sutton	
(France)	A	L2-3	Hartson, Sutton	
Anderlecht	A	L0-1		
(Belgium)	H	W3-1	Larsson, Miller, Sutton	
		UEFA		
Teplice	H	W3-0	Larsson 2, Sutton	3
(Czech Republic)	A	L0-1		
Barcelona	H	W1-0	Thompson	4
(Spain)	A	D0-0		
Villarreal	H	D1-1	Larsson	QF
(Spain)	A	L0-2		
		2004-05 EC		
		GROUP STAGE		
Barcelona	H	L1-3	Sutton	
(Spain)	A	D1-1	Hartson	
AC Milan	A	L1-3	Varga	
(Italy)	H	D0-0		
Shakhtar Dontesk	A	L0-3		
(Ukraine)	H	W1-0	Thompson	
		2005-2006 EC		
Artmedia Bratislava	A	L0-5		Q2
(Slovakia)	H	W4-0	Thompson pen, Hartson, McManus, Beattie	
		2006-2007 EC		
		GROUP STAGE		
Manchester Utd	H	W1-0	Nakamura	
(England)	A	L2-3	Vennegoor, Nakamura	
FC Copenhagen	H	W1-0	Miller	
(Denmark)	A	L1-3	Jarosik	
Benfica	H	W3-0	Miller 2, Pearson	
(Portugal)	A	L0-3		

Opponents	Venue	Res	Scorers	Rnd
		LAST 16		
AC Milan	H	D0-0		
(Italy)	A	D0-0		
		(AC Milan win 1-0 after extra-time)		
		2007-08 EC		
Spartak Moscow	A	D1-1	Hartley	Q2
(Russia)	H	D1-1	McDonald	
		GROUP STAGE		
Shakhtar Donetsk	A	L0-2		
(Ukraine)	H	W2-1	Jarosik, Donati	
AC Milan	H	W2-1	McManus, McDonald	
(Italy)	A	L0-1		
Benfica	A	L0-1		
(Portugal)	H	W1-0	McGeady	
		LAST 16		
Barcelona	H	L2-3	Vennegoor, Robson	
(Spain)	A	L0-1		
		2008-09 EC		
		GROUP STAGE		
Aalborg BK	H	D0-0		
(Denmark)	A	L1-2	Robson	
Villarreal	A	L0-1		
(Spain)	H	W2-0	Maloney, McGeady	
Manchester United	A	L0-3		
(England)	H	D1-1	McDonald	
		2009-10 EC		
Dinamo Moscow	H	L0-1		Q3
(Russia)	A	W2-0	McDonald, Samaras	
Arsenal	H	L0-2		Play-off
(England)	A	L1-3	Donati	
		UEFA Europa League		
		GROUP STAGE		
Hapoel Tel-Aviv	A	L1-2	Samaras	
(Israel)	H	W2-0	McDonald, Robson	
Rapid Vienna	H	D1-1	McDonald	
(Austria)	A	D3-3	Fortune 2, McGowan	
Hamburg	H	L0-1		
(Germany)	A	D0-0		
		2010-11 EC		
Braga	A	L0-3		Q3
(Portugal)	H	W2-1	Hooper, Juarez	
		UEFA Europa League		
		Play-off Round		
Utrecht	H	W2-0	Juarez, Samaras	
(Holland)	A	L0-4		

Opponents	Venue	Res	Scorers	Rnd
		2011-12 UEFA Europa League		
		Play-off Round		
FC Sion	H	D0-0		
(Switzerland)	A	DL1-3	Mulgrew	
(Celtic were awarded 3-0 wins in both legs after Sion were found guilty by UEFA of fielding five ineligible players over the two games)				
		GROUP STAGE		
Atletico Madrid	A	L0-2		
(Spain)	H	L0-1		
Udinese	H	D1-1	Ki	
(Italy)	A	D1-1	Hooper	
Rennes	A	D1-1	Ledley	
(France)	H	W3-1	Hooper, Stokes 2	
		2012-13 EC		
HJK Helsinki	H	W2-1	Hooper, Mulgrew	Q3
(Finland)	A	W2-0	Ledley, Samaras	
		Play-off Round		
Helsingborg	A	W2-0	Commons, Samaras	
(Sweden)	H	W2-0	Hooper, Wanyama	
		Group Stage		
Benfica	H	D0-0		
(Portugal)	A	L1-2	Samaras	
Spartak Moscow	A	W3-2	Hooper, Kombarov (og), Samaras	
(Russia)	H	W2-1	Hooper, Commons	
Barcelona	A	L1-2	Samaras	
(Spain)	H	W2-1	Wanyama, Watt	
		Round of 16		
Juventus	H	L0-3		
(Italy)	A	L0-2		

DUNDEE

Opponents	Venue	Res	Scorers	Rnd
		1962-63 EC		
FC Cologne	H	W8-1	Gilzean 3, Wishart, Smith	P
(West Germany)			Robertson, Penman, og	
	A	L0-4		
Sporting Lisbon	A	L0-1		1
(Portugal)	H	W4-1	Gilzean 3, Cousin	
Anderlecht	A	W4-1	Gilzean 2, Cousin, Smith	QF
(Belgium)	H	W2-1	Cousin, Smith	
AC Milan	A	L1-5	Cousin	SF
(Italy)	H	W1-0	Gilzean	
		1964-65 ECWC		
Bye				1
Real Zaragossa	H	D2-2	Murray, Houston	2
(Spain)	A	L1-2	Robertson	
		1967-68 FC		
DWS Amsterdam	A	L1-2	McLean	1
(Holland)	H	W3-0	Wilson, McLean 2, 1 pen	

Opponents	Venue	Res	Scorers	Rnd
FC Liege	H	W3-1	Stuart 2, Wilson	2
(Belgium)	A	W4-1	McLean 4	
		Bye in Round 3		
Zurich	H	W1-0	Easton	QF
(Switzerland)	A	W1-0	Wilson	
Leeds United	H	D1-1	Wilson	SF
(England)	A	L0-2		
		1971-72 UEFA		
Akademisk	H	W4-2	Bryce 2, Wallace, Lambie	1
(Denmark)	A	W1-0	Duncan	
Cologne	A	L1-2	Kinninmonth	2
(West Germany)	H	W4-2	Duncan 3, Wilson	
AC Milan	A	L0-3		3
(Italy)	H	W2-0	Wallace, Duncan	
		1973-74 UEFA		
Twente Ensch.	H	L1-3	Stewart	1
(Holland)	A	L2-4	Johnston, Scott	
		1974-75 UEFA		
RWD Molenbeek	A	L0-1		1
(Belgium)	H	L2-4	Duncan, Scott	
		2003-04 UEFA		
Vllaznia Shkoder	A	W2-0	Lovell, Novo	Q
(Albania)	H	W4-0	Novo 2, Sara, Rae	
Perugia	H	L1-2	Novo	1
(Italy)	A	L0-1		

DUNDEE UNITED

Opponents	Venue	Res	Scorers	Rnd
		1966-67 FC		
Bye				1
Barcelona	A	W2-1	Hainey, Seeman	2
(Spain)	H	W2-0	Mitchell, Hainey	
Juventus	A	L0-3		3
(Italy)	H	W1-0	Dossing	
		1969-70 FC		
Newcastle Utd	H	L1-2	Scott	1
(England)	A	L0-1		
		1970-71 FC		
Grasshoppers	H	W3-2	Reid I, Markland, Reid A	1
(Switzerland)	A	D0-0		
Sparta Prague	A	L1-3	Traynor	2
(Czechoslovakia)	H	W1-0	Gordon	
		1974-75 ECWC		
Jiul Petrosani	H	W3-0	Narey, Copland, Gardner	1
(Romania)	A	L0-2		
Bursaspor	H	D0-0		2
(Turkey)	A	L0-1		
		1975-76 UEFA		
Keflavik	A	W2-0	Narey 2	1
(Iceland)	H	W4-0	Hall 2, Hegarty, pen, Sturrock	
Porto	H	L1-2	Rennie	2
(Portugal)	A	D1-1	Hegarty	

Opponents	Venue	Res	Scorers	Rnd
		1977-78 UEFA		
KB Copenhagen	H	W1-0	Sturrock	1
(Denmark)	A	L0-3		
		1978-79 UEFA		
Standard Liege	A	L0-1		1
(Belgium)	H	D0-0		
		1979-80 UEFA		
Anderlecht	H	D0-0		1
(Belgium)	A	D1-1	Kopel	
Diosgyor	H	L0-1		2
(Hungary)	A	L1-3	Kopel	
		1980-81 UEFA		
Slask Wroclaw	A	D0-0		1
(Poland)	H	W7-2	Dodds 2, Pettigrew 3, Stark, Payne pen	
Lokeren	H	D1-1	Pettigrew	
(Belgium)	A	D0-0		
		1981-82 UEFA		
Monaco	A	W5-2	Bannon 2, 1 pen, Dodds 2, Kirkwood	1
(France)	H	L1-2	Milne	
Borussia M.	A	L0-2		2
(West Germany)	H	W5-0	Milne, Kirkwood, Hegarty, Sturrock, Bannon	
Winterslag	A	D0-0		3
(Belgium)	H	W5-0	Bannon, Narey, Hegarty Milne 2	
Radnicki Nis	H	W2-0	Narey, Dodds	QF
(Yugoslavia)	A	L0-3		
		1982-83 UEFA		
PSV Eindhoven	H	D1-1	Dodds	1
(Holland)	A	W2-0	Kirkwood, Hegarty	
Viking Stavanger	A	W3-1	Milne 2, Sturrock	2
(Norway)	H	D0-0		
Werder Bremen	H	W2-1	Milne, Narey	3
(West Germany)	A	D1-1	Hegarty	
Bohemians	A	L0-1		QF
(Czechoslovakia)	H	D0-0		
		1983-84 EC		
Hamrun Spartans	A	W3-0	Reilly, Bannon, Stark	1
(Malta)	H	W3-0	Milne, Kirkwood 2	
Standard Liege	A	D0-0		2
(Belgium)	H	W4-0	Milne 2, Hegarty, Dodds	
Rapid Vienna	A	L1-2	Stark	QF
(Austria)	H	W1-0	Dodds	
AS Roma	H	W2-0	Dodds, Stark	SF
(Italy)	A	L0-3		
		1984-85 UEFA		
AIK Stockholm	A	L0-1		1
(Sweden)	H	W3-0	Sturrock, Milne 2	

Opponents	Venue	Res	Scorers	Rnd
ASK Linz	A	W2-1	Kirkwood, Bannon pen	2
(Austria)	H	W5-1	Hegarty, Coyne 2, Gough Beaumont	
Manchester Utd	A	D2-2	Hegarty, Sturrock	3
(England)	H	L2-3	Dodds, Hegarty	
		1985-86 UEFA		
Bohemians	A	W5-2	Sturrock 3, Bannon 2	1
(Rep of Ireland)	H	D2-2	Milne, Redford	
Vardar Skopje	H	W2-0	Redford, Gough	2
(Yugoslavia)	A	D1-1	Hegarty	
Neuchatel Xamax	H	W2-1	Dodds, Redford	3
(Switzerland)	A	L1-3	Redford	
		1986-87 UEFA		
Lens	A	L0-1		1
(France)	H	W2-0	Milne, Coyne	
Uni. Craiova	H	W3-0	Redford 2, Clark	2
(Romania)	A	L0-1		
Hadjuk Split	H	W2-0	McInally, Clark	3
(Yugoslavia)	A	D0-0		
Barcelona	H	W1-0	Gallacher	QF
(Spain)	A	W2-1	Clark, Ferguson	
Borussia Moench.	H	D0-0		SF
(West Germany)	A	W2-0	Ferguson, Redford	
IFK Gothenburg	A	L0-1		F
(Sweden)	H	D1-1	Clark	
		1987-88 UEFA		
Coleraine	A	W1-0	Sturrock	1
(Northern Ireland)	H	W3-1	Gallacher, Sturrock, Clark	
Vitkovice	H	L1-2	Ferguson	2
(Czechoslovakia)	A	D1-1	og	
		1988-89 ECWC		
Floriana	A	D0-0		1
(Malta)	H	W1-0	Meade	
Din. Bucharest	H	L0-1		2
(Romania)	A	D1-1	Beaumont	
		1989-90 UEFA		
Glentoran	A	W3-1	Cleland, McInally, Hinds	1
(Northern Ireland)	H	W2-0	Clark, Gallacher	
Antwerp	A	L0-4		2
(Belgium)	H	W3-2	Paatelainen, O'Neill, Clark	
		1990-91 UEFA		
FH Hafnafjordur	A	W3-1	Jackson, Cleland, og	1
(Iceland)	H	D2-2	Connolly, og	
Arnhem	A	L0-1		2
(Holland)	H	L0-4		
		1993-94 UEFA		
Brondby	A	L0-2		1
(Denmark)	H	W3-1	McKinlay, Crabbe, Clark	

Opponents	Venue	Res	Scorers	Rnd
		1994-95 ECWC		
Tatran Presov	H	W3-2	Petric, Nixon, Hannah	1
(Slovakia)	A	L1-3	Nixon	
		1997-98 UEFA		
C E Principat	A	W8-0	Zetterlund, Winters 4, McSwegan 3	Q
(Andorra)	H	W9-0	Olofsson, Zetterlund, Winters 2, McLaren, McSwegan 3, Thompson	
Trabzonspor	A	L0-1		Q
(Turkey)	H	D1-1	McLaren	
		2005-06 UEFA		
MyPa 47	A	D0-0		Q2
(Finland)	H	D2-2	Kerr, Samuel	
		2010-11 UEFA Europa League Play-off Round		
AEK Athens	H	L0-1		
(Greece)	N	D1-1	Daly	
(Matched moved to Panionios due to pitch problems)				
		2011-12 UEFA Europa League		
Slask Wroclaw	A	L0-1		Q2
(Poland)	H	W3-2	Watson, Goodwillie, Daly	
(Slask Wroclaw through on away goals)				
		2012-13 UEFA Europa League		
Dynamo Moscow	H	D2-2	Flood, Watson	Q3
(Russia)	A	L0-5		

DUNFERMLINE

Opponents	Venue	Res	Scorers	Rnd
		1961-62 ECWC		
St Patrick's Ath	H	W4-1	Melrose, Peebles, Dickson, Macdonald	1
(Rep of Ireland)	A	W4-0	Peebles 2, Dickson 2	
Vardar Skopje	H	W5-0	Smith, Dickson 2, Melrose, Peebles	2
(Yugoslavia)	A	L0-2		
Ujpest Dozsa	A	L3-4	Smith, Macdonald 2	QF
(Hungary)	H	L0-1		
		1962-63 FC		
Everton	A	L0-1		1
(England)	H	W2-0	Miller, Melrose	
Valencia	A	L0-4		2
(Spain)	H	W6-2	Melrose, Sinclair 2 McLean, Peebles, Smith	
	N	L0-1		
		1964-65 FC		
Oergryte	H	W4-2	McLaughlin 2, Sinclair 2	1
(Sweden)	A	D0-0		
Stuttgart	H	W1-0	Callaghan	2
(West Germany)	A	D0-0		
Athletico Bilbao	A	L0-1		3

(Spain)	H	W1-0	Smith	
	A	L1-2	Smith	
		1965-66 FC		
Bye				1
KB Copenhagen	H	W5-0	Fleming, Paton 2, Robertson, Callaghan	2
(Denmark)	A	W4-2	Edwards, Paton, Fleming, Ferguson	
Spartak Brno	H	W2-0	Paton, Ferguson, pen	3
(Czechoslovakia)	A	D0-0		
Real Zaragossa	H	W1-0	Paton	QF
(Spain)	A	L2-4	Ferguson 2	
		1966-67 FC		
Frigg Oslo	A	W3-1	Fleming 2, Callaghan	1
(Norway)	H	W3-1	Delaney 2 Callaghan	
Dynamo Zagreb	H	W4-2	Delaney, Edwards, Ferguson 2	2
(Yugoslavia)	A	L0-2		
		1968-69 ECWC		
Apoel	H	W10-1	Robertson 2, Renton 2 Barry, Callaghan W 2, Gardner Edwards, Callaghan T	1
(Cyprus)	A	W2-0	Gardner, Callaghan W	
Olymp. Piraeus	H	W4-0	Edwards 2, Fraser, Mitchell	2
(Greece)	A	L0-3		
West Bromwich	H	D0-0		QF
(England)	A	W1-0	Gardner	
Slovan Bratislava	H	D1-1	Fraser	SF
(Czechoslovakia)	A	L0-1		
		1969-70 FC		
Bordeaux	H	W4-0	Paton 2, Mitchell, Gardner	1
(France)	A	L0-2		
Gwardia Warsaw	H	W2-1	McLean, Gardner	2
(Poland)	A	W1-0	Renton	
Anderlecht	A	L0-1		3
(Belgium)	H	W3-2	McLean 2, Mitchell	
		2004-05 UEFA		
FH Hafnarfjordur	A	D2-2	Brewster, Skerla	Q2
(Iceland)	H	L1-2	Dempsey	
		2007-08 UEFA		
BK Hacken	H	D1-1	Hamilton	Q2
BK Hacken	A	L0-1		

FALKIRK

Opponents	Venue	Res	Scorers	Rnd
		2009-10 UEFA Europa League		
Vaduz	H	W1-0	Flynn	Q2
(Liechtenstein)	A	L0-2		

GRETNA

Opponents	Venue	Res	Scorers	Rnd
		2006-07 UEFA		
Derry City	H	L1-5	McGuffie	Q
(Ireland)	A	D2-2	Graham, Baldacchino	

HEARTS

Opponents	Venue	Res	Scorers	Rnd
		1958-59 EC		
Standard Liege	A	L1-5	Crawford	P
(Belgium)	H	W2-1	Bauld	
		1960-61 EC		
Benfica	H	L1-2	Young	P
(Portugal)	A	L0-3		
		1961-62 FC		
Union St Gilloise	A	W3-1	Blackwood, Davidson 2	1
(Belgium)	H	W2-0	Wallace, Stenhouse	
Inter Milan	H	L0-1		2
(Italy)	A	L0-4		
		1963-64 FC		
Lausanne	A	D2-2	Traynor, Ferguson	1
(Switzerland)	H	D2-2	Cumming, Hamilton J	
	A	L2-3	Wallace, Ferguson	
		1965-66 FC		
Bye				1
Valerengen	H	W1-0	Wallace	2
(Norway)	A	W3-1	Kerrigan 2, Traynor	
Real Zaragossa	H	D3-3	Anderson, Wallace, Kerrigan	3
(Spain)				
	A	D2-2	Anderson, Wallace	
	A	L0-1		
		1976-77 ECWC		
Lokomotiv Leipzig	A	L0-2		1
(East Germany)	H	W5-1	Kay, Gibson 2, Brown, Busby	
SV Hamburg	A	L2-4	Park, Busby	2
(West Germany)	H	L1-4	Gibson	
		1984-85 UEFA		
Paris St Germain	A	L0-4		1
(France)	H	D2-2	Robertson 2	
		1986-87 UEFA		
Dukla Prague	H	W3-2	Foster, Clark, Robertson	1
(Czechoslovakia)	A	L0-1		
		1988-89 UEFA		
St Patrick's Ath	A	W2-0	Foster pen, Galloway	1
(Rep of Ireland)	H	W2-0	Black, Galloway	
FK Austria	H	D0-0		2
(Austria)	A	W1-0	Galloway	

Opponents	Venue	Res	Scorers	Rnd
Velez Mostar (Yugoslavia)	H	W3-0	Bannon, Galloway, Colquhoun	3
	A	L1-2	Galloway	
Bayern Munich	H	W1-0	Ferguson	QF
(West Germany)	A	L0-2		
		1990-91 UEFA		
Dnepr	A	D1-1	Robertson	1
(USSR)	H	W3-1	McPherson, Robertson 2	
Bologna	H	W3-1	Foster 2, Ferguson	2
(Italy)	A	L0-3		
		1992-93 UEFA		
Slavia Prague	A	L0-1		1
(Czech Rep)	H	W4-2	Mackay, Baird, Levein, Snodin	
Standard Liege	H	L0-1		2
(Belgium)	A	L0-1		
		1993-94 UEFA		
Atletico Madrid	H	W2-1	Robertson, Colquhoun	1
(Spain)	A	L0-3		
		1996-97 ECWC		
Red Star Belgrade	A	D0-0		1
(Yugoslavia)	H	D1-1	McPherson	
		1998-99 ECWC		
Lantana	A	W1-0	Makel	Q
(Estonia)	H	W5-0	Hamilton, Fulton, McCann, Flogel, Holmes	
Real Mallorca	H	L0-1		1
(Spain)	A	D1-1	Hamilton	
		2000-2001 UEFA		
IBV	A	W2-0	Severin, Jackson	Q
(Iceland)	H	W3-0	McSwegan, Tomaschek, O'Neil	
Stuttgart	A	L0-1		
(Germany)	H	W3-2	Pressley, Petric, Cameron pen	1
		2003-2004 UEFA		
Zeljeznicar	H	W2-0	de Vries, Webster	1
(Bosnia)	A	D0-0		
Bordeaux	A	W1-0	de Vries	2
(France)	H	L0-2		
		2004-05 UEFA		
Sporting Braga	H	W3-1	Webster, Hartley, Kisnorbo	1
(Portugal)	A	D2-2	de Vries 2	

Opponents	Venue	Res	Scorers	Rnd
			GROUP STAGE	
Feyenoord (Hol)	A	L0-3		
Shalke (Ger)	H	L0-1		
FC Basel (Swi)	A	W2-1	Wyness, Neilson	
Ferencvaros (Hun)	A	L0-1		
			2006-07 EC	
NK Siroki Brijeg	H	W3-0	o.g, Tall, Bednar	Q
(Bosnia)	A	D0-0		
AEK Athens	H	L1-2	Mikoliunas	Q
(Greece)	A	L0-3		
			UEFA	
Sparta Prague	H	L0-2		1
(Czech Rep)	A	D0-0		
			2009-10 UEFA Europa League	
Dinamo Zagreb	A	L0-4		Play-off
(Croatia)	H	W2-0	Stewart, Zaliukas	
			2011-12 UEFA Europa League	
Paksi	A	D1-1	Hamill	Q3
(Hungary)	H	W4-1	Stevenson 2, Driver, Skacel	
			Play-off Round	
Tottenham	H	L0-5		
(England	A	D0-0		
			2012-13 UEFA Europa League	
Liverpool	H	L0-1		Play-off
(England)	A	D1-1	Templeton	

HIBERNIAN

Opponents	Venue	Res	Scorers	Rnd
			1955-56 EC	
Rot-Weiss Essen	A	W4-0	Turnbull 2, Reilly, Ormond	1
(West Germany)	H	D1-1	Buchanan J	
Djurgaarden	H	W3-1	Combe, Mulkerrin, og	QF
(Sweden)	A	W1-0	Turnbull pen	
Reims	A	L0-2		SF
(France)	H	L0-1		
			1960-61 FC	
Barcelona	A	D4-4	McLeod, Preston Baker 2	QF
(Spain)	H	W3-2	Kinloch 2, 1 pen, Baker	
AS Roma	H	D2-2	Baker, McLeod	SF
(Italy)	A	D3-3	Baker 2, Kinloch	
	A	L0-6		
			1961-62 FC	
Belenenses	H	D3-3	Fraser 2, Baird pen	1
(Portugal)	A	W3-1	Baxter 2, Stevenson	
Red Star Belgrade	A	L0-4		2
(Yugoslavia)	H	L0-1		
			1962-63 FC	
Stavenet	H	W4-0	Byrne 2, Baker, og	1
(Denmark)	A	W3-2	Stevenson 2, Byrne	

Opponents	Venue	Res	Scorers	Rnd
DOS Utrecht	A	W1-0	Falconer	2
(Holland)	H	W2-1	Baker, Stevenson	
Valencia	A	L0-5		QF
(Spain)	H	W2-1	Preston, Baker	
		1965-66 FC		
Valencia	H	W2-0	Scott, McNamee	1
(Spain)	A	L0-2		
	A	L0-3		
		1967-68 FC		
Porto	H	W3-0	Cormack 2, Stevenson	1
(Portugal)	A	L1-3	Stanton pen	
Napoli	A	L1-4	Stein	2
(Italy)	H	W5-0	Duncan, Quinn, Cormack Stanton, Stein	
Leeds United	A	L0-1		3
(England)	H	D1-1	Stein	
		1968-69 FC		
Ljubljana	A	W3-0	Stevenson, Stein, Marinello	1
(Yugoslavia)	H	W2-1	Davis 2	
Lokomotiv Leipzig	H	W3-1	McBride 3	2
(East Germany)	A	W1-0	Grant	
SV Hamburg	A	L0-1		3
(West Germany)	H	W2-1	McBride 2	
		1970-71 FC		
Malmo FF	H	W6-0	McBride 3 Duncan 2, Blair	1
(Sweden)	A	W3-2	Duncan, McEwan, Stanton	
Vitoria Giumaraes	H	W2-0	Duncan, Stanton	2
(Portugal)	A	L1-2	Graham	
Liverpool	H	L0-1		3
(England)	A	L0-2		
		1972-73 ECWC		
Sporting Lisbon	A	L1-2	Duncan	1
(Portugal)	H	W6-1	Gordon 2, O'Rourke 3, og	
Besa	H	W7-1	Cropley, O'Rourke 3, Duncan 2, Brownlie	2
(Albania)				
	A	D1-1	Gordon	
Hadjuk Split	H	W4-2	Gordon 3, Duncan	QF
(Yugoslavia)	A	L0-3		
		1973-74 UEFA		
Keflavik	H	W2-0	Black, Higgins	1
(Iceland)	A	D1-1	Stanton	
Leeds United	A	D0-0		2
(England)	H	D0-0		
		1974-75 UEFA		
Rosenborg	A	W3-2	Stanton, Gordon, Cropley	1
(Norway)	H	W9-1	Harper 2, Munro 2, Stanton 2, Cropley 2 pens, Gordon	

Opponents	Venue	Res	Scorers	Rnd
Juventus	H	L2-4	Stanton, Cropley	2
(Italy)	A	L0-4		
		1975-76 UEFA		
Liverpool	H	W1-0	Harper	1
(England)	A	L1-3	Edwards	
		1976-77 UEFA		
Sochaux	H	W1-0	Brownlie	1
(France)	A	D0-0		
Osters Vaxjo	H	W2-0	Blackley, Brownlie pen	2
(Sweden)	A	L1-4	Smith	
		1978-79 UEFA		
Norrkoping	H	W3-2	Higgins 2, Temperley	1
(Sweden)	A	D0-0		
Strasbourg	A	L0-2		2
(France)	H	W1-0	McLeod pen	
		1989-90 UEFA		
Videoton	H	W1-0	Mitchell	1
(Hungary)	A	W3-0	Houchen, Evans, Collins	
FC Liege	H	D0-0		
(Belgium)	A	L0-1		
		1992-93 UEFA		
Anderlecht	H	D2-2	Beaumont, McGinlay	1
(Belgium)	A	D1-1	Jackson	
		2001-02 UEFA		
AEK Athens	A	L0-2		1
(Greece)	H	W3-2 (aet)	Luna 2, Zitelli	
		2005-06 UEFA		
Dnipro	H	D0-0		1
(Ukraine)	A	L1-5	Riordan	
		2010-11 UEFA Europa League		
Maribor	A	L0-3		3
(Slovenia)	H	L2-3	De Graaf 2	

KILMARNOCK

Opponents	Venue	Res	Scorers	Rnd
		1964-65 FC		
Eintracht Frankfurt	A	L0-3		1
(West Germany)	H	W5-1	Hamilton, McIlroy, Sneddon McFadzean, McInally	
Everton	H	L0-2		2
(England)	A	L1-4	McIlroy	
		1965-66 EC		
Nendori Tirana	A	D0-0		P
(Albania)	H	W1-0	Black	
Real Madrid	H	D2-2	McLean pen, McInally	1
(Spain)	A	L1-5	McIlroy	

Opponents	Venue	Res	Scorers	Rnd
		1966-67 FC		
Bye				1
Antwerp	A	W1-0	McInally	2
(Belgium)	H	W7-2	McInally 2, Queen 2 McLean 2, Watson	
La Gantoise	H	W1-0	Murray	3
(Belgium)	A	W2-1	McInally, McLean	
Lokomotiv Leipzig	A	L0-1		QF
(East Gemany)	H	W2-0	McFadzean, McIlroy	
Leeds United	A	L2-4	McIlroy 2	SF
(England)	H	D0-0		
		1969-70 FC		
Zurich	A	L2-3	McLean J, Mathie	1
(Switzerland)	H	W3-1	McGrory, Morrison, McLean T	
Slavia Sofia	H	W4-1	Mathie 2, Cook, Gilmour	2
(Bulgaria)	A	L0-2		
Dynamo Bacau	H	D1-1	Mathie	3
(Romania)	A	L0-2		
		1970-71 FC		
Coleraine	A	D1-1	Mathie	1
(Northern Ireland)	H	L2-3	McLean T, Morrison	
		1997-98 ECWC		
Shelbourne	H	W2-1	Wright 2	Q
(Rep of Ireland)	A	D1-1	McIntyre	
Nice	A	L1-3	Wright	1
(France)	H	D1-1	Reilly	
		1998-99 UEFA		
Zeljeznicar	A	D1-1	McGowne	P
(Bosnia)	H	W1-0	Mahood	
Sigma Olomouc	A	L0-2		P
(Czech Rep)	H	L0-2		
		1999-2000 UEFA		
KR Reyjkavic	A	L0-1		Q
(Iceland)	H	W2-0	Wright, Bagan	
Kaislerslautern	A	L0-3		1
(Germany)	H	L0-2		
		2001-2002 UEFA		
Glenavon	A	W1-0	Innes	Q
(Northern Ireland)	H	W1-0	Mitchell	
Viking Stavanger	H	D1-1	Dargo	1
(Norway)	A	L0-2		

LIVINGSTON

Opponents	Venue	Res	Scorers	Rnd
		2002-2003 UEFA		
Vaduz	A	D1-1	Rubio	Q
(Liechtenstein)	H	D0-0		
Sturm Graz	A	L2-5	Zarate, Lovell	1
(Austria)	H	W4-3	Wilson 2 (1 pen), Xausa, Andrews	

MORTON

Opponents	Venue	Res	Scorers	Rnd
		1968-69 FC		
Chelsea	A	L0-5		1
(England)	H	L3-4	Thorop, Mason, Taylor	

MOTHERWELL

Opponents	Venue	Res	Scorers	Rnd
		1991-92 FC		
Katowice	A	L0-2		1
(Poland)	H	W3-1	Kirk 2, Cusack	
		1994-95 UEFA		
Hanvar	H	W3-0	Coyne, McGrillen, Kirk	P
(Faroe Islands)	A	W4-1	Kirk 2, Davies, Burns	
Bor Dortmund	A	L0-1		1
(Germany)	H	L0-2		
		1995-96 UEFA		
My-Pa 47	H	L1-3	McSkimming	P
(Finland)	A	W2-0	Burns, Arnott	
		2008-09 UEFA		
AS Nancy	A	L0-1		1
(France)	H	L0-2		
		2009-10 UEFA Europa League		
Llanelli	H	L0-1		Q1
(Wales)	A	W3-0	Sutton 2, Murphy	
Flamurtari Vlorë	A	L0-1		Q2
(Albania)	H	W8-1	Murphy 3, Slane, Forbes 2, Hutchinson, McHugh	
Steaua Bucharest	A	L0-3		Q3
(Romania)	H	L1-3	Forbes	
		2010-11 UEFA Europa League		
Breidablik	H	W1-0	Forbes	2
(Iceland)	A	W1-0	Murphy	
Aalesunds	A	D1-1	Murphy	3
(Norway)	H	W3-0	Murphy, Sutton, Page	
Odense	A	L1-2	Hateley	Play-off
(Denmark)	H	L0-1		
		2012-13 EC		
Panathinaikos	H	L0-2		3
(Greece)	A	L0-3		
		2012-13 UEFA Europa League		
Levante	H	L0-2		Play-off
(Spain)	A	L0-1		

PARTICK THISTLE

Opponents	Venue	Res	Scorers	Rnd
		1963-64 FC		
Glentoran	A	W4-1	Hainey, Yard 2, Wright	1
(Northern Ireland)	H	W3-0	Smith 2, Harvey, pen,	
Spartak Brno	H	W3-2	Yard, Harvey, pen,	2
(Czechoslovakia)			Ferguson	
	A	L0-4		
		1972-73 UEFA CUP		
Honved	A	L0-1		1
(Hungary)	H	L0-3		

QUEEN OF THE SOUTH

Opponents	Venue	Res	Scorers	Rnd
		2008-09 UEFA		
FC Nordsjaelland	H	L1-2	O'Connor	Q
(Denmark)	A	L1-2	Harris	

RAITH ROVERS

Opponents	Venue	Res	Scorers	Rnd
		1995-96 UEFA		
Gotu	H	W4-0	Dair, Rougier, Cameron	P
(Faroe Islands)			McAnespie	
	A	D2-2	Lennon, Crawford	
Akranes	H	W3-1	Lennon 2, Wilson	1
(Iceland	A	L0-1		
Bayern Munich)	H	L0-2		2
(Germany)	A	L1-2	Lennon	

RANGERS

Opponents	Venue	Res	Scorers	Rnd
		1956-57 EC		
Bye				P
Nice	H	W2-1	Murray, Simpson	1
(France)	A	L1-2	Hubbard pen	
	N	L1-3	og	
		1957-58 EC		
St Etienne	H	W3-1	Kichenbrand, Scott,	P
(France)			Simpson	
	A	L1-2	Wilson	
AC Milan	H	L1-4	Murray	1
(Italy)	A	L0-2		
		1959-60 EC		
Anderlecht	H	W5-2	Millar, Scott, Matthew,	P
(Belgium)			Baird 2	
	A	W2-0	Matthew, McMillan	

Opponents	Venue	Res	Scorers	Rnd
Red Star	H	W4-3	McMillan, Scott, Wilson	1
Bratislava			Millar	
(Czechoslovakia)	A	D1-1	Scott	
Sparta Rotterdam	A	W3-2	Wilson, Baird, Murray	QF
(Holland)	H	L0-1		
	N	W3-2	Baird 2, og	
Eintracht Frankfurt	A	L1-6	Caldow pen	SF
(West Germany)	H	L3-6	McMillan 2, Wilson	
		1960-61 ECWC		
Ferencvaros	H	W4-2	Davis, Millar 2, Brand	P
(Hungary)	A	L1-2	Wilson	
Borussia Moench	A	W3-0	Millar, Scott, McMillan	QF
(West Germany)	H	W8-0	Baxter, Brand 3, Millar 2	
			Davis, og	
Wolves	H	W2-0	Scott, Brand	SF
(England)	A	D1-1	Scott	
Fiorentina	H	L0-2		F
(Italy)	A	L1-2	Scott	
		1961-62 EC		
Monaco	A	W3-2	Baxter, Scott 2	P
(France)	H	W3-2	Christie 2, Scott	
Vorwaerts	A	W2-1	Caldow pen, Brand	1
(East Germany)	H	W4-1	McMillan 2 Henderson, og	
Standard Liege	A	L1-4	Wilson	
(Belgium)	H	W2-0	Brand, Caldow	
		1962-63 ECWC		
Seville	H	W4-0	Millar 3, Brand	1
(Spain)	A	L0-2		
Tottenham	A	L2-5	Brand, Millar	2
(England)	H	L2-3	Brand, Wilson	
		1963-64 EC		
Real Madrid	H	L0-1		P
(Spain)	A	L0-6		
		1964-65 EC		
Red Star Belgrade	H	W3-1	Brand 2, Forrest	P
(Yugoslavia)	A	L2-4	Greig, McKinnon	
	N	W3-1	Forrest 2, Brand	
Rapid Vienna	H	W1-0	Wilson	1
(Austria)	A	W2-0	Forrest, Wilson	
Inter Milan	A	L1-3	Forrest	QF
(Italy)	H	W1-0	Forrest	
		1966-67 ECWC		
Glentoran	A	D1-1	McLean	1
(Northern Ireland)	H	W4-0	Johnston, Smith D,	
			Setterington, McLean	

Opponents	Venue	Res	Scorers	Rnd
Bor Dortmund	H	W2-1	Johansen, Smith A	2
(West Germany)	A	D0-0		
Real Zaragoza	H	W2-0	Smith, Willoughby	QF
(Spain)	A	L0-2		
Slavia Sofia	A	W1-0	Wilson	SF
(Bulgaria)	H	W1-0	Henderson	
Bayern Munich	N	L0-1		F
(West Germany)				
		1967-68 FC		
Dynamo Dresden	A	D1-1	Ferguson	1
(East Germany)	H	W2-1	Penman, Greig	
FC Cologne	H	W3-0	Ferguson 2, Henderson	2
(West Germany)	A	L1-3	Henderson	
Bye				3
Leeds United	H	D0-0		QF
(England)	A	L0-2		
		1968-69 FC		
Vojvodina	H	W2-0	Greig pen, Jardine	1
(Yugoslavia)	A	L0-1		
Dundalk	H	W6-1	Henderson 2, Greig	2
(Rep of Ireland)			Ferguson 2, og	
	A	W3-0	Mathieson, Stein 2	
DWS Amsterdam	A	W2-0	Johnstone, Henderson	3
(Holland)	H	W2-1	Smith, Stein	
Athletic Bilbao	H	W4-1	Ferguson, Penman,	QF
(Spain)			Persson, Stein	
	A	L0-2		
		1969-70 ECWC		
Steaua Bucharest	H	W2-0	Johnston 2	1
(Romania)	A	D0-0		
Gornik Zabrze	A	L1-3	Persson	2
(Poland)	H	L1-3	Baxter	
		1970-71 FC		
Bayern Munich	A	L0-1		1
(West Germany)	H	D1-1	Stein	
		1971-72 ECWC		
Rennes	A	D1-1	Johnston	1
(France)	H	W1-0	MacDonald	
Sporting Lisbon	H	W3-2	Stein 2, Henderson	2
(Portugal)	A	L3-4	Stein 2, Henderson	
Torino	A	D1-1	Johnston	QF
(Italy)	H	W1-0	MacDonald	
Bayern Munich	A	D1-1	og	SF
(West Germany)	H	W2-0	Jardine, Parlane	
Dynamo Moscow	N	W3-2	Johnston 2, Stein	F
(USSR)				

Opponents	Venue	Res	Scorers	Rnd
		1972-73 European Super Cup		
Ajax	H	L1-3	MacDonald	
(Holland)	A	L2-3	MacDonald, Young	
		1973-74 ECWC		
Ankaragucu	A	W2-0	Conn, McLean	1
(Turkey)	H	W4-0	Greig 2, O'Hara, Johnstone	
Borussia Moench.	A	L0-3		2
(West Germany)	H	W3-2	Conn, Jackson, MacDonald	
		1975-76 EC		
Bohemians	H	W4-1	Fyfe, Johnstone, O'Hara	1
(Rep of Ireland)			og	
	A	D1-1	Johnstone	
St Etienne	A	L0-2		2
(France)	H	L1-2	MacDonald	
		1976-77 EC		
Zurich	H	D1-1	Parlane	1
(Switzerland)	A	L0-1		
		1977-78 ECWC		
Young Boys	H	W1-0	Greig	P
(Switzerland)	A	D2-2	Johnstone, Smith	
Twente Enschede	H	D0-0		1
(Holland)	A	L0-3		
		1978-79 EC		
Juventus	A	L0-1		1
(Italy)	H	W2-0	MacDonald, Smith	
PSV Eindhoven	H	D0-0		2
(Holland)	A	W3-2	MacDonald, Johnstone	
			Russell	
FC Cologne	A	L0-1		QF
(West Germany)	H	D1-1	McLean	
		1979-80 ECWC		
Lillestrom	H	W1-0	Smith	P
(Norway)	A	W2-0	MacDonald A, Johnstone	
Fortuna Dusseldorf	H	W2-1	MacDonald A, McLean	1
(West Germany)	A	D0-0		
Valencia	A	D1-1	McLean	2
(Spain)	H	L1-3	Johnstone	
		1981-82 ECWC		
Dukla Prague	A	L0-3		1
(Czechoslovakia)	H	W2-1	Bett, MacDonald J	
		1982-83 UEFA		
Borussia Dortmund	A	D0-0		1
(West Germany)	H	W2-0	Cooper, Johnstone	
FC Cologne	H	W2-1	Johnstone, McClelland	2
(West Germany)	A	L0-5		

Opponents	Venue	Res	Scorers	Rnd
		1983-84 ECWC		
Valetta	A	W8-0	Paterson, McPherson 4	1
(Malta)			MacDonald, Prytz 2	
	H	W10-0	Mitchell 2, MacDonald 3	
			Dawson, MacKay, Davis 2,	
			Redford	
Porto	H	W2-1	Clark, Mitchell	2
(Portugal)	A	L0-1		
		1984-85 UEFA		
Bohemians	A	L2-3	McCoist, McPherson	1
(Rep of Ireland)	H	W2-0	Paterson, Redford	
Inter Milan	A	L0-3		2
(Italy)	H	W3-1	Mitchell, Ferguson 2	
		1985-86 UEFA		
Osasuna	H	W1-0	Paterson	1
(Spain)	A	L0-2		
		1986-87 UEFA		
Ilves	H	W4-0	Fleck 3, McCoist	1
(Finland)	A	L0-2		
Boavista	H	W2-1	McPherson, McCoist	2
(Portugal)	A	W1-0	Ferguson	
Borussia Moench.	H	D1-1	Durrant	3
(West Germany)	A	D0-0		
		1987-88 EC		
Dynamo Kiev	A	L0-1		1
(USSR)	H	W2-0	Falco, McCoist	
Gornik Zabrze	H	W3-1	McCoist, Durrant, Falco	2
(Poland)	A	D1-1	McCoist pen	
Steaua Bucharest	A	L0-2		QF
(Romania)	H	W2-1	Gough, McCoist pen	
		1988-89 UEFA		
Katowice	H	W1-0	Walters	1
(Poland)	A	W4-2	Butcher 2, Durrant	
			Ferguson	
FC Cologne	A	L0-2		2
(West Germany)	H	D1-1	Drinkell	
		1989-90 EC		
Bayern Munich	H	L1-3	Walters, pen	1
(West Germany)	A	D0-0		
		1990-91 EC		
Valetta	A	W4-0	McCoist, Hateley,	1
(Malta)			Johnston 2	
	H	W6-0	Dodds, Spencer,	
			Johnston 3, McCoist	
Red Star Belgrade	A	L0-3		2
(Yugoslavia)	H	D1-1	McCoist	

Opponents	Venue	Res	Scorers	Rnd
		1991-92 EC		
Sparta Prague	A	L0-1		1
(Czechoslovakia)	H	W2-1	McCall 2	
		1992-93 EC		
Lyngby	H	W2-0	Hateley, Huistra	1
(Denmark)	A	W1-0	Durrant	
Leeds United	H	W2-1	og, McCoist	2
(England)	A	W2-1	Hateley, McCoist	
		GROUP STAGE		
Marseille (France)	H	D2-2	McSwegan, Hateley	
CSKA Moscow (Russia)	A	W1-0	Ferguson	
FC Bruges (Belgium)	A	D1-1	Huistra	
FC Bruges	H	W2-1	Durrant, Nisbet	
Marseille	A	D1-1	Durrant	
CSKA Moscow	H	D0-0		
		1993-94 EC		
Levski Sofia	H	W3-2	McPherson, Hateley 2	1
(Bulgaria)	A	L1-2	Durrant	
		1994-95 EC		
AEK Athens	A	L0-2		1
(Greece)	H	L0-1		
Anorthosis	H	W1-0	Durie	P
(Cyprus)	A	D0-0		
		1995-96 EC		
		GROUP STAGE		
Steaua Bucharest (Romania)	A	L0-1		
Borussia Dort (Germany)	H	D2-2	Gough, Ferguson	
Juventus (Italy)	A	L1-4	Gough	
Juventus	H	L0-4		
Steaua Bucharest	H	D1-1	Gascoigne	
Borussia Dort	A	D2-2	Laudrup, Durie	
		1996-97 EC		
Vladikavkaz	H	W3-1	McInnes, McCoist, Petric	Q
(Russia)	A	W7-2	McCoist 3, van Vossen Laudrup 2, Miller	
		GROUP STAGE		
Grasshoppers (Switzerland)	A	L0-3		

Opponents	Venue	Res	Scorers	Rnd
Auxerre (France)	H	L1-2	Gascoigne	
Ajax (Holland)	A	L1-4	Durrant	
Ajax	H	L0-1		
Grasshoppers	H	W2-1	McCoist 2, 1 pen	
Auxerre	A	L1-2	Gough	
		1997-98 EC		
Gotu	A	W5-0	Negri, Durie 2, McCoist 2	Q
(Faroe Islands)	H	W6-0	Durie, Negri 2, McCoist Albertz, Ferguson	
Gothenburg	A	L0-3		Q
(Sweden)	H	D1-1	Miller	
		UEFA		
Strasbourg	A	L1-2	Albertz	1
(France)	H	L1-2	Gattuso	
		1998-99 UEFA		
Shelbourne (Rep of Ireland)	A	W5-3	Albertz 2, 1 pen, Amato 2, van Bronckhorst	Q
	H	W2-0	Johansson 2	
PAOK Salonika	H	W2-0	Kanchelskis, Wallace	Q
(Greece)	A	D0-0		
Beitar	A	D1-1	Albertz	1
(Israel)	H	W4-2	Gattuso, Porrini, Johansson, Wallace	
Bayer Leverkusen (Germany)	A	W2-1	van Bronckhorst, Johansson	2
	H	D1-1	Johansson	
Parma	H	D1-1	Wallace	3
(Italy)	A	L1-3	Albertz	
		1999-2000 EC		
FC Haka (Finland)	A	W4-1	Amoruso, Mols 2 Johansson	Q
	H	W3-0	Wallace, Mols, Johansson	
Parma	H	W2-0	Vidmar, Reyna	Q
(Italy)	A	L0-1		
		GROUP STAGE		
Valencia	A	L0-2		
(Spain)	H	L1-2	Moore	
Bayern Munich	H	D1-1	Albertz	
(Germany)	A	L0-1		
PSV Eindhoven	A	W1-0	Albertz	
(Holland)	H	W4-1	Amoruso Mols 2, McCann	

Opponents	Venue	Res	Scorers	Rnd
		UEFA		
Bor Dortmund	H	W2-0	Kohler og, Wallace	
(Germany)	A	L0-2		
(Dortmund won 3-1 on penalties)				
		2000-2001 EC		
Zalgiris Kaunas	H	W4-1	Johnston, Albertz, Dodds 2	Q2
(Lithuania)	A	D0-0		
Herfolge BK	A	W3-0	Albertz, Dodds, Amoruso	Q3
(Denmark)	H	W3-0	Wallace, Johnston, Kanchelskis	
		GROUP STAGE		
Sturm Graz	H	W5-0	Mols, de Boer, Albertz, van Bronckhorst, Dodds	
(Austria)	A	L0-2		
Monaco	A	W1-0	van Bronckhorst	
(France)	H	D2-2	Miller, Mols	
Galatasaray	A	L2-3	Kanchelskis, van Bronckhorst	
(Turkey)	H	D0-0		
		UEFA		
Kaiserslautern	H	W1-0	Albertz	3
(Germany)	A	L0-3		
		2001-2002 EC		
NK Maribor	A	W3-0	Flo 2, Nerlinger	Q2
(Slovenia)	H	W3-1	Caniggia 2, Flo	
Fenerbahce	H	D0-0		Q3
(Turkey)	A	L1-2	Ricksen	
		UEFA		
Anzhi	N	W1-0	Konterman	1
(Russia)				
Moscow Dynamo	H	W3-1	Amoruso, Ball, de Boer	2
(Russia)	A	W4-1	de Boer, Ferguson, Flo Lovenkrands	
PSG	H	D0-0		3
(France)	A	D0-0		
(aet, Rangers won 4-3 on penalties)				
Feyenoord	H	D1-1	Ferguson pen	4
(Holland)	A	L2-3	McCann, Ferguson pen	
		2002-2003 UEFA		
Viktoria Zizkov	A	L0-2		1
(Czech Republic)	H	W3-1	de Boer 2, McCann	
(aet, 2-0 after 90 mins. Zizkov won on away goals)				
		2003-2004 EC		
FC Copenhagen	H	D1-1	Lovenkrands	Q3
(Denmark)	A	W2-0	Arteta, Arveladze	
		GROUP STAGE		
VfB Stuttgart	H	W2-1	Nerlinger, Lovenkrands	
(Germany)	A	L0-1		

Opponents	Venue	Res	Scorers	Rnd
Panathinaikos	A	D1-1	Emerson	
(Greece)	H	L1-3	Mols	
Manchester Utd	H	L0-1		
(England)	A	L0-3		
		2004-05 EC		
CSKA Moscow	A	L1-2	Novo	Q3
(Russia)	H	D1-1	Thompson	
		UEFA		
Maritimo	A	L0-1		1
(Portugal)	H	W1-0	Prso	
		(aet, Rangers win 4-2 on penalties)		
		GROUP STAGE		
Amica Wronki (Pol)	A	W5-0	Lovenkrands, Novo, Ricksen, Arveladze, Thompson	
Graz AK (Aut)	H	W3-0	Novo, Arveladze, Namouchi	
AZ Alkmaar (Hol)	A	L0-1		
Auxerre (Fra)	H	L0-2		
		2005-06 EC		
A Famagusta	A	W2-1	Novo, Ricksen	Q3
(Cyprus)	H	W2-0	Buffel, Prso	
		GROUP STAGE		
Porto	H	W3-2	Lovenkrands, Prso, Kyrgiakos	
(Portugal)	A	D1-1	McCormack	
Inter Milan	A	L0-1		
(Italy)	H	D1-1	Lovenkrands	
Artmedia Bratislava	H	D0-0		
(Slovakia)	A	D2-2	Prso, Thompson	
		LAST 16		
Villarreal	H	D2-2	Lovenkrands, Pena og	
(Spain)	A	D1-1	Lovenkrands	
		2006-07 UEFA		
Molde	H	W2-0	Buffel, Ferguson	1
(Denmark)	A	D0-0		
		GROUP STAGE		
Livorno (Italy)	A	W3-2	Adam, Boyd, Novo,	
Maccabi Haifa (Is)	H	W2-0	Novo, Adam	
Auxerre (Fra)	A	D2-2	Novo, Boyd	
P. Belgrade (Cro)	H	W1-0	Hutton	
		LAST 32		
Hapoel Tel Aviv	H	W4-0	Ferguson 2, Boyd, Adam	
(Israel)	A	L1-2	Novo	
		LAST 16		
Osasuna	H	D1-1	Hemdani	
(Spain)	A	L0-1		
		2007-08 EC		
Zeta	H	W2-0	Weir, McCulloch	
(Montenegro)	A	W1-0	Beasley	

Opponents	Venue	Res	Scorers	Rnd
Red Star	H	W1-0	Novo	
(Serbia)	A	D0-0		
		GROUP STAGE		
VfB Stuggart	H	W2-1	Adam, Darcheville	
(Germany)	A	L2-3	Adam, Ferguson	
Lyon	A	W3-0	McCulloch, Cousin, Beasley	
(France)	H	L0-3		
Barcelona	H	D0-0		
(Spain)	A	L0-2		
		UEFA		
		LAST 32		
Panathinaikos	H	D0-0		
(Greece)	A	D1-1	Novo	
		LAST 16		
Werder Bremen	H	W2-0	Cousin, Davis	
(Germany)	A	L0-1		
		QUARTER-FINAL		
Sporting Lisbon	H	D0-0		
(Portugal)	A	W2-0	Darcheville, Whittaker	
		SEMI-FINAL		
Fiorentina	H	D0-0		
Fiorentina	A	D0-0	(aet, Rangers win 4-2 on penalties)	
		FINAL		
Zenit St Petersburg	N	L0-2		
		2008-09 EC		
FBK Kaunas	H	D0-0		Q
(Lithuania)	A	L1-2	Thomson	
		2009-10 EC		
		GROUP STAGE		
Stuttgart	A	D1-1	Bougherra	
(Germany)	H	L0-2		
Sevilla	H	L1-4	Novo	
(Spain)	A	L0-1		
Unirea Urziceni	H	L1-4	Gomes og	
(Romania)	A	D1-1	McCulloch	
		2010-11 EC		
		GROUP STAGE		
Manchester Utd	A	D0-0		
(England)	H	L0-1		
Bursapor	H	W1-0	Naismith	
(Turkey)	A	D1-1	Miller	
Valencia	H	D1-1	Edu	
(Spain)	A	L0-3		
		UEFA EUROPA LEAGUE		
		LAST 32		
Sporting Lisbon	H	D1-1	Whittaker	
(Portugal)	A	D2-2	Diouf, Edu	

(Rangers through on away goals)

Opponents	Venue	Res	Scorers	Rnd
		LAST 16		
PSV Eindhoven	A	D0-0		
(Holland)	H	L0-1		
		2011-12 EC		
Malmo	H	L0-1		Q
(Sweden)	A	D1-1	Jelavic	
		UEFA Europa League Play-off Round		
NK Maribor	A	L1-2	Ortiz	
(Slovenia)	H	D1-1	Bocanegra	

ST JOHNSTONE

Opponents	Venue	Res	Scorers	Rnd
		1971-72 UEFA		
SV Hamburg	A	L1-2	Pearson	1
(West Germany)	H	W3-0	Hall, Pearson, Whitelaw	
Vasas Budapest	H	W2-0	Connolly pen, Pearson	2
(Hungary)	A	L0-1		
Zeljeznicar	H	W1-0	Connolly	3
(Yugoslavia)	A	L1-5	Rooney	
		1999-2000 UEFA		
VPS Vaasa	A	D1-1	Lowndes	Q
(Finland)	H	W2-0	Simao 2	
Monaco	A	L0-3		1
(France)	H	D3-3	Leonard og, Dasovic, O'Neil	
		2012-13 UEFA Europa League		
Eskişehirspor	A	L0-2		Q2
(Turkey)	H	D1-1	Tade	

ST MIRREN

Opponents	Venue	Res	Scorers	Rnd
		1980-81 UEFA		
Elfsborg	A	W2-1	Somner, Abercromby	1
(Sweden)	H	D0-0		
St Etienne	H	D0-0		2
(France)	A	L0-2		
		1983-84 UEFA		
Feyenoord	H	L0-1		1
(Holland)	A	L0-2		
		1985-86 UEFA		
Slavia Prague	A	L0-1		1
(Czechoslovakia)	H	W3-0	Gallagher, McGarvey 2	
Hammarby	A	D3-3	Gallagher 3	2
(Sweden)	H	L1-2	McGarvey	
		1987-88 ECWC		
Tromso	H	W1-0	McDowall	1
(Norway)	A	D0-0		
Mechelen	A	D0-0		2
(Belgium)	H	L0-2		

SCOTTISH JUNIOR CUP

Season	Winner		Runner-up	
1886-87	Fairfield (Govan)	3	Edinburgh Woodburn	1
	(after protest)			
1887-88	Wishaw Thistle	3	Maryhill	1
1888-89	Burnbank Swifts	4	W Benhar Violet	1
1889-90	Burnbank Swifts	3	Benburb 1	
	(after protest)			
1890-91	Vale of Clyde	2	Chryston Ath	0
	(after a draw)			
1891-92	Minerva	5	W Benhar Violet	2
1892-93	Vale of Clyde	3	Dumbarton Fern	2
	(after a draw)			
1893-94	Ashfield	3	Renfrew V	0
1894-95	Ashfield	2	West Calder Wan.	1
	(after a draw)			
1895-96	Cambuslang Hibs	3	Parkhead	1
1896-97	Strathclyde	2	Dunfermline Juniors	0
	(after protest)			
1897-98	Dalziel Rovers	2	Parkhead	1
1898-99	Parkhead	4	Westmarch XI	1
1899-00	Maryhill	3	Rugby XI	2
1900-01	Burnbank Ath	2	Maryhill	0
1901-02	Glencairn	1	Maryhill	0
	(after a draw)			
1902-03	Parkhead	3	Larkhall Th	0
1903-04	Vale of Clyde	3	Parkhead	0
1904-05	Ashfield	2	Renfrew Vic.	1
1905-06	Dunipace Juniors	1	Rob Roy	0
	(after a draw)			
1906-07	Strathclyde	1	Maryhill XI	0
	(after two draws)			
1907-08	Larkhall Th	1	QP Hampden XI	0
1908-09	Kilwinning R	1	Strathclyde	0
	(after a draw)			
1909-10	Ashfield	3	Kilwinning R.	0
	after protest)			
1910-11	Burnbank Ath	1	Petershill	0
	(after a draw)			
1911-12	Petershill	5	Denny Hibs	0
1912-13	Inverkeithing Utd	1	Dunipace Juniors	0
1913-14	Larkhall Th	1	Ashfield	0
	(after two draws)			
1914-15	Parkhead	2	Port Glasgow Ath	0
1915-16	Petershill	2	Parkhead	0
1916-17	St Mirren Juniors	1	Renfrew Juniors	0
	(after a draw)			
1917-18	Petershill awarded cup, no final tie			

1918-19	Glencairn	1	St Anthony's	0
	(after a draw)			
1919-20	Parkhead	2	Cambuslang R	0
1920-21	Rob Roy	1	Ashfield	0
1921-22	St Roch's	2	Kilwinning R	1
	(after protest)			
1922-23	Musselb'gh Bruntonian	2	Arniston R	0
1923-24	Parkhead	3	Baillieston Juniors	1
	(after a draw)			
1924-25	Saltcoats Vics	2	St Anthony's	1
	(after two draws)			
1925-26	Strathclyde	2	Bridgeton Wav.	0
	(after a draw)			
1926-27	Glencairn	2	Cambuslang R	1
1927-28	Maryhill Hibs	6	Burnbank Ath	2
1928-29	Dundee Violet	4	Denny Hibs	0
1929-30	Newtongrange Star	3	Hall Russell's	0
1930-31	Denny Hibs	1	Burnbank Ath	0
	(replay ordered, Denny failed to appear)			
1931-32	Perthshire	2	Rob Roy	1
1932-33	Yoker Ath	4	Tranent Juniors.	2
	(after a draw)			
1933-34	Benburb	3	Bridgeton Wav	1
1934-35	Tranent	6	Petershill	1
1935-36	Benburb	1	Yoker Ath	0
	(after a draw)			
1936-37	Arthurlie	5	Rob Roy	1
1937-38	Cambuslang R	3	Benburb	2
1938-39	Glencairn	2	Shawfield	1
1939-40	Maryhill	1	Morton Juniors	0
1940-41	Perthshire	3	Armadale Th	1
	(after two draws)			
1941-42	Clydebank	4	Vale of Clyde	2
1942-43	Rob Roy	3	Benburb	1
	(after two draws)			
1943-44	Perthshire	1	Blantyre Vics	0
1944-45	Burnbank Ath	3	Cambuslang R	1
	(after protest)			
1945-46	Fauldhouse Utd	2	Arthurlie	0
1946-47	Shawfield	2	Bo'ness Utd	1
	(after a draw)			
1947-48	Bo'ness Utd.	2	Irvine Meadow	1
1948-49	Auchinleck Talbot	3	Petershill	2
1949-50	Blantyre Vics	3	Cumnock	0
1950-51	Petershill	1	Irvine Meadow	0
1951-52	Kilbirnie Ladeside	1	Camelon	0
1952-53	Vale of Leven	1	Annbank Utd	0
1953-54	Sunnybank	2	Lochee Harp	1

Season	Winner	Score	Runner-up	Score
1954-55	Kilsyth R	4	Duntocher Hibs	1
	(after a draw)			
1955-56	Petershill	4	Lugar Boswell Th	1
1956-57	A'deen Bnks o' Dee	1	Kilsyth R	0
1957-58	Shotts Bon Accord	2	Pumpherston	0
1958-59	Irvine Meadow	2	Shettleston	1
1959-60	St Andrew's	3	Greenock	1
1960-61	Dunbar United	2	Cambuslang R	0
	(after a draw)			
1961-62	Rob Roy	1	Renfrew	0
	(after a draw)			
1962-63	Irvine Meadow	2	Glenafton Ath	1
1963-64	Johnstone Burgh	3	Cambuslang R	0
	(after a draw)			
1964-65	Linlithgow Rose	4	Baillieston	1
1965-66	Bonnyrigg Rose	6	Whitburn	1
	(after a draw)			
1966-67	Kilsyth R	3	Glencairn	1
	(after a draw)			
1967-68	Johnstone Burgh	4	Glenrothes	3
	(after a draw)			
1968-69	Cambuslang R	1	Rob Roy	0
1969-70	Blantyre Vics	1	Penicuick Ath	0
	(ater a draw)			
1970-71	Cambuslang R	2	Newtongrange Star	1
1971-72	Cambuslang R	3	Bonnyrigg Rose	2
	(after 1-1 draw)			
1972-73	Irvine Meadow	1	Cambuslang R	0
	(after two draws)			
1973-74	Cambuslang R	3	Linlithgow Rose	1
1974-75	Glenrothes	1	Glencairn	0
1975-76	Bo'ness Utd	3	Darvel	0
1976-77	Kilbirnie Ladeside	3	Rob Roy	1
1977-78	Bonnyrigg Rose	1	Stonehouse Violet	0
1978-79	Cumnock	1	Bo'ness Utd	0
1979-80	Baillieston	2	Benburb	0
	(after a draw)			
1980-81	Pollok	1	Arthurlie	0
1981-82	Baillieston	0	Blantyre Vics	1
1982-83	East Kilbride Th	2	Bo'ness Utd	0
1983-84	Baillieston	0	Bo'ness Utd	2
1984-85	Pollok	3	Petershill	1
	(after 1-1 draw)			
1985-86	Auchinleck Talbot	3	Pollok	2
1986-87	Auchinleck Talbot	1	Kilbirnie Ladeside	0
	(after 1-1 draw)			
1987-88	Auchinleck Talbot	1	Petershill	0
1988-89	Cumnock	1	Ormiston Primrose	0
1989-90	Hill o' Beath	1	Lesmahagow	0

1990-91	Auchinleck Talbot	1	Newtongrange Star	0
1991-92	Auchinleck Talbot	4	Glenafton	0
1992-93	Glenafton	1	Tayport	0
1993-94	Largs Thistle	1	Glenafton	0
1994-95	Camelon	2	Whitburn	0
1995-96	Camelon	0	Tayport	2
	(after extra time)			
1996-97	Pollok	3	Tayport	1
1997-98	Arthurlie	4	Pollok	0
1998-99	Kilwinning Rangers	1	Kelty Hearts	0
1999-2000	Johnstone Burgh	2	Whitburn	2
	(aet, 2-2 full time. Whitburn won 4-3 on penalties)			
2000-01	Renfrew	0	Carnoustie Panmure	0
	(aet, Renfrew won 6-5 on penalties)			
2001-02	Linlithgow Rose	1	Auchinleck Talbot	0
2002-03	Tayport	1	Linlithgow Rose	0
	(after extra time)			
2003-04	Carnoustie Panmure	0	Tayport	0
	(aet, Carnoustie won 4-1 on penalties)			
2004-05	Lochee United	0	Tayport	2
2005-06	Auchinleck Talbot	2	Bathgate Thistle	1
2006-07	Kelty Hearts	1	Linlithgow Rose	2
	(after extra time)			
2007-08	Bathgate Thistle	2	Cumnock	1
2008-09	Auchinleck Talbot	2	Clydebank	1
2009-10	Largs Thistle	0	Linlithgow Rose	1
2010-11	Auchinleck Talbot	2	Musselburgh	1
	(after extra time)			
2011-12	Auchinleck Talbot	1	Shotts Bon Accord	2
2012-13	Auchinleck Talbot	1	Linlithgow Rose	0

AUCHINLECK TALBOT raise the Scottish Junior Cup for the third time in five years after defeating Linlithgow

JUNIOR CONTACTS

ANNBANK UTD .... J Currie, 07595 609325
ARDEER THISTLE .... P McBlain, 07767 898818
ARDROSSAN WINTON ROVERS ... B Macnamara, 07969 241895
ARTHURLIE .... A Pollock, 07547 676262
ASHFIELD .... T Robertson, 07801 394259
AUCHINLECK TALBOT .... H Dumigan, 07929 525494
BEITH .... R McCarter, 07501 897050
BELLSHILL .... W Ward, 07543 677932
BENBURB .... A Wiseman, 07969 954415
BLANTYRE VICS .... D Sinclair, 07831 327483
CAMBUSLANG RANGERS .... S Wilson, 07951 595710
CARLUKE ROVERS .... Ms T Cranston, 07909 548465
CLYDEBANK .... M Bamford, 07817 619286
CRAIGMARK BURNTONIANS .... D Conway, 07748 550589
CUMBERNAULD UTD .... A Robertson, 07533 194432
CUMNOCK .... G Morton, 07966 767405
DALRY .... H Aitken, 07968 862364
DARVEL .... J MacLachlan, 07858 430200
DUNIPACE .... I Duncan, 01324 813463
EAST KILBRIDE THISTLE .... J Stewart, 07766 116496
FORTH WANDERERS .... J Kelly, 07715 054638
GIRVAN .... R Hutcheson, 077618 67717
GLASGOW PERTHSHIRE .... Ms C Cunningham, 07854 183775
GLENAFTON ATHLETIC .... J Stewart, 07831 232638
GREENOCK .... L Faulkner, 07833 098858
HURLFORD .... W McMahon, 01563 821047
IRVINE MEADOW .... Mrs L McFarlane, 07854 767 062
IRVINE VICTORIA .... Ms S Thomson, 07980 875410
JOHNSTONE BURGH .... R Cantwell, 07719 323744
KELLO ROVERS .... Ms G Keggans, 07800 864158
KILBIRNIE LADESIDE .... G Ronney, 07889 403298
KILSYTH RANGERS .... R McKay, 07946 261384
KILWINNING RANGERS .... D Martin, 07427 507078
KIRKINTILLOCH ROB ROY .... C O'Brien, 07955 095707
LANARK UNITED .... T Anderson, 07721 047708
LARGS THISTLE .... Ms M Soutter, 07533 238655
LARKHALL THISTLE .... Mrs F Tierney, 07706 681274
LESMAHAGOW .... A Irving, 07963 770172
LUGAR BOSWELL THISTLE .... K Young, 07812 046194
MARYHILL .... G Anderson, 07693 804869

MAYBOLE ...... A Meek, 01655 883419
MUIRKIRK ...... B Tait, 07596 089828
NEILSTON ...... H Blair, 0141 881 8282
NEWMAINS UTD COMMUNITY FC ...... J Devine, 07833 187781
PETERSHILL ...... D Crozier, 07711 867748
POLLOK ...... F McNeill, 07847 542590
PORT GLASGOW ...... P Loughlin, 07946 814951
ROSSVALE ...... A Sandilands, 07908 713302
RENFREW ...... G Johnston, 07724 807774
ROYAL ALBERT ATHLETIC ...... P Higgins, 01698 888498
RUTHERGLEN GLENCAIRN ...... A Forbes, 07787 737654
SALTCOATS VICTORIA ...... G Hunter, 07505 488430
ST ANTHONY'S ...... F McKenna, 07790 169666
ST ROCH'S ...... C McMenamin, 07786 528920
SHETTLESTON ...... A McCulloch, 07429 119989
SHOTTS BON ACCORD ...... A Hendry, 07760 571381
THORNIEWOOD UTD ...... I McLaughlin, 07758 249811
TROON ...... Ms S Hamilton, 07932 214639
VALE OF CLYDE ...... J Wilson, 07772 973091
VALE OF LEVEN ...... A Wallace, 07950 075210
WHITLETTS VICTORIA ...... J Shields, 07918 030175
WISHAW ...... R Watson, 07764 223057
YOKER ATHLETIC ...... C Bissland, 07850 150681

Annbank Utd (New Pebble Pk), **Ardeer Thistle** (Ardeer Stdm), **Ardrossan Winton Rovers** (Winton Pk), **Arthurlie** (Dunterlie Pk), **Ashfield** (Saracen Pk), **Auchinleck Talbot** (Beechwood Pk), **Beith Juniors** (Bellsdale Pk), **Bellshill Ath** (sharing Fullarton Pk), **Benburb** (Tinto Pk), **Blantyre V** (Castle Pk), **Cambuslang Rangers** (Somervell Pk), **Carluke Rov** (John Cumming Stdm), **Clydebank** (sharing Holm Pk), **Craigmark Burtonians** (Station Pk), **Cumbernauld Utd** (Guy's Meadow), **Cumnock** (Townhead Pk), **Dalry Th** (Merksworth Pk), **Darvel** (Recreation Pk), **Dunipace** (Westfield Pk), **East Kilbride Th** (Show Park), **Forth W** (Kingshill Pk), **Girvan** (Hamilton Park), **Glasgow Perthshire** (Keppoch Pk), **Glenafton Athletic** (Loch Pk), **Greenock** (Ravenscraig Stadium), **Hurlford Utd** (Blair Pk), **Irvine Meadow** (Meadow Pk), **Irvine Vics** (Victoria Pk), **Johnstone Burgh** (Keanie Pk), **Kello Rovers** (Nithside Pk), **Kilbirnie Ladeside** (Valefield), **Kilsyth Rangers** (Duncansfield), **Kilwinning Rangers** (Abbey Pk), **Kirkintilloch Rob Roy** (Adamslie Pk), **Lanark Utd** (Moor Pk), **Largs Th** (Barrfields Stdm), **Larkhall Th** (Gasworks Pk), **Lesmahagow** (Craighead Pk), **Lugar Boswell Th** (Rosebank Pk), **Maryhill** (Lochburn Pk), **Maybole** (Ladywell Stadium), **Muirkirk** (Burnside Pk), **Neilston** (Brig o'Lea Stadium), **Newmains United Community FC** (Victoria Pk), **Petershill** (New Petershill Pk), **Pollok** (Newlandsfield Pk), **Port Glasgow** (Port Glasgow Community Stadium), **Renfrew** (Western Pk), **Rossvale FC** (New Petershill Park), **Royal Albert** (TBC), **Rutherglen Glencairn** (Clyde Gateway Stadium), **Saltcoats Vics** (Campbell Pk), **St Anthony's** (McKenna Pk), **St Roch's** (Provanmill Pk), **Shettleston** (Greenfield Pk), **Shotts Bon Accord** (Hannah Pk), **Thorniewood Utd** (Robertson Pk), **Troon** (Portland Pk), **Vale of Clyde** (Fullarton Pk), **Vale of Leven** (Millburn Pk), **Whitletts Vics** (Dam Park Stadium), **Wishaw** (The Beltane).

FA CUP WINNERS

1872 Wanderers 1 Royal Engineers 0
1873 Wanderers 2 Oxford Uni 0
1874 Oxford Uni 2 Royal Enginers 0
1875 Royal Enginers 2 Old Etonians 0 (after 1-1 draw)
1876 Wanderers 3 Old Etonians 0 (after 1-1 draw)
1877 Wanderers 2 Oxford Uni 1 (aet)
1878 Wanderers 3 Royal Enginers 1
1879 Old Etonians 1 Clapham Rovers 0
1880 Clapham Rovers 1 Oxford Uni 0
1881 Old Carthusians 3 Old Etonians 0
1882 Old Etonians 1 Blackburn R 0
1883 Blackburn Oly 2 Old Etonians 1 (aet)
1884 Blackburn R 2 Queen's Park 1
1885 Blackburn R 2 Queen's Park 0
1886 Blackburn R 2 WBA 0 (after a 0-0 draw)
1887 Aston V 2 WBA 0
1888 WBA 2 Preston 1
1889 Preston 3 Wolves 0
1890 Blackburn R 6 Sheff Wed 1
1891 Blackburn R 3 Notts Co 1
1892 WBA 3 Aston V 0
1893 Wolves 1 Everton 0
1894 Notts Co 4 Bolton 1
1895 Aston V 1 WBA 0
1896 Sheff Wed 2 Wolves 1
1897 Aston V 3 Everton 2
1898 Notts Forest 3 Derby 1
1899 Sheff Utd 4 Derby 1
1900 Bury 4 Southampton 0
1901 Tottenham H 3 Sheff U 1 (after 2-2 draw)
1902 Sheff U 2 Southampton 1 (after 1-1 draw)
1903 Bury 6 Derby 0
1904 Man City 1 Bolton 0
1905 Aston V 2 Newcastle 0
1906 Everton 1 Newcastle 0
1907 Sheff W 2 Everton 1
1908 Wolves 3 Newcastle 1
1909 Man U 1 Bristol C 0
1910 Newcastle 2 Barnsley 0 (after 1-1 draw)
1911 Bradford C 1 Newcastle 0 (after 0-0 draw)
1912 Barnsley 1 West Brom 0 (aet, after 0-0 draw)
1913 Aston Villa 1 Sunderland 0
1914 Burnley 1 Liverpool 0
1915 Sheff U 3 Chelsea 0
1920 Aston V 1 Huddersfield 0 (aet)
1921 Tottenham 1 Wolves 0
1922 Huddersfield 1 Preston 0
1923 Bolton 2 West Ham 0
1924 Newcastle 2 Aston Villa 0
1925 Sheff U 1 Cardiff 0
1926 Bolton 1 Man City 0
1927 Cardiff 1 Arsenal 0
1928 Blackburn 3 Huddersfield 1
1929 Bolton 2 Portsmouth 0
1930 Arsenal 2 Huddersfield 0
1931 West Brom 2 Birmingham 1
1932 Newcastle 2 Arsenal 1
1933 Everton 3 Man City 0
1934 Man City 2 Portsmouth 1
1935 Sheffield W 4 West Brom 2
1936 Arsenal 1 Sheffield U 0
1937 Sunderland 3 Preston 1
1938 Preston 1 Huddersfield 0 (after extra time)

1939 Portsmouth 4 Wolves 1
1946 Derby 4 Charlton 1 (aet)
1947 Charlton 1 Burnley 0 (aet)
1948 Man Utd 4 Blackpool 2
1949 Wolves 3 Leicester 1
1950 Arsenal 2 Liverpool 0
1951 Newcastle 2 Blackpool 0
1952 Newcastle 1 Arsenal 0
1953 Blackpool 4 Bolton 3
1954 WBA 3 Preston 2
1955 Newcastle 3 Man City 1
1956 Man City 3 Birmingham 1
1957 Aston Villa 2 Man Utd 1
1958 Bolton 2 Man Utd 0
1959 Notts Forest 2 Luton 1
1960 Wolves 3 Blackburn 0
1961 Tottenham 2 Leicester 0
1962 Tottenham 3 Burnley 1
1963 Man Utd 3 Leicester 1
1964 West Ham 3 Preston 2
1965 Liverpool 2 Leeds 1 (aet)
1966 Everton 3 Sheff Wed 2
1967 Tottenham 2 Chelsea 1
1968 West Brom 1 Everton 0 (aet)
1969 Man City 1 Leicester 0
1970 Chelsea 2 Leeds 1 (aet, first game a 2-2 draw)
1971 Arsenal 2 Liverpool 1 (aet)
1972 Leeds 1 Arsenal 0
1973 Sunderland 1 Leeds 0
1974 Liverpool 3 Newcastle 0
1975 West Ham 2 Fulham 0
1976 Southampton 1 Man U 0
1977 Man Utd 2 Liverpool 1
1978 Ipswich 1 Arsenal 0
1979 Arsenal 3 Man Utd 2
1980 West Ham 1 Arsenal 0
1981 Tottenham 3 Man City 2 (after 1-1 draw)
1982 Tottenham 1 QPR 0 (after 1-1 draw)
1983 Man Utd 4 Brighton 0 (after 2-2 draw)
1984 Everton 2 Watford 0
1985 Man Utd 1 Everton 0 (aet)
1986 Liverpool 3 Everton 1
1987 Coventry 3 Tottenham 2 (aet)
1988 Wimbledon 1 Liverpool 0
1989 Liverpool 3 Everton 2 (aet)
1990 Man Utd 1 Crystal P 0 (after 3-3 draw)
1991 Tottenham 2 Notts Forest 1 (aet)
1992 Liverpool 2 Sunderland 0
1993 Arsenal 2 Sheff Wed 1 (aet, first game 1-1)
1994 Man Utd 4 Chelsea 0
1995 Everton 1 Man Utd 0
1996 Man Utd 1 Liverpool 0
1997 Chelsea 2 Middlesboro 0
1998 Arsenal 2 Newcastle 0
1999 Man Utd 2 Newcastle 0
2000 Chelsea 1 Aston V 0
2001 Liverpool 2 Arsenal 1
2002 Arsenal 2 Chelsea 0
2003 Arsenal 1 Southampton 0
2004 Man Utd 3 Millwall 0
2005 Arsenal 0 Man Utd 0 (aet, Arsenal won 5-4 on penalties)
2006 Liverpool 3 West Ham 3 (aet, Liverpool won 3-1 on penalties)
2007 Chelsea 1 Man Utd 0 (aet)
2008 Portsmouth 1 Cardiff 0
2009 Chelsea 2 Everton 1
2010 Chelsea 1 Portsmouth 0
2011 Manchester City 1 Stoke 0
2012 Chelsea 2 Liverpool 1
2013 Manchester City 0 Wigan 1

Shaun Maloney was part of Wigan's FA Cup-winning side

ENGLISH LEAGUE CHAMPIONS

Season	Champions
1888-89	Preston NE
1889-90	Preston NE
1890-91	Everton
1891-92	Sunderland
1892-93	Sunderland
1893-94	Aston Villa
1894-95	Sunderland
1895-96	Aston Villa
1896-97	Aston Villa
1897-98	Sheffield United
1898-99	Aston Villa
1899-1900	Aston Villa
1900-01	Liverpool
1901-02	Sunderland
1902-03	The Wednesday
1903-04	The Wednesday
1904-05	Newcastle United
1905-06	Liverpool
1906-07	Newcastle United
1907-08	Manchester United
1908-09	Newcastle United
1909-10	Aston Villa
1910-11	Manchester United
1911-12	Blackburn Rovers
1912-13	Sunderland
1913-14	Blackburn Rovers
1914-15	Everton
1919-20	West Bromwich Albion
1920-21	Burnley
1921-22	Liverpool
1922-23	Liverpool
1923-24	Huddersfield Town
1924-25	Huddersfield Town
1925-26	Huddersfield Town
1926-27	Newcastle United
1927-28	Everton
1928-29	Sheffield Wednesday
1929-30	Sheffield Wednesday
1930-31	Arsenal
1931-32	Everton
1932-33	Arsenal
1933-34	Arsenal
1934-35	Arsenal
1935-36	Sunderland
1936-37	Manchester City
1937-38	Arsenal
1938-39	Everton
1946-47	Liverpool
1947-48	Arsenal
1948-49	Portsmouth
1949-50	Portsmouth
1950-51	Tottenham Hotspur
1951-52	Manchester United
1952-53	Arsenal
1953-54	Wolves
1954-55	Chelsea
1955-56	Manchester United
1956-57	Manchester United
1957-58	Wolves
1958-59	Wolves
1959-60	Burnley
1960-61	Tottenham Hotspur
1961-62	Ipswich Town
1962-63	Everton
1963-64	Liverpool
1964-65	Manchester United
1965-66	Liverpool
1966-67	Manchester United
1967-68	Manchester City
1968-69	Leeds United
1969-70	Everton
1970-71	Arsenal
1971-72	Derby County
1972-73	Liverpool
1973-74	Leeds United
1974-75	Derby County
1975-76	Liverpool
1976-77	Liverpool
1977-78	Nottingham Forest
1978-79	Liverpool
1979-80	Liverpool
1980-81	Aston Villa
1981-82	Liverpool
1982-83	Liverpool
1983-84	Liverpool
1984-85	Everton
1985-86	Liverpool
1986-87	Everton
1987-88	Liverpool

1988-89	Arsenal
1989-90	Liverpool
1990-91	Arsenal
1991-92	Leeds United
PREMIER LEAGUE	
1992-93	Manchester United
1993-94	Manchester United
1994-95	Blackburn Rovers
1995-96	Manchester United
1996-97	Manchester United
1997-98	Arsenal
1998-99	Manchester United
1999-00	Manchester United
2000-01	Manchester United
2001-02	Arsenal
2002-03	Manchester United
2003-04	Arsenal
2004-05	Chelsea
2005-06	Chelsea
2006-07	Manchester United
2007-08	Manchester United
2008-09	Manchester United
2009-10	Chelsea
2010-11	Manchester United
2011-12	Manchester City
2012-13	Manchester United

ENGLISH LEAGUE CUP WINNERS

1961	Aston Villa
1962	Norwich City
1963	Birmingham City
1964	Leicester City
1965	Chelsea
1966	WBA
1967	Queen's Park Rangers
1968	Leeds United
1969	Swindon Town
1970	Manchester City
1971	Tottenham Hotspur
1972	Stoke City
1973	Tottenham Hotspur
1974	Wolves
1975	Aston Villa
1976	Manchester City
1977	Aston Villa
1978	Nottingham Forest
1979	Nottingham Forest
1980	Wolves
1981	Liverpool
1982	Liverpool
1983	Liverpool
1984	Liverpool
1985	Norwich City
1986	Oxford United
1987	Arsenal
1988	Luton Town
1989	Nottingham Forest
1990	Nottingham Forest
1991	Sheffield Wed.
1992	Manchester United
1993	Arsenal
1994	Aston Villa
1995	Liverpool
1996	Aston Villa
1997	Leicester City
1998	Chelsea
1999	Tottenham Hotspur
2000	Leicester City
2001	Liverpool
2002	Blackburn Rovers
2003	Liverpool
2004	Middlesbrough
2005	Chelsea
2006	Manchester United
2007	Chelsea
2008	Tottenham Hotspur
2009	Manchester United
2010	Manchester United
2011	Birmingham City
2012	Liverpool
2013	Swansea City

KI helped Swansea City to glory against Bradford City

FORMER Scotland defender Malky Mackay led his Cardiff City side to promotion from the Championship

SIR Alex Ferguson retired from the game with his Manchester United side clinching the title

DAVID MOYES in 1982 after being drafted into Celtic's squad. He now faces a huge challenge at Old Trafford

PAUL Lambert helped Aston Villa avoid relegation after a tough first year at the Premier League side

NOTES

NOTES